EVIL ON THE ROOF OF THE WORLD

EVIL ON THE ROOF OF THE WORLD

A Cycling Trip That Ended in Terror

WILLIAM ELLIOTT HAZELGROVE

BLOOMSBURY ACADEMIC
NEW YORK • LONDON • OXFORD • NEW DELHI • SYDNEY

BLOOMSBURY ACADEMIC

Bloomsbury Publishing Inc, 1359 Broadway, New York, NY 10018, USA
Bloomsbury Publishing Plc, 50 Bedford Square, London, WC1B 3DP, UK
Bloomsbury Publishing Ireland, 29 Earlsfort Terrace, Dublin 2, D02 AY28, Ireland

BLOOMSBURY, BLOOMSBURY ACADEMIC and the Diana logo are trademarks of Bloomsbury Publishing Plc

First published in the United States of America 2025

Copyright © William Elliott Hazelgrove, 2026

Cover design: Sally Rinehart
Cover image © Lauren Geoghegan and Jay Austin, Simply Cycling blog, 2021

All rights reserved. No part of this publication may be: i) reproduced or transmitted in any form, electronic or mechanical, including photocopying, recording or by means of any information storage or retrieval system without prior permission in writing from the publishers; or ii) used or reproduced in any way for the training, development or operation of artificial intelligence (AI) technologies, including generative AI technologies. The rights holders expressly reserve this publication from the text and data mining exception as per Article 4(3) of the Digital Single Market Directive (EU) 2019/790.

Bloomsbury Publishing Inc does not have any control over, or responsibility for, any third-party websites referred to or in this book. All internet addresses given in this book were correct at the time of going to press. The author and publisher regret any inconvenience caused if addresses have changed or sites have ceased to exist, but can accept no responsibility for any such changes.

Library of Congress Cataloging-in-Publication Data Available

ISBN: HB: 979-8-8818-0038-3
ePDF: 979-8-8818-6551-1
eBook: 979-8-8818-0039-0

Typeset by Deanta Global Publishing Services, Chennai, India
Printed and bound in the United States of America

For product safety related questions contact productsafety@bloomsbury.com.

To find out more about our authors and books visit www.bloomsbury.com andسign up for our newsletters.

You watch the news, and you read the papers, and you're led to believe that the world is a big, scary place. People, the narrative goes, are not to be trusted. People are bad. People are evil. . . . I don't buy it. Evil is a make-believe concept we've invented to deal with the complexities of fellow humans holding values and beliefs and perspectives different than our own. . . . Badness exists, sure, but even that's quite rare. By and large, humans are kind. Self-interested sometimes, myopic sometimes, but kind. Generous and wonderful and kind. No greater revelation has come from our journey than this.

—JAY AUSTIN

They are killing us . . . they are killing us all.

—MARIE CLAIRE, SURVIVOR OF TAJIKISTAN ATTACK

"Thou Mayest."

—TIMS

For Jay and Lauren

CONTENTS

Author's Note ix
Foreward x
Prologue: Pamir Highway, The Roof of the World, July 29, 2018 xiii

1 Getting Ready, Washington, DC, May 2017 1

PART I Africa 11

2 South Africa, June 9, 2017 13
3 Georgetown, 2012 19
4 Namibia, The Great Karoo Desert, July 2017 27
5 Miles from Nowhere, 1977 35
6 Botswana, August 2017 41
7 The Under Five Gang, 2015 47
8 Zambia, September 2017 55
9 The Georgetown Gang, 2025 61
10 Tanzania, November 2017 67
11 The Tiny House, 2012 75

PART II Europe 81

12 Spain, December 2017 83
13 Into the Wild, 1992 91

14 Valencia, Spain, January 2018 99

15 The New York Bicycle Murders, 2017 105

16 France, February 2018 109

17 The Adventures of Huckleberry Finn, 1871 115

18 Croatia and Montenegro, April 2018 121

19 Wild, 1995 127

20 On the Road to Kazakhstan, May 2018 135

PART III **Central Asia** 139

21 Selga, Khatlong Province, Tajikistan, 1985 141

22 Kazakhstan, June 2018 145

23 The Pamirs, "The Roof of the World," July 17, 2018 151

24 The Lost City of Z, 1925 163

25 Sixty Miles to Dushanbe, July 28, 2018 167

26 Collision, July 29, 2018 173

27 The Aftermath, July 29, 2018 179

PART IV **Home** 187

28 United States, July 30, 2018 189

29 Evil on the Roof of the World 197

30 Endings 203

31 The Walden Pondo Coffee House 205

Acknowledgments 209
Appendix 210
Bibliography 213
Index 216
About the Author 220

AUTHOR'S NOTE

Out of respect for the families some names were changed or omitted. I put together the chronology of Jay and Lauren's trip from uploaded blogs, Instagram posts, and interviews with friends, family, and people who were with them before and during the attack. The blogs and Instagram posts were uploaded sporadically during their trip, sometimes months after they were written. Some Instagram and blog posts were found in Jay's phone after his death. I have done my best to piece together the various social media posts into a coherent chronology, but the dates at times do not correspond with the timeline of their trip. In the interest of telling their story, I have had to use the rules of all historians and writers in creating a cogent narrative.

Common sense.

FOREWARD

Lauren Geoghegan and Jay Austin quit their Washington jobs and on July 17, 2017, began a bike trip around the world. On July 29, 2018, they biked along Highway A 385 in the Danghara District after biking through the Pamir Mountains of Tajikistan along with five other cyclists. The Pamir Highway climbs to elevations of 15,000 feet and was once known as the Silk Road. One hundred kilometers south of the capital of Tajikistan, Dushanbe, five ISIS terrorists ran the cyclists down with a South Korean Daewoo sedan and brutally murdered the two Americans along with a Dutch national and a Swiss citizen.

Newspapers, radio stations, and television stations in the United States and around the world would pick up the story of the two twenty-nine-year-old Americans and speculate how two highly educated, well-connected millennials from Washington, DC, had crashed into the homicidal sights of ISIS terrorists on a remote mountain highway in Tajikistan. I read Jay and Lauren's story in the *New York Times* in 2018, shortly after it happened. I was intrigued. Not so much by the horrifying way they died, but the crashing together of different cultures on a deserted mountain highway in Tajikistan. I was also intrigued by what motivated Jay and Lauren to leave well-paying Washington jobs and take the road less traveled.

After writing a proposal for the publisher and digging into some research, I found Jay's declaration that "he didn't want to waste his years in front of a small rectangular screen at the Department of Housing and Urban Development, retire at sixty-five, and then die ten years later."[1] This resonated with me; it fit in with Americans who have thrown a conventional life aside to pursue a life less certain. Jay and Lauren's desire for adventure or a different American dream fits the pantheon of people looking for something beyond the safe confines of a world without risk. American history is littered with adventurers, from Amelia Earhart's daring aerial exploration to Teddy Roosevelt heading West to the Badlands, to Jack London's famous trek into the Yukon, to Mark Twain lighting out for the territories, to Thomas Stevens, who in 1887 biked around the world on a big wheel bicycle, all the way back to Thoreau, and up to the present day of Chris McCandless's journey into the wilds of Alaska.

FOREWARD

And because Jay and Lauren's journey was a trip around the world on a bike, I might as well get this out of the way: I am a biker, too. After discovering the bike trails on the outer rim of the exurbs of Chicago over twenty years ago, I have never looked back. Central to Jay and Lauren's story is their love of biking. This love of biking propelled their trip around the world along with their ethos that it was now or never. Jay was convinced that now was the time to enjoy life, not when they were too old to pull off an around-the-world bike trip. "I've missed too many sunsets while my back was turned. Too many thunderstorms went unwatched, too many gentle breezes unnoticed . . . there's magic out there, in this great big, beautiful world and I've long since scooped up the last of the scraps to be found in my cubicle,"[2] he wrote in his Simply Cycling blog.

Jay and Lauren set out on their journey believing that the world was a good place and evil was an aberration. "That is why we're traveling," Austin wrote. "Not to be given things but to be given hope, confirmation that the oft-maligned batch of humans that occupy this planet are largely good and kind."[3] The online vitriol after the attack was intense. Many people taunted Jay's belief that evil was a human construct. Many people felt that Jay and Lauren were entitled millennials who should have never entered old Soviet-aligned countries like Tajikistan. The armchair quarterbacks had an online field day.

Years passed, and the more I read about Lauren and Jay, how their lives played out in blog posts, and people who knew them, the more I felt this was a story of two people who did not identify with consumer culture, capitalism, materialism, but believed a gentler way of living in sync with the world was the answer. The very system the ISIS-inspired terrorists were attacking was a system Jay and Lauren had abandoned by living a lifestyle free of convention. Unlike the ISIS terrorists at the bottom of the food chain in Tajikistan with Afghanistan just over the border, leaking cleric-led men willing to die for Allah, Jay and Lauren were at the top of the American pyramid: Georgetown University graduates, both working in Washington, DC, at well-paid jobs, after interning for a congressman and the administration. The men who attacked them wouldn't have understood people who left privileged lives to pursue an aesthetic ideal.

Like Christopher Johnson McCandless, who left the middle-class world to go live off the land in Alaska in 1992, chronicled in the book *Into the Wild* by Jon Krakauer, Jay and Lauren accepted the risks of their actions and knew there was a possibility fate might turn against them. "Risk is the singular inherent quality in adventure, and so without risk—without fear of that risk—there is no adventure,"[4] Jay wrote in his blog five weeks before they left. Lauren had told her mother the State Department had Tajikistan as "a low risk" and pointed out that people were killed every year in New York. Jay was two years from having his student loans forgiven if he stayed at his job at the Department of Housing and Urban Development. When I asked Jay's mother why her son didn't wait it out for two years, she replied, "Jay said he was never going to pay off his student loans and was not going to wait any longer."[5]

Lauren had been working for seven years in Georgetown University admissions when she gave notice. After quitting their jobs, they were ready to go around the world on their bikes. Jay and Lauren's bike trip was supposed to be a four-year journey. Their plan was to begin in South Africa and end in South America. Between these two points would be flights from Africa to Europe, then from Turkey to Central Asia, possibly India, Australia, where their bikes would be disassembled, crated, then reassembled. They made it one year and twelve days when their trip ended with the terrorist attack in Tajikistan.

One night over dinner, I was telling my wife about their incredible journey and the remarkable people Jay and Lauren met as they biked through Africa, Europe, the Eastern European countries, and finally the Pamir Mountains. She paused and looked at me and spoke quietly: "It is like they led a whole life in one year."

I couldn't have said it better.

This is their story.

Notes

1. Austin, Jay, Simply Cycling Blog.
2. Ibid.
3. Ibid.
4. Ibid.
5. Jea Santovasco Interview.

PROLOGUE

PAMIR HIGHWAY, THE ROOF OF THE WORLD, JULY 29, 2018

Parts of the highway are a cold, barren, snow blowing hell. Other parts are a roasting, sweating, climb with heat radiating from scorched blacktop. The exhilaration of the snow-crested peaks and the Godlike panorama of the Pamir Mountains spreading into infinity is breathtaking. The British and Russians fought it out for a century over control of this hostile barrier. The military department of the Russian empire built the road to transfer troops from Fergana to the Alay Valley. The Soviet Union called the highway M4,1, but to the rest of the world the road transecting the Pamir Mountains through Afghanistan, Uzbekistan, Tajikistan, and Kyrgyzstan of 1,200 kilometers was the Pamir Highway. It is the only continuous route through the twisting elevation of the Pamir Mountains and the biking destination for cyclists from all over the world. The route begins in Tajikistan and ends in Osh Kyrgyzstan. Between these two points are passes of 15,000-feet elevation with air so thin it is hard to breathe, to think, and almost impossible to cycle. Acclimation is key, but the human brain rebels against the lack of oxygen and demands whatever it can get for the organs and heart and leaves the muscles gasping for more. Many cyclists are reduced to walking their bikes up to the high passes.

Lauren Geoghegan was one of those cyclists walking her bike and having trouble just doing that. The altitude had left her with a headache and red blood cells depleted. The mountainous highway was going higher and higher, and with every push of her pedal, she felt a throbbing headache right between her eyes. The icy, frigid wind cut down between snow-crested mountains and went right through her Patagonia biking jacket, thermal Under Armour, another layer of a thick biking jersey, and a T-shirt. Layers were the key; this usually did the trick, but this wind was brutal. Her eyes were watering, her cheeks felt like ice, and all she could think of was going home. She had been cycling for over a year.

The trip around the world began on July 17, 2017. No. She didn't want to desert Jay, but more than that, quitting now felt like defeat. "I would get WhatsApp messages, oh my God this is so hard I don't know if I can keep going,"[1] recalled her friend and roommate at Georgetown University, Molly Scalise. "Then she would stick it out."[2] Jay was biking steadily ahead, unaffected, it seemed, by weather or fatigue since they had entered the Pamir Mountains. But Jay had the insulation of the zealot. Some would say later that Lauren was on his bike trip around the world, and that Jay would have gone with or without her. That would ignore the fact that Lauren Geoghegan had traveled to Beirut, Damascus, and Lebanon in college and evaluated the trip a full year before she decided to bike around the world.

Lauren looked down the Pamir Highway, bisecting the mountains in Tajikistan. There was a beauty to the bleak path with mountains in the distance. The gray rock of the snow-crested mountains broken by scraggly Juniper trees would have been impressive if she didn't feel so miserable. The highway climbed to an elevation until cyclists and hikers felt like they were suffocating. Insomnia and nausea were also symptoms of the high elevation. Lauren had been fighting gastrointestinal issues on and off for the last month.

She looked out again. The vista was breathtaking if pedaling up steep grades hadn't taken all her breath away. But the rocky mountainous landscape was also psychologically challenging. There was a cold, foreboding quality that pushed down on cyclists as they pedaled toward the roof of the world with the only thought of reaching the top.

The Silk Highway running through the Pamir Mountains in Tajikistan was Mecca as far as bikers were concerned. Camel caravans had once carried silk from East to West, beginning in 500 BC to the early sixteenth century along with wool, coal, porcelain, and bronze. The plodding caravans passing through snowy mountains on the Silk Road was legendary for being the historical artery for religious pilgrims, missionaries, and explorers. The route from Badakhshan to Tajikistan has become fabled in the West with Marco Polo describing the region as the "highest place in the world." Marking the Southern boundary of Central Asia, it is the crossroad of empires with crevasses, glaciers, and snowy peaks. British explorers mapped the high passes into British India, while Russian explorers let the world know about the great peaks of northern Pamir. The high elevations, the breathtaking view from the mountains, makes it the Everest for the cycling community. Persians know the Pamir Mountains as Bam-I-Dunya or *"the roof of the world."*

Jay and Lauren labored to move their loaded-down Salsa Marrakesh bikes up the road. The fatigue of oxygen-starved blood and the thump of pounding headaches kept time with the push of every pedal. Add to this the topography of the mountains bordering Afghanistan. "It is cold and windy and mountainous

PROLOGUE   xv

and most of all very, very high,"[3] Jay wrote in an Instagram post on July 25, 2018. On a zoom call from Amsterdam, six years later, Kim Postma, fifty-eight, thinks back on biking the Pamirs. She talks with a clipped accent, her long blond hair tossed back. She has made a life out of traveling with her life partner, Rene Wokke, a fifty-six-year-old psychologist from the Netherlands. They had traveled to over 130 countries and were on a trip from Thailand to Iran when they met the two twenty-nine-year-old Americans in Kyrgyzstan. They had veered around Afghanistan, thinking it was too dangerous and biked the Pamir instead. Kim is the only witness capable of talking about the attack on the Pamir Highway. "Those memories are hard,"[4] she emails back. Still, she agrees to talk with me.

Kim and Rene had joined Lauren and Jay as they crossed the Pamir. A Dutch couple who lived on a houseboat and took in wayward children, they loved biking the mountains and were on their way to the Pamir Highway. "My parents were very adventurous, and I was raised independently,"[5] Kim said nodding. The couple were constantly planning their next trip where "you never know where you will end up."[6] When the two couples met up again two weeks later, they agreed to cross the Pamir Mountains together. As they entered the mountains, a Swiss couple, Marie Clarie Diemand, fifty-nine, and Markus Hummel, sixty-two, joined them along with a young Frenchman Guillaume Kazabat. They were now a group of seven cyclists entering the toughest cycling highway in the world. "Lauren was having a hard time . . . couldn't eat . . . couldn't cycle at all," Kim Postma recalled. "We stopped by a river and on other side was Afghanistan. We could see people. . . . Lauren asked me if I was afraid. Jay talked about going to the other side, but she would not. She asked me several times if I was scared. I could see she was afraid." [7]

Lauren had double-checked the state department's risk assessment that had Tajikistan at Level One, *Exercise Normal Precautions*. Tajikistan was a poor Muslim country with an autocratic government, and as many as 1,300 young men had fought with ISIS in Syria. But there was no direct history of terrorists attacking Westerners. Now, after several days in the mountains, the weather had changed again. The group had biked to a lower elevation and the sun was hot, and they were looking to refill their water bottles. Water is precious to the biker even in cold climates. The body loses water from long-distance biking, and hydration is a constant battle. Without water, fatigue sets in, grogginess happens, muscles cramp, senses dull. Add to this the very thin air, and biking goes from the thrill of being one with nature and breathing in the cold clean air of the mountains, to an unbearable slog where each push of the pedal becomes an effort. Jay had to walk Lauren's bike up several mountain passes and posted again on July 25, "Laurens having a bit of difficulty."[8]

Kim Postma described the trip through the Pamir as "taking two or three steps, then take a breath, then walk some more."[9] Beyond having the panic attack, Lauren was having doubts about continuing. "Lauren was thinking of flying back to the States, seeing friends and family, earning a little money, and maybe rejoining Jay,"[10] Postma recollected. On another pass at 14,000 feet, Jay walked back down and pushed Lauren's bike up as she hiked to the top.

A few days later, the weather changed again. They had cleared the high passes and descended to the lower elevations. It was hot again, and they all peeled the clothes that seemed ridiculous as the temperature hit 80 degrees Fahrenheit. Biking shorts and T-shirts along with bandannas became the uniform as the sun beat down. Jay and Lauren rode in a line. They were in front, then the Swiss couple, Markus Hummel, Marie Clarie Dieman, then Kim Postma, and Rene Wokke, and Guillaume Kazabat, the French cyclist, quickly fell behind with stomach issues.

The cyclists turned onto a deserted stretch on Highway A 385 with sand-colored land spreading out on both sides except for spidering high-tension towers on the left side. It was 3:30 in the afternoon, and the sun had cleared the earlier clouds. Jay and Lauren rode at the head of the group. The temperature had warmed further with heat radiating up from the two-lane blacktop. They had air pods in and listened to music or podcasts. Lauren was feeling better about the ride. The altitude sickness had abated, and they were sixty miles from hot showers and a warm bed in the capital, Dushanbe. Lauren was listening to Taylor Swift. Jay was listening to a podcast. No one saw the five men clutching knives and meat cleavers in the approaching white South Korean Daewoo sedan.

Notes

1. Molly Scalise Interview by William Hazelgrove.
2. ibid.
3. Jay Austin Instagram @simplycycling, July 25, 2018.
4. Kim Postma Email.
5. Kim Postma Interview by William Hazelgrove, April 29, 2024.
6. Ibid.
7. Ibid.
8. Jay Austin Instagram @simplycycling, July 25, 2018.
9. Kim Postma Interview by William Hazelgrove, April 29, 2024.
10. Ibid.

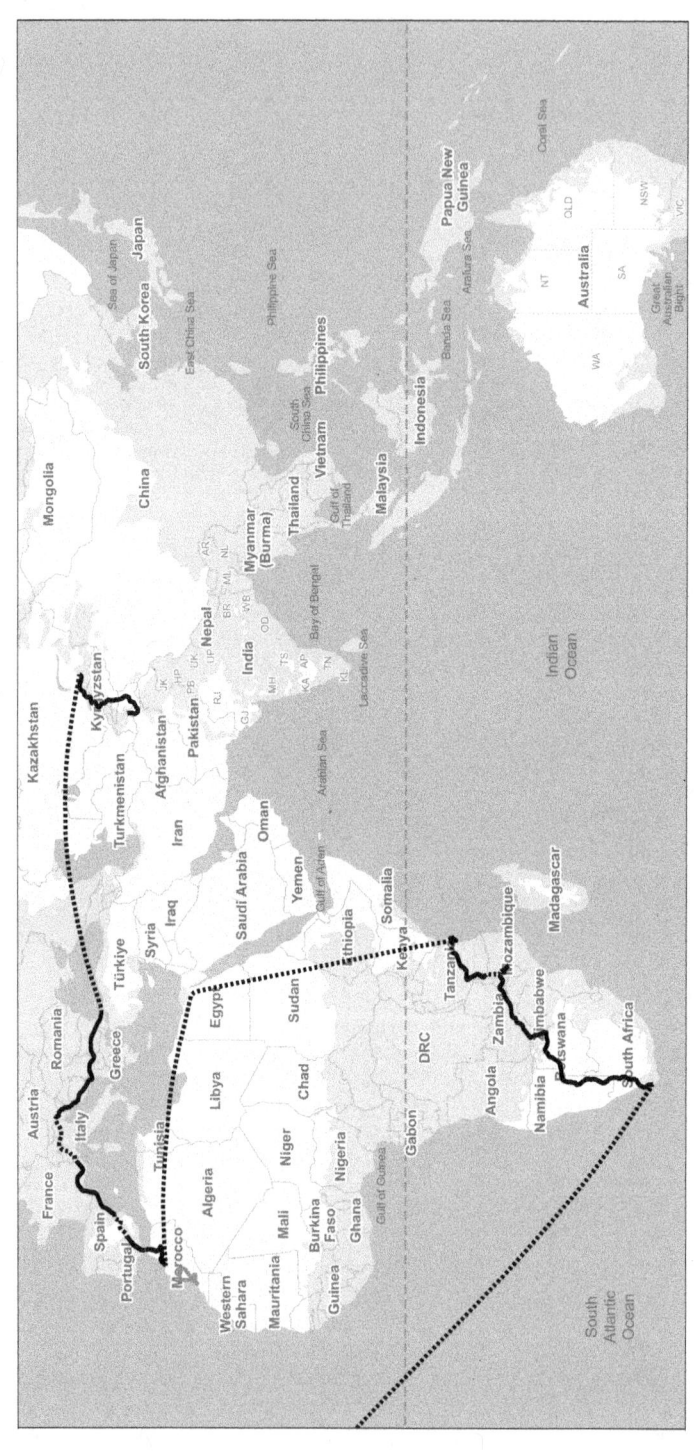

Map 1 Jay and Lauren's approximate cycling route

1
GETTING READY

WASHINGTON, DC, MAY 2017

On May 15, 2017, Jay Austin posted on Instagram:

> HEY FRIENDS! Big news. In 6 weeks, Lauren and I are quitting our jobs and leaving DC to go bike around the world for the next few years. I'm really excited, but also terribly sad to be leaving so many beautiful, familiar faces for so long. I'd love to see y'all (if you are in DC) or catch up on the phone (if you're not) before heading out, so let me know if/when you're around . . . we leave July 6. We're flying into South Africa and plan on biking north through eastern Africa, then onwards to Europe and Asia and if we make it this far, Australia and the Americas.[1]

It is the American dream for many to quit their job and live the life they have wanted. The great moment came for Jay Austin at the Department of Housing and Urban Development (HUD) on June 14, 2017, when he walked out with his cardboard box and freed himself from the shackles of his nine-to-five. In a blog post, entitled "I Quit My Job Today," he writes:

> I quit my job today. I'm terrified. I'm thrilled. I feel like I felt when I stepped off a plane at ten thousand feet some years back, tumbling head over heels, plummeting toward the earth. . . . I know there's a parachute. I know it will be ok . . . I've spent almost seven years—seven years-going to the same place at the same time on the same days of the week. . . . the people were wonderful, the work was service-orientated, the hours were flexible, the salary was good. I got health insurance and paid time off and a whole lot of autonomy. I had some patient bosses who put up with me taking three-month long sabbaticals every year.[2]

A case might be made that in 2016 quitting a government job wasn't a big shock for a progressive like Jay Austin, but it was a long time coming. Jay had been the nonconformist at the Department of Housing and Urban Development, wearing V-necked T-shirts, shorts, and flip-flops to work while brewing kombucha in his cubicle and building a Cornhole set in the hallway. "Jay was a master at learning the rules and then exploiting the holes," Abby Miller, a coworker at HUD, recalled in a later interview. "He came up with the telework request at a time when no one was working at home."[3]

But the discontent grew with each passing year. In another blog post, Jay wrote:

> I am young and white and American and living awfully close to the world's shining beacon on a hill, or something like that. . . . I've grown tired of spending the best hours of my day in front of a glowing rectangle . . . coloring the best years of my life in swaths of grey and beige. I've missed too many sunsets while my back was turned. Too many thunderstorms went unwatched, too many gentle breezes unnoticed. There's magic out there in this great big, beautiful world.[4]

Jay early on had begun planning his escape. He began taking extended vacations and returned from a scooter trip across the country more determined to break free. He cut his costs and moved out of his apartment at age twenty-three and built "a tiny house" in a tiny house community. His 145-square-foot house, "the matchbox," lowered his fixed costs, allowing him to plow more money into traveling, cycling in Morocco, backpacking in Europe, and spending four weeks in India. Abby Miller went on a trip to Eastern Europe with Jay. Abby has short brown shaved hair and bright eyes, and now lives with her wife. She paused during our interview. "To be honest with you Jay and I split up in 2015. It was never anything romantic, I was gay then too, but we had a knock down drag out fight in the Slovenian forest over the pros and cons of the Chinese government with Jay taking the position China was a much more efficient form of government." Abby pulled her hand through her short hair. "He was the most obtuse frustrating white man I've ever known." She shook her head. "He was like a verbal hammer and after that we didn't see each other for years."[5]

After each of the trips, Jay increasingly questioned his work life at HUD. I am not interested in this pot at the end of the rainbow sort of existence, because I don't believe it to exist. I am interested in the pursuit of everyday happiness . . . the kind where we embrace Mondays as an amazing fucking day in which the sun is still shining . . . not as a day we churn through in route to Friday.[6] Jay passed up promotions at the Department of Housing and Urban Development, not wanting the extra responsibility. All during this time, he socked money away into his bank account from his six-figure job for the day he would quit.

"He was able to walk away from his job, but most people can't,"[7] Molly Scalise, Lauren Geoghegan's roommate in Georgetown said later. She noted that Lauren did not have the same savings, and it was a much bigger decision to leave her job. "Lauren didn't make a snap decision . . . she actually thought about the trip for a full year before deciding to go."[8]

During the Christmas holidays of 2017, Lauren and Jay formalized their plan to bike around the world. They told family and friends that they were quitting their jobs and didn't have a time frame or even a set travel plan. "I was shocked she was quitting her job," Lauren's childhood friend, Kendall O'Connor said shaking her head. "I was like this is crazy and I asked my mom if she was serious about biking around the world because she talked to Lauren's mom almost every day. To me . . . it was scary."[9]

Jay expressed his own private doubts in his blog and the cost of the trip:

Every week I spend on the road may mean (a lot) less money in my bank account and fewer bullets on my résumé, but every week I spend tucked away in an office, staring at a computer, doing roughly the same thing I've done for the past seven years—that's foregoing a whole lot . . . it's foregoing a worldly education and a worldly adventure; it's giving up the privilege to forget what day of the week it is or what date of the month it is. It's giving up my fundamental freedom: the freedom to be anywhere I want in the world.[10]

During our interview, Kendall is keeping an eye on her children in bib overalls. She leans forward, pulling back her blond hair. I was getting ready for my wedding and Lauren was getting ready to bike around the world. I mean she had one job for seven years. A job that made her happy at Georgetown University and here she was . . . this smart hardworking driven young woman who was going to quit her job . . . to what . . . go bike around the world?[11]

"We all thought it was kind of crazy," Molly Scalise said later. She knew Lauren was adventurous, but she was nowhere near the explorer Jay was with his minimalist ethos embracing the hardships of doing without. To Molly, Lauren enjoyed friendly hotels, good food, and jewelry. "Lauren loved the things that she had."[12]

Jay's friends took comfort that Lauren was going with him. She would ground Jay from what some saw as impulsive idealism for the man who had gone skydiving and then ran a marathon barefoot after reading how marathons were meant to be run. "Once we were on his scooter and went to the beach," Abby, his coworker from HUD, said laughing. "And he had read a book about how to handle traffic and the book said to go slow and steady on a highway . . . we had traffic backed up for miles and I'm like, it's not working Jay, but he believed that this way was better."[13]

Jay's initial plan was nebulous and ambitious.

> Now, we don't really have a firm route, and we don't even know if we'll be making it "around the world" (whatever that means), but we'd certainly like to have the option to move ever eastward. So, I've tried to get a sense of where spontaneity won't be a problem (Europe, Latin America), and where it most certainly would be a problem (Central Asia). I compiled a long, 66-country spreadsheet filled with columns of information—information cobbled together from embassy websites, traveler forums, and comment sections—about things like maximum stay, visa validity, visa costs, and the all-important how-and-when-and-where-one-would-actually-go-about-applying-for-a-visas.[14]

Many countries such as Iran and China were problematic in getting visas, so the trip was whittled down. Jay and Lauren plotted a general route for their trip that would begin at the Southern tip of Africa, head north into Europe, cut east into Central and South Asia, fly over to India, then to South America, and then finally pedal back home to the United States. Australia might be added later. A budget of $23 a day was settled on.

For Jay, quitting his job was the jump-off point into a new life.

> I'd like to wake up every morning and expect that this day may well be the best day of my life and to not be delusional in thinking so. At the very least, I'd like to close the day by having learned something, having been moved, having been happy in the moment. I'd like to die pursuing one of those days, not in a cubicle pursuing the happiness that may not rest on the horizon of a retirement I may never reach.[15]

Lauren was ready to shake up her life. She had worked in the Georgetown University admission office for seven years and was considering returning to school for a graduate degree. This around-the-world journey seemed like the opportunity to break with her job and join the man she loved on a grand adventure. Her coworker at Georgetown University, Kristen Robinson, said later. "that trip was the ultimate show of love, to quit your job and go off with someone. You have to be committed then."[16]

Jay had written about his plan to bike around the world early on in his blog. "Right now, there's something I want to do, and it's the same thing I've wanted to do since I was young: to live the life of an astronaut, to float, quietly, through time and space to see the whole world and watch it turn slowly beneath my feet. I want to bike around the world."[17] Jay Austin's blog posts speak of someone planning to leave the world behind. After he had quit his job, he wrote, "I think I've found freedom, an escape from enslaving and an escape from being enslaved.

An escape from the whole rotten system, articulated in a way much darker than intended, but hey, it's a pretty dark system. I think I've found freedom—for me, for now, and I think it looks like this."[18]

Jay threw himself into planning his four-year trip around the world. The clothes, camping equipment, electronics, and biking gear Lauren and Jay gathered would be extensive. A man named Thomas Stevens, in 1884, rode a black enameled big-wheel bike from San Francisco to Boston and then to New York. He took a steamer to Liverpool and went East until he had gone around the world and returned to San Francisco in December 1886. *Adventure Cyclist* described him "as a man of medium height, wearing an oversized blue flannel shirt over blue overalls which were tucked into a pair of leggings at the knee and tanned as a nut. A mustache protruded from his face."[19]

This was Steven's biking attire for his ride around the world. Born in Berkhamsted, England, the son of a laborer, he came to America with his father in 1868 and settled in Missouri. His mother would not come over for two years, and the family would drift from Denver to San Francisco, where Thomas learned to ride a bike. He worked for two years in a Wyoming mill, and then while working in a Colorado mine, he formulated the idea to bike around the world. His bike, known as a "Penny Farthing" and built by the Pope Manufacturing Company of Chicago, would carry a handlebar bag that contained Thomas's socks, a spare shirt, a raincoat that doubled as a tent and bedroll, and a Bulldog revolver. Thomas Steven's journey would eventually produce a thousand-page book, *Around the World on a Bicycle.* Jay listed what they would bring on their journey in a spreadsheet. Jay's bike, a Salsa Marrakesh Flat bar Deore modified for the journey, was not cheap. Starting at $2,000, the modifications added like a car cranked up to the final price. Jay listed the bike this way. "A sturdy steel frame clearance for 500 mm tires, a triple crankset, disc brakes, downshift tubers, a kickstand plate, and tons of braze-ons for bottle cages, the Marrakesh is built for world expeditions."[20]

Biking is an expensive sport. My own bike costs less than a thousand dollars. I have had people ride by me and say, "hey you're doing pretty good with a bike like that." These are the triathletes blowing by me with $5,000–10,000 custom-fitted bikes with electronic gear shifting. But as one bike store mechanic told me, "it's not the bike: it's the engine." Lauren's bike was also a $2,000 Salsa Marrakesh. The equipment each bike carried was spare bike pads, security keys, rags, toothbrush, chain lube, pump, multitool, spoke wrench, spoke repair kit, spare spokes, spare cables, cassette remover, patch kit, super glue, inner tubes, spare nuts and bolts, tape, cable ties, bike locks, daypack, bottle cages, front light, rear rack, front basket, helmets, and cycling vest. The biking equipment and bikes were quickly a $5,000 expenditure. Biking around the world can be done on a budget. Lauren and Jay's planned budget of $23 a day is spartan, but there would be flights at several junctures, which would cost thousands. Additional equipment included Patagonia and Under Armor shirts, Vasque Grand Traverse hiking shoes, sandals, socks, underwear, Under Armour Launch 7 shorts, Decathlon Kanani tights, multifunctional scarf, Vancrown headbands, Suncloud Causeway sunglasses, Patagonia Nano Air Hoody, Patagonia Nano Puff, the North Face Wicked Beanie, Buff Merino Wool Thermal Beanie, Showers Pass Club Waterproof shoes, Marmot Minimalist Pants, and Marmot Minimalist Jacket.

Biking shirts can run $120, and the same goes for thermal tights. One does not go to a bike store lightly. Jay and Lauren augmented their well-appointed bikes with the latest electronics: Sony RX100MIII camera Sunpak mini tripod, Lensmate filter adapter, Sony NP-BX1 batteries, SanDisk Micro SDXC cards, Vastar Cell Phone Tripod Mount, DJI Spark, and extra DJI Intelligent battery; a Kindle Paperwhite with Ayto case, Black Diamond Revolt headlamp with Black Diamond AAA Rechargeable batteries, Huawei Mate SE phone, KuGI case, Vodafone earbuds, Moko Foldable Bluetooth Keyboard, USB Battery Bank Anker Astro E8, Travel adapter, and USB brick. The equipment also included two Katabatic Alsek 22 F sleeping bags and Therm A Rest NeoAir XTherm sleeping pads, as well as innovative camping gear along with a Big Agnes Copper Spur HV tent, first aid kit, antibiotics, surgical gloves, malarial treatment, passports, an MSR Dragonfly stove, and GSI Outdoors Pinnacle Backpacker Nested Cook set.

And since Jay and Lauren had to carry everything themselves, they focused with laser-like attention on each object they planned to bring. One reporter who dropped by to write a profile of Jay Austin found him in front of a scale, weighing the possessions he planned to pack—hat: 2 ounces; tablet: 11 ounces. They found a deck of cards online measuring just 1 inch by 1 inch.

Unlike Chris McCandless (*Into the Wild*), who went into the wilderness with a sack of rice and a twenty-two-scope rifle, or Thomas Stevens, who carried five items with him, Lauren and Jay were going on their around-the-world trip with the best equipment money could buy. The five ISIS terrorists who would attack them in Tajikistan couldn't afford one of their $500 sleeping bags. Lauren and Jay had more earning power than 90 percent of Muslim families in Tajikistan. The equipment would mitigate hardships, but the risks were still there. In a blog post, Jay acknowledged the risk of his looming adventure before he left.

"Over the tens of thousands of kilometers, we're likely to travel, it only takes one mistake, a hungry animal, a wild dog, a distracted driver, an angry individual, a slippery patch of ice . . . ."[21] He was aware he would be putting Lauren at risk as well. "I am comfortable assuming that risk for myself, but this time, I'm not traveling by myself. When you love someone, you want to keep them safe. . . . I worry about something happening and not being able to stop it from happening."[22]

GETTING READY 7

There was risk. The State Department's assessment of risk in Tajikistan in 2024 *"recommends US citizens exercise caution due to terrorism, unexploded landmines, and occasional violence near the border with Kyrgyzstan."*[23]

When Lauren and Jay set out in 2017, the risk was at the lowest level. Still, the post-9/11 world is anything but stable, and their proposed route would take them close to the border of Afghanistan. Suddenly, they were in the home stretch of arranging to leave for possibly four years. Jay wrote in his blog, "We are just five weeks away from embarking on the biggest, scariest, and most rewarding journey of our lives. There's not much left to do now: move a house, pack a few bikes, see some friends for the last time for a while, get on a plane, and hope for the best."

They had spent the last month "getting jabbed in the arms with all sorts of vaccinations." Jay listed the vaccines in his blog:

- Hepatitis A
- Hepatitis B
- Influenza
- Measles, mumps, and rubella
- Typhoid
- Tetanus, diphtheria, acellular pertussis
- Yellow fever
- Chickenpox
- Polio
- Meningitis
- Japanese encephalitis
- Rabies[24]

They loaded 400 books into their kindles and cancelled credit cards. They set a budget of $7,000 to $7,200 per year with $3,000 of self-insurance. Jay posted in his blog. "Having a cheap trip is easy and having a comfortable trip is easy but having a cheap comfortable trip is pretty hard."[25] Jay then listed his concerns before leaving. He had a fear of the trip not living up to their expectations, of not wanting to return to their former lives after being on the road for four years, and then under the headline, *Something Goes Wrong*, there is an eerie prescience to his blog post:

Perhaps the greatest fear is the most immediate and the most physical. This isn't the first adventure I've taken that I know those would deem risky.

But those past adventure were always shorter . . . always pretty close to civilization and needed supplies and a return home . . . this will not be one of those adventures . . . it only takes one mistake—I worry about something happening and not being able to stop it from happening or not being able to do anything once it does happen. It's a terrifying fear.[26]

They set up their blogs on Instagram with the handle @simplycycling. In an introductory post, they write, "We're Jay and Lauren, two Americans from Washington, DC (by way of New York and California, respectively). We'll both be 28 when we set off on our bike ride around the world, giving up a pair of comfortable, full-time jobs (in government and education, respectively) for way more uncertainty, way more discomfort, and—we hope—way more fun."[27] Jay had his *Tiny House* towed to a friend's backyard, and Lauren arranged to rent her room in the house she was living with three other women. In Jay's blog, he posts a picture of himself following his trailered house down the street on a bike. A case of poison ivy from the new location gave him a week of itching and burning. A blog post the year before they leave gives a quick answer as to why they have decided to bike around the world.

> We're young and healthy and we won't always be young and healthy, so it seems like a good time. Our jobs are comfortable and all, but we've both been at them a while, and we know what the next year of employed life looks like for us: lots of days in an office, lots of rushed evenings and rushed mornings, lots of routine and maybe a few short adventures to break things up, but overall not much different than the year before, or the one before that. A bike ride around the world sounds like a hell of an adventure.[28]

On June 8, 2017, Jay Austin and Lauren Geoghegan boarded a plane to fly to South Africa for the first leg of their around-the-world trip. In another blog post, Jay reevaluated the risk and concluded that the concept of evil might be a matter of trust. "We live in a world where your life is dictated largely by how you trust. If you do not trust others, if you believe human nature to be something dark and rotten, you close yourself off to a whole lot. If you do not open the shutters, all you get is darkness, no matter what's outside . . . there's no way to let the light in unless you open your shutters to a wider world." [29]

They were two twenty-eight-year-olds with the best education money could buy, the best bikes and equipment money could buy, and who worked in the power and money capital of the world, Washington DC. They were walking away from their jobs, their families, their friends, their lives, and plunging into the unknown. Mr. Thomas Stevens, in 1886, carried one tool on his trip that Jay Austin and Lauren Geoghegan never considered, but to Mr. Stevens, who

GETTING READY

would be imprisoned, chased, and arrested several times, a snub-nosed Bulldog British revolver was as important as a bicycle pump.

Notes

1. @simplycycling, June 14, 2017.
2. Jay Austin Blog, June 14, 2017.
3. Abby Miller Interview by William Hazelgrove, April 30, 2024.
4. Jay Austin Blog, June 14, 2017.
5. Abby Miller Interview by William Hazelgrove, April 30, 2024.
6. Jay Austin Blog, June 14, 2017.
7. Molly Scalise Interview by William Hazelgrove, March 12, 2024.
8. Ibid.
9. Kendall O'Connor Interview by William Hazelgrove, May 6, 2024.
10. Simplycycling.com blog, Jay Austin, October 12, 2016.
11. Kendall O'Connor Interview by William Hazelgrove, May 6, 2024.
12. Molly Scalise Interview by William Hazelgrove, March 12, 2024.
13. Abby Miller Interview by William Hazelgrove, April 30, 2024.
14. Jay Austin Blog, April 18, 2017.
15. Jay Austin Blog.
16. Kristen Robinson Interview by William Hazelgrove, April 12, 2024.
17. Santovasco, Jea, My Stories Since the Death of My Son, Jay Austin, Simply Be Kind Foundation, Manalapan NJ, 20.
18. Jay Austin Blog.
19. Stevens, Thomas, Around the World on a Bicycle, Thomas G. Clark, 2019.
20. Simplycycling. Org, May 2018.
21. Ibid., January 10, 2017.
22. Jay Austin Blog.
23. US Department of State (gov), https://travel.state.gov>traveladvisories>traveladvisories
24. Simplycycling.org, April 18, 2017.
25. Simplycycling.org Reflections, January 10, 2017.
26. Ibid.
27. Ibid., October 6, 2016.
28. Ibid.
29. Simplycycling.org Valencia, January 2018.

PART I
AFRICA

2
SOUTH AFRICA

JUNE 9, 2017

Jay and Lauren's plane landed in Cape Town, South Africa, on June 9, 2017. They are now in the postapartheid world of South Africa, which began in 1974 and ended in 1990, but the country is still highly segregated. Unemployment is rampant and centered mostly in the 80 percent Black population. Economic crisis, along with low business investment and rising levels of violent crime, have some leaders warning the country is in danger of collapsing into a failed state. The International Monetary Fund determined South Africa was suffering from massive corruption in 2017.

The two Americans emerge in the hot, steamy weather and face the task of putting their bikes back together after rescuing them from baggage claim. The giant cardboard boxes they shipped their bikes in are "heavy, misshapen, bulging with the abuse of handlers and conveyor belts and the unrelenting rain." Jay and Lauren set about reassembling their bikes. "We connect handlebar to stem, hub to fork, pedal to crank . . . and ready these twenty-five pound hunks of steel, aluminum and rubber."[1] After they have assembled the bikes, they set out on a highway and are beset by blaring truckers and speeding drivers. The shoulder is littered with debris and glass. Lauren's tire quickly goes flat. It is a sickening feeling every cyclist knows when suddenly the speeding rim hits the asphalt. Jay flips his bike over, levers off the rubber tire from the rim, and swaps out the inner tube. It is a greasy, sweaty affair. By the time Jay finishes, it is evening, and they decide to camp along a rest stop.

Jay, for being a meticulous planner, had left their route open.

Wherever the winds and weather and our own whims take us. We think we'll start in Botswana—though that too might change—and head north from there, to Ethiopia or Sudan or Egypt . . . we may wait out the winter in southern Europe before setting out east, navigating a mess of tricky visas and geopolitical issues to cross central Asia and work our way down to southeast Asia. At some point we'll catch a flight (if not a few)—from Thailand or Malaysia or Indonesia or Australia—and pick up down in South America, steering back toward the States.

Then he leaves himself an out. "We're not opposed to cutting things short or taking a different way around, or catching a train, plane, or ferry if certain stretches become just too difficult."[2]

Jay will write most of his blog posts on simplycycling.org, and both he and Lauren have Instagram accounts. The posts on Instagram and the blog are uploaded when they enter a Wi-Fi zone, with many posts uploaded together. Lauren's first Instagram picture shows their bikes on a bleak two-lane highway with the caption, "taken after getting a flat on the first day."[3]

Jay describes their first campsite as "a small cut out from the main road with a few picnic tables and some dying shrubs." It is essentially a rest stop. "Beyond that there's a fence, protecting a large nature reserve, that is in itself a buffer zone for a power plant further back."[4] Jay and Lauren pitch their tent behind some shrubs along a chain-link fence. Camping at any rest stop in any country is dangerous, with people flowing through all night long. They hope their tent won't be noticed behind the shrubs. Jay and Lauren blow up their inflatable pads, open their sleeping bags, and climb in. It is unsettling to camp at night. It is unnerving to camp in a foreign country. A stick breaking, a noise in the woods, or the sound of a car pulling up conjures up nightmares. Jay and Lauren lay in the darkness. South Africa pierces the silence with the call of birds and the strange cackles of monkeys.

In a cycling article posted in 2021, bike hijackings were cited in South Africa. A common method used by criminals is "to bump or knock the cyclist down with a vehicle at which point they jump out and steal the bike and the belongings of the injured individual."[5] Another biker online suggests skipping South Africa because of the crime and the narrow highways. All cyclists are advised to be vigilant and not bike at night. Jay and Lauren's bright orange tent pitched by a fence at a rest stop is an invitation to trouble. Still, they try and get some sleep, but soon their sleep is interrupted by "the sound of whining combustion and crunching gravel that interrupts the relative silence then doors open . . . doors close."[6]

Jay sits up quickly, pulls on his shoes, unzips the tent, and meets a man with *Eskom* emblazoned on his shirt. The man asks for identification. He is a security guard for the power plant and explains he is concerned about how close their tent is to the fence. Jay explains the situation with Lauren's flat tire, and the man takes his passport and radios the information in. He then allows Jay and Lauren to remain. Jay goes back into the tent, and they eat some peanut butter

SOUTH AFRICA

sandwiches. Jay feels too jittery to sleep, so he flips on his headlamp and starts reading a book. The night has grown colder, and he snuggles deeper into his sleeping bag. The silence feels less oppressive.

Headlights cut through the orange nylon of the tent. Lauren sits up quickly as the sound of hard shoes on gravel reaches them. Jay turns off his lamp as a voice calls from behind the fence. "You must come with us. You cannot stay." Jay scrambles out of the tent to another man with Eskom on his shirt. "It will get very cold tonight," he explains. "You do not understand how cold it will get. And it is not safe. Truckers stop here during the night, and it is not safe. It has all been sorted out. A truck will come by and pick you up and give you a ride back into town."[7]

They are at the mercy of men they don't know. Jay and Lauren don't want to pack up their tent again and load their bikes into a van; "but we don't feel we have much of a choice,"[8] Jay writes later. They pack up the tent and their bikes and go to the road and stand in the cold darkness for half an hour. Finally, a truck and a sedan turn off the road, and two more Eskom men load their bikes into the truck. Lauren and Jay climb into the car and are taken to an unknown destination. The driver tells them, "This will really be much better. You would just be so cold. And robbed, definitely. They would have robbed you. You see, this little town here," he gestures to a small bundle of lights. "It's a colored town. The people . . . well, you wouldn't understand."[9]

Jay and Lauren are transported to a campground that costs 160 rand for a night. "We feel duped and defeated," Jay posts later, but they pay the fee and set up their campsite by the toilets. They pitch their tent again, unroll sleeping bags, blow up their inflatable mats, and climb back in. They are tired and cold, and before sleep comes, they hear footsteps by the tent again. Jay scrambles once again to a man standing by the tent. It is the campground warden. "You're supposed to be at that site over there. This site is for camper vehicles." Jay explains this is where they were dropped off, and they don't speak Afrikaans. The man shrugs. "I see. I see, but you understand this is the caravan spot."[10]

Jay is exasperated and tired. They are looking at breaking down their tent for the third time. "I look around. It's pitch black well after 9 PM. It's a Tuesday in a sleepy beachside town in winter. There are dozens of vacant campsites all around us." Jay looks at the man and pleads his case. In frustration, he asks, "Are you expecting many more caravans to roll in tonight?"[11]

The man stares at Jay, then shrugs and walks away. Jay goes back into the tent and tells Lauren they can stay. Lauren's Instagram post sums up their night as "being relocated by individuals with good intentions."[12] Jay and Lauren pack up the next morning and continue. Biking is hard. Camping is hard. Jay and Lauren are suddenly together twenty-four seven with eight hours of biking a day, and then setting up camp and fixing food while carrying all their worldly belongings in panniers (oblong cloth carry bags) slung to the side of their bikes. Fifty or sixty pounds of gear on a bike makes cycling slow and arduous. Lauren's muscles aren't used to cycling, and her early Instagram posts celebrate the distance biked for the day.

Jay's coworker from HUD, Abby Miller, later commented in an interview, "I was very surprised to hear Lauren was going. She was quiet, kind, interested, but her energy was not off the board. She and Jay were very up and down in their relationship and my impression was he was not super into her at that time."[13] Neither Lauren nor Jay had trained for biking all day and adjusting to a very different diet. "We begin cooking food," Jay notes in his blog. "Basic things. Spaghetti typically. Our diet consists mainly of peanut butter sandwiches and bread, but sometimes we get a bag of chips. We drink plenty of water."[14]

Jay and Lauren's first week in South Africa didn't improve. The next two nights, they spent camping near a dam in the mountains. Lauren posts on Instagram a picture of their tent in a landscape that looks like the moon. Their orange and white tent stands out. Lauren's posts are more measured than Jay's. She notes they had been looking for a wild camping spot, but they found Africa has been fenced in. "Everything is locked away," Jay posts. "From Cape Town onwards there is the road and maybe three meters of rock on each side of it, and then there are fences tall and spiky . . . some evenings, we pedal for ten or twenty or thirty kilometers in frustration, just looking for a place to lay our heads."[15]

Jay's blog is more honest, and many of his posts don't involve Lauren.

> This is the point where I'm supposed to say that life on the road is glorious. That we're having the time of our lives, living free, relishing these moments. That I don't know why we didn't do this sooner . . . but things are hard. At times we're not really having much fun. I can only speak for myself, but we seem to share a disappointment about our first week on the road. I feel tired. Stretched thin. Rushed. I wake up with a feeling of dread, of pointlessness. I see little purpose in getting out of my sleeping bag just to be cold. I have little motivation to pack all my things into two overstuffed smelly bags, strap them to an assemblage of non-motorized transport and pedal further from the civilization I know with no real aim, no real destination.[16]

The fantasy of the trip around the world has fallen. There is no audience now except the disembodied feed of their blogs and Instagram posts. The rigor of wild camping is tough, uncomfortable, cold, hot, exhausting, and unsettling. Biking down the side of highways, rough dirt or sand roads, is hard. And being away from friends and family is tough. "We've climbed two passes, and no one cares," Jay writes. "We're bumping along dozens of kilometers on wash boarded road enroute to our third, and it doesn't really matter."[17] There are no high-fives or energy drinks. No audience to play to. There is only the ceaseless and mostly boring slow pace of loaded-down bikes that barely reach 10 miles an hour.

The trip didn't improve, and Jay wrote later that week, "We bicker. We say mean things to each other when the going gets tough. Our happiness and our connection feel inversely correlated to the grade of the road in front of us. Smiles turn downward as the road turns upward. There are sparks of joy, sure, but they feel like short bursts of light in a dark room."[18] They reach Loeriesfontein up in the Northern Cape and fill eight water bottles and an eight-liter water bladder. They load up with almonds with oatmeal and halva and instant noodles, and peanut butter and bread and spaghetti. Exhausted, stressed, doubting, barely getting along, Lauren and Jay are headed into the Great Karoo Desert. As Jay would later write, it is "a vast expanse of some of earth's driest, most desolate landscapes. And we've been warned not to underestimate the Karoo."[19]

Lauren and Jay are fighting. The biking and camping have been hard and tiring. One could not blame Lauren for wondering how she had gone from the bucolic enclave of Georgetown to a hot, dusty road in South Africa.

Notes

1. Ibid. South Africa, July 22, 2017.
2. Simplycycling.org, October 6, 2016.
3. Instagram Post Lauren Geoghegan, July 7, 2017.
4. Simplycycling.org, Cape Town, July 23, 2017.
5. Secura online article, Cycling in South Africa, www.secura.co.za>5 best safety tips for cycling in South Africa.
6. Ibid.
7. Ibid.
8. Ibid.
9. Ibid.
10. Ibid.
11. Ibid.
12. Instagram Post, Lauren Geoghegan, July 24, 2017.
13. Interview with Abby Miller by William Hazelgrove, April 30, 2024.
14. Simplycycling.org #3, South Africa, July 24, 2017.

15 Ibid.
16 Ibid.
17 Ibid.
18 Ibid.
19 Ibid., #4, July 30, 2017.

3
GEORGETOWN
2012

In 1745, George Gordon built a tobacco inspection house along the Potomac River. The tobacco trading post was nearby, and quickly wharves and warehouses sprung up, and the small community thrived as a port for shipment of goods. In 1751, Maryland purchased 60 acres from George Gordon and George Beall, and by 1752, the town survey was completed. Georgetown had arrived and was incorporated in 1789 by the Maryland legislature. In 1800, the capital of the United States moved from Philadelphia to Washington DC, and Georgetown became a municipal government within the District of Columbia. Ships sailing up the Potomac from the Atlantic Ocean could no further than Georgetown.

Washington's power brokers and elites settled in Georgetown, which became the unofficial residence of senators, presidents, and lobbyists. It is the crown of the powerband today that runs up along the East Coast from the feeder prep schools and then dropping off students at Yale, Princeton, and Harvard, and then picking them up again and dropping them in New York and Washington in places like the upper East Side or Georgetown.

Jay Austin graduated from the University of Delaware in just three years and was in the graduate program at Georgetown University. He was wonky and slight. Lauren was an undergraduate and was introduced to Jay through a mutual friend. There was no great bolt of lightning. He was five-six with close cropped hair, dark brown eyes, and getting his master's. Lauren had been at Georgetown for four years, and the minimalistic fast-talking graduate student intrigued her. "Lauren had a slow start with relationships,"[1] her childhood friend, Kendall O'Connor recalled. "She had fallen for this tall dark handsome Southern dude, very preppy, Georgetown dude, very different from Jay, but he regarded her as a friend. Jay was a unique wind that blew in. Not like anyone she had met before."[2] Molly Scalise, her roommate in Georgetown, paused when I asked her about Lauren before she met Jay:

> She liked fruity drinks, margaritas daiquiris, liked nice clothes, going out for drinks. We went to the Tombs, a basement bar Chaplains, Ethiopian restaurants. She had a huge social network and did some online dating on Tinder. She went on those dates but nobody serious, lot of doctors lawyers, lot of people in tech, consulting, lot of government people. When she met Jay . . . he was something different.

Georgetown University was a Jesuit college dating back to 1789 invoking the mission, as Molly Scalise put it, "to become a global citizen."[3] The Jesuits were members of the Society of Jesus and make a profession of "perpetual poverty, chastity, and obedience and promise a special obedience to the sovereign pontiffs . . . to accept orders to go anywhere in the world, even if required to live in extreme conditions."[4]

Lauren Geoghegan arrived in Georgetown in the fall of 2012 and loved the historic neighborhood founded in 1751 in Washington, DC, with its small restaurants and bohemian coffee houses. Majoring in government with minors in Spanish and Arabic, she met Molly Scalise and moved in with four other girls in a rangy apartment. Lauren flourished in the progressive atmosphere of Georgetown. "She had a bohemian style, we would go to happy hours, dancing, concerts, find poetry readings, long walks around the city," Molly recalled. "She was more spontaneous than me, she was an adventurer . . . and yet at the same time she loved to stay home and bake cookies."[5]

Lauren Geoghegan grew up in Glendale, California, a community that sits in the shadow of the Verdugo Mountains in the San Fernando Valley. The suburb is the fourth largest city in Los Angeles County with a population of 196,543. The mostly white enclave bordering Hollywood studios was once a Sundown City. In the 1960s, Blacks had to leave the city limits before dark or risk arrest or violence. The Civilian Conservation Corps in the 1930s was prevented from stationing African American workers in a local park, and, in 1964, for a time the American Nazi Party was stationed there. But the city changed along with the country, and for people like Kendall O'Connor, who grew up there down the street from the Geoghegans, it was Norman Rockwell middle-class haven.

"Lauren's parents didn't even get air conditioning until a few years ago," Kendall continued while carrying her computer to another room during our interview:

> They used fans. I mean her dad was a doctor, head of Psychiatry and her mom was able to stay home with the kids . . . she was a social worker in

psychiatry. But Glendale was this sleepy town at that time. Her parents had birthday parties in the backyard and every time the barbecue was hamburgers and hotdogs with a pinata and a big cake at the end.

Kendall lands at a table during our interview and adjusts the camera on her computer. She pulls back her hair. "We were the Jewish family on the street, but we were dragged along for the Christmas Caroling."[6]

Lauren attended Immaculate Heart Catholic girls' school and refused to take prep courses because this would be unfair to people who couldn't afford the courses. This goes along with the refusal to take the SAT for college because it was biased against minorities. She loved to travel, and traveling across the Mideast in college allowed her to perfect her Arabic. She studied abroad in Beirut, Egypt, and Jordan and then went to Damascus on a weekend trip. Coming back to a hostel with her girlfriend in Egypt, someone attacked her friend and Lauren fought him off.

Kendall paints a picture of Lauren's childhood with movie nights, Winchell Donut Saturdays, and weekly family meetings. High school was in the Hollywood Hills, where Tyra Bank and Megan Markle had attended. Lauren had a high school locker plastered with Hollywood heartthrobs Keith Ledger and Jonathan Taylor Thomas. She screamed first when she and Kendall had their ears pierced. Kids rode their bikes in the streets and walked from one house to another where every family was a family of three.

With two Ivy League degrees herself, leaning close to the screen in a farmer's bib over a striped shirt, Kendall reels off Lauren's accomplishments. "No one told us we had to do our homework, we were self-starters all the way."[7] Lauren showed a flair for drama in high school and was in theater and musicals. She was admitted to Georgetown University, and the two friends kept in contact. Kendall navigated advanced degrees and the American Teacher program, and Lauren left for Georgetown in Washington, DC. After moving to San Francisco and getting married, Kendall was hired for a teaching profession in Atlanta. "We wanted to live in California, but it was just too expensive, we couldn't afford the neighborhood that I had grown up in. So, we packed everything into POD containers and the only things we had left in our 650 square foot apartment was a futon and a suitcase."[8]

When Lauren went to work for Georgetown University admissions, it seemed like a natural fit. Kristen Robinson worked in admissions, and they went to see Senator Obama speak one night. Kristen now has children and still works for Georgetown University. She shakes her head, speaking in a measured tone:

> Seeing people at the height of their power was amazing. I know Lauren worked on the Hill for Senator Adam Schiff for a time. She was an incredible listener,

and we would have deep conversations. When she started in admissions she worked in the phone room answering hundreds of calls, then she started traveling around the country talking to applicants. She really wanted to get diverse students into Georgetown and had a gift of making you feel like you were the most important person in the world.[9]

Kristen paused. "Admissions can be grueling and after work we would go to *The Tunes* a local Georgetown undergraduate bar or go to a jazz club or to the mall for Fourth of July fireworks, shows at the Kennedy Center, the sculpture garden," Kristen smiles. "She was good at picking shows off the beaten path. We went to lots of Indian restaurants with her favorite drinks a vodka cranberry and whiskey sours."[10]

Jay and Lauren's paths kept crossing, and Lauren came to hear Jay's political views, his view of the environment, his dedication to minimalism. Jay interned in the Obama administration while she worked for Congressman Shiff. They started dating on and off. After graduation, Jay landed at HUD, while Lauren continued working in admissions at Georgetown. Nights began to blend together with wine, beer, and pizza around a fire pit outside Jay's new Tiny House.

They broke up several times over the next five years. One breakup was over Lauren putting students into loans that they could never pay back. "The breaking up was hard on Lauren," Kristen commented later and paused. "Lauren liked things, she liked food, and Jay had embraced this ascetic lifestyle and was into this minimalism thing. That wasn't Lauren at all. She loved clothes and had these beautiful Mexican clothes from her mother. She wanted to have a family with children." Kristen had reservations about Lauren's plan to quit her job and bike around the world. "I know she loved him." She paused. "But I knew it would be really challenging for Lauren."[11]

After starting at HUD, Jay began devoting his time to *The Homeless Children's Playtime Project*, where he became a "Play Ranger" and interacted with the kids. Jay was the only male volunteer, and after his death a book of testimonials was created. In every picture in the book, Jay is fully engaged with the homeless children, and his coworkers' tributes to him are inspiring. In 2013, he bought a Honda 250 scooter and decided to cross the country on a three-month trip. In a blog that would later become *The Scooter Diaries*, Jay recognizes the risks of going across the country on a small motorcycle. "I'm set to depart. And the truth is it is really really terrifying. More than 10,000 miles of battling awful drivers on cell phones and trying not to get run over I find myself most anxious about the simple act of not knowing where I am going."[12] Then he writes a farewell entry before leaving:

Friends, as I board my bike, start my engine, and drive down 395, across the 14th Street bridge and away from the District of Columbia—my home, my community, my family for these past four years—I want to take a moment to thank you. . . . I am the sum of the people I've met and these adventures have been made possible by caring and listening to my crazy schemes and philosophies with an honest ear and not a judgmental stare.[13]

Jay's ride was fraught with near accidents, getting lost in the Grand Canyon, nearly being drowned in a flash flood, and camping in the woods on freezing nights along the highways. But during his trip he discovers another world:

> I raced across the continent finding all sorts of things. I found canyons and buffalo and rivers you could still drink from and people who still drank from them. I found the sky was still beautiful on Tuesday afternoons and Friday mornings and that there was so much going on that I'd been missing while facing a glowing rectangle in the depths of a federal office building.[14]

His rides through the Adirondacks at night in freezing rain become a near-death experience.

> Gusts of wind, bouts of hail, splashes from cars speeding by, and my own chilled fatigue all conspired to knock me from my scooter, to lay me out along the highway as a warning to any other bikers naive enough to confront such a storm head-on. For hours, I gripped the handlebars, gripped them so tight I lost feeling in both arms.[15]

In one blog entry, Jay writes about not expecting to survive. "So many dangers physical dangers crammed into so short a time span and I was okay with that for I knew I'd rather live a life short and splendid than slow and stale."[16]

Stranded in Yellowstone National Park with a flat tire, Jay finally gets going again only to be chased by some wild bulls. It is during his trip he questions the ethos of traveling alone.

> Loneliness, maybe, was another factor that help set my brisk pace across the continent. Beyond a brief bout of angst in New Orleans, I never found traveling alone to be lonely; later, I'll discuss just how liberating I found it to be. But I would not doubt that somewhere, on the outskirts of my mind, I was running away from loneliness, confident that the sights and sensations of a new location would keep my mind too occupied to feel that stinging sadness, the sadness of not being able to share such remarkable experiences with another, a sadness that would, maybe, catch up with me after a day or two in the same spot, but not if I moved quickly, not if I always raced away from it just as it neared. I don't know if loneliness was truly a factor, for I never consciously caught it on.

By the time he reaches San Francisco, he is burned out and tired. "I felt angry, bitter, hopeless. I was still at least two thousand miles from home, and I had lost the stamina to go on."[17] Toward the end of the trip, Jay began to fantasize about his own death. "In stunning detail, I'd visualize myself weightlessly catapulting from Rousseau (his scooter) flying twenty feet forward in the air before hitting the ground and bouncing once, twice, eight times, then sliding into a ditch with forty-seven broken bones . . . the skin from my right torso, shredded along the asphalt, arm contorted beyond recognition." [18]

And then sixty days later, Jay arrived back home in DC. He sums up his trip covering 15,167 miles, 28 states, 3 provinces, 3 countries, and 29 national parks:

> I felt freedom I could never hope to describe, limitless liberation that awakened the adventurer, the child, the vagabond within me. I lost myself to the spirit of the traveler, I felt my very being subsumed by something greater. I was born anew and born better, a new self within me . . . perhaps some can live with subtle texture, a simple pattern, the routine and repeated shapes of a routine . . . but for me nothing but the brightest canvas will do, a screaming mess of passion and paint splatter, vivacious variety, every inch of my narrow dimensions covered with dirt and grime and blood and tears of well-worn life.[19]

It is on this trip that Jay develops a biking philosophy:

> Cycling through lands foreign or domestic is a sign of trust. I feel safe here and I thank you for safe passage. The cycle tourist makes herself vulnerable to all external threats, and at times must rely on not just the safety but the kindness of strangers, and this sends a very different message to the community than the noisy cars that rattle by, doors locked and windows rolled, leaving nothing but fumes and dust for the people to hold on to. In the saddle, there's time for a *salaam* for each and every individual. In the saddle, you move more slowly. You talk more and you learn more and you hear more and, importantly, you spend more: you stop for water and for snacks and for lodging far more often.[20]

Jay continues through Africa filling his blog with quotes from naturalists and philosophers, and then it's time to go home. "I'll miss this, the Atlas out my window, the tireless drumbeat percussing from the medina. . . . I'll miss that motion of the pedals, that work of instant reward, uninterrupted for hours. But I'll be going home, to a comfortable city of gentle familiarities and some welcome rest, home to friends I miss and a girl I love."[21]

With Lauren and Jay, biking became part of their life together. They rode all the fifty streets of Washington and took a cycling trip to Iceland, where they biked all over the country. Lauren adopted Jay's attitude toward biking to see the world. "Cars create the expectation that disaster can be averted, just trust the car," he wrote. "Bikes create the expectation that disaster is pretty much inevitable and should be embraced; just trust the universe and the people that inhabit it."[22] The month-long biking trip to Iceland is a warm-up for Jay and Lauren's trip around the world:

> It's only the first full day of twenty-six straight days traveling Iceland at the speed of tranquility, twenty-six straight days of camping under crisp, twilit skies. Between our arrival in Keflavik and our final few days of relaxation in Reykjavik, we'll have cycled well over a thousand kilometers across black deserts of volcanic ash, through glacier-chiseled fjords and desolate lava fields, past ice caps and milky blue lagoons, over little hills and great big mountains, under ominous rain clouds and fierce Arctic terns and blazing sunlight, down dazzling descents and rock-ridden gravel roads.[23]

Ferocious trucks on highways and fierce winds plague the trip in Iceland along with freezing nights in their tent, but the routine of biking all day and camping at night is established:

> We get up, slowly, and set about our still-fresh routine of deflating the sleeping pads, stuffing away the bags, disassembling the tent. We pack our panniers and load them onto our bicycles and push everything we have with us, which isn't much, really—up from the overgrown field onto the smooth road. . . . I heave the bike forward, step on the left pedal and begin rolling, throw my foot around to the right pedal and press down. We're off.[24]

They have wild camped in Iceland and dealt with severe headwinds and dangerous traffic. Jay crossed America on a scooter and biked Africa. In a final blog post about fear on their trip, he wrote: "Fear of the weather is well founded; fear of people is not. Coming from the states, we've perhaps never felt safer than we did in Iceland . . . outside of Reykjavik, petty theft or violent crime is virtually unheard of."[25]

At the end of twenty six days, Lauren and Jay return to Washington and feel they are ready for the trip of their lives. A biking trip around the world.

Notes

1. Kendall O'Connor Interview with William Hazelgrove, May 6, 2024.
2. Ibid.
3. Molly Scalise Interview by William Hazelgrove, March 12, 2024.
4. Vacher, Marguerite, Nuns Without Cloister, University Press, NY, 2010, 345.
5. Molly Scalise Interview by William Hazelgrove, March 12, 2024.
6. Kendall O'Connor Interview with William Hazelgrove, May 6, 2024.
7. Ibid.
8. Ibid.
9. Interview with Kristen Robinson by William Hazelgrove, April 12, 2024.
10. Ibid.
11. Interview with Kristen Robinson by William Hazelgrove, April 12, 2024.
12. Scooter Diaries undated.
13. Ibid.
14. Ibid.
15. Ibid.
16. Ibid.
17. Ibid.
18. Ibid.
19. Ibid.
20. Jay Austin Blog undated.
21. Ibid.
22. Simplycycling.org Reflections, November 17, 2016.
23. Simplycycling.org Iceland, January 25, 2017.
24. Ibid.
25. Ibid., October 27, 2016.

4
NAMIBIA

THE GREAT KAROO DESERT, JULY 2017

When Lauren and Jay were warned by the security guards about crime, racism might have motivated the warnings. But the postapartheid world of South Africa did have the highest crime rate in the world. From April 2017 to March 2018, 57 murders were committed each day in South Africa along with a reported 43,195 rapes. More importantly, there were 500 xenophobic attacks against foreigners between 1994 and 2018. Lauren had told her mother that New York was more dangerous than where they were biking, but no one was pitching a tent in the middle of New York.

Now they were biking through the Great Karoo Dessert. The Karoo was known as "an almost impenetrable barrier to the interior from Cape Town, and the early adventurers, explorers, hunters, and travelers on the way to the Highveld unanimously denounced it as a frightening place of great heat, great frosts, great floods, and great droughts." Today, it is still a place of great heat and frosts with low rainfall, heat, and cloudless skies the dominant features of the Karoo. Jay writes, "It's our fourth day here in the desert . . . up until when a few trucks came barreling by this afternoon, we hadn't *seen* another human in a day or two. There is profound emptiness all around us that's eerie but not altogether unenjoyable."[1]

Biking is an art best performed in perfect circumstances of low wind and low temperature, but the art of cycling is also adapting to the worst of circumstances. Heat. Heat brings fatigue. Muscles tire easily. Breathing is labored. Dehydration sets in quickly. Sunscreen becomes liquid and blinds the eyes with an agonizing sting. A cyclist puts their head down and pushes on thinking about their destination. The world becomes small then. Just a cycling computer that tells the cyclist, he or she is going nowhere fast. Six, seven, eight, ten miles an hour. The trick is to drink copious water as the sweat pours out. A cyclist wishes they were anywhere but where they are. You bike on because that is all you can do.

Lauren and Jay are now in the middle of the Great Karoo. "A vast expanse of some of earths driest most desolate landscape. . . . We've been warned not to underestimate the Karoo, nor the few roads daring enough to cut through it. Don't expect people . . . don't expect shops, nor guesthouses, nor cell service,"[2] Jay writes in a blog post. They have entered a gravel road that "is all flats and descents, yet it feels like pedaling uphill."[3]

The next day they pedal by a salt flat and camp along the side of the road. The Instagram photos are of a bleak, barren, sandy landscape. The sun beats down. Jay writes:

> We wake up in the same place most mornings under the familiar canopy of our tent. It's a predictable temperature, freezing. We lie in bed for a little while, talking . . . we usually skip breakfast. We get ready for the world outside, which involves dressing and packing a bag or two. We greet the day with a task to work toward, then we stop for the evening and make ourselves dinner and wash our dishes. If we're not too tired, we'll read a little before bed. It's a routine that grows familiar and its comforting in its simplicity.

Jay then quotes Cameau, "The master in the art of living makes little distinction between his work and his play, his labor and his leisure, his mind and his body, his education and his recreation, his love and his religions, he simply pursues his vision of excellence in whatever he does."[4]

Jay's next post on Instagram shows sunbaked land with Lauren sitting in the middle of the dirt road. "The Karoo was even more desolate than we anticipated, we went one twenty-four hour stretch without seeing another person or vehicle and another forty-eight hours without actually talking to anyone other than each other."

They carry seventy-seven pounds of water strapped to their bikes for the crossing. Loose sandy roads continually stop their bikes, and they are forced to walk to higher ground. Flies descend along with headwinds.

> Our muscles ache. Our lips chap. Our spirits, high the prior evening, begin to flag. After five or more hours of pedaling, we call it an early day. We've made it about thirty kilometers. We eye our rations closely. We'd packed more water and food than we thought we'd need, but if this headwind continues, we're woefully unprepared. We drink carefully and hope for easier pedaling in the days to come.[5]

Camping in the desert they "look up at the stars, spot satellites sailing along earth's orbit."[6] Lauren and Jay finally reach the town of Koes and realize Lauren has lost her phone. She had already lost her cycling gloves, and a pannier bounced off her bike. She posts on Instagram and admits the desert riding had been tough:

> My bicycle would sink into the deep sand and topple over. Weighed down by my gear and 12 liters of water plus food I had to use all my strength to right the bicycle and push it to better ground. At the end of our third day after eight hours of biking I realized that the 5 liter jug of water I was carrying on my bike rack had fallen off and I started experiencing ulnar nerve palsy in my right dominant hand then I lost my phone in (the town) Koes.[7]

In Koes, they go into a rowdy bar where men push shots on them and lecture about the advantages of Apartheid. Jay writes later:

> We're told in frank terms that apartheid wasn't so bad for the blacks and the Colored's of South Africa. There was free education, and free healthcare, and thus nothing to complain about, some in the group assert. A Bulgarian immigrant tells us that he considers himself more African than the Africans here, because it was his choice to live in this place . . . they're broadly crass and repulsive and cast a dirty sheen over the earlier lighter moments of the evening.[8]

A woman returns Lauren's phone and demands a five hundred Nambian dollar reward. They pay the woman. Lauren posts on Instagram,

> Saturday marked our first full month on the road since departing Cape Town . . . for many of these kilometers we've been alone biking and camping on quiet roads through vast open spaces. Our stay in Koes was the first time in 3.5 weeks that we had sustained conversations and interactions with other people here. I hadn't realized the extent to which my spirit was in need of quality connection.[9]

The local people insist Lauren use their landline to call her parents. Already the desolation of "quiet roads through vast open spaces"[10] is taking its toll. They leave Koes and pedal 160 kilometers to the next town. They take on steep hills, heat, and the flies, and Lauren falls ill.

Fifteen hours of illness in the tent begins as Jay records in his blog that night:

> It's been a hard day, and her stomach is in knots. In the early evening, she rushes out of the tent and vomits on the ground nearby. Her insides empty after the next few hours and that night, she curls into the fetal position and rests, eyes closed, fighting chills and nausea and fatigue. There is little we can

do at the moment. I give her some ibuprofen. Her symptoms don't call for Imodium or an antibiotic. Just water, which her body refuses to drink.[11]

The early signs of heat exhaustion are nausea and vomiting. The roads have been dirt and gravel with the weather very hot and dry. In an Instagram post on July 23, Lauren posts a picture of herself by the 117-kilometer mark. Her arms are raised in victory.

> Sometimes you can bike 100 km in a day and sometimes it takes three days to bike a 117 stretch. My experience was the latter with this road. It was really really difficult for me . . . the scenery was beautiful but there were also moments of *why am I doing this again?* And a few tears. I was happy to return to a sealed road at the 117km mark . . . we have more climbs and unpaved roads in our future. Onwards.[12]

They have been biking for just over two weeks. In the morning, Lauren feels better. As they are packing up their tent, a truck rolls up and a man gets out. "Oh, good morning, I was just curious who it was that was camping here on my land."[13] Jay looks at the man and then at the uncultivated empty land. Jay doesn't believe in the concept of private property and quotes the words of Jean Jacques Rousseau in his blog. "To establish the right of the first occupier over a plot of ground, the following conditions are necessary; first, the land must not yet be inhabited, secondly a man must only take the amount he needs for his subsistence and in the third place, possession must be taken, not by empty ceremony, but by labor and cultivation."[14] The man asked them to exit by the gate next to his house. Jay keeps his thoughts on private property to himself while filling up their water bottles at his house.

They pedal another 12 kilometers, and Lauren is still feeling weak. They find a campground, and Jay falls ill with an onset of nausea, chills, and fatigue. In his sleeping bag he feels like he is burning up and begins to shake. He stumbles out of the tent and to the toilets that are just "a bowl on a cement platform with a canvas roof and walls of bamboo reeds." Jay writes later, "I open the door, mind spinning and all strength leaving my legs. I collapse onto the cold concrete, lying my head on the smooth ground. I feel unable to move."[15] Jay spends most of the night lying on the cement pedestal by the toilet. The gastrointestinal issues go on for several days, and Lauren gets sick again.

They finally get better and pedal on. Besides wild camping, they stay with people found through sites called *couchsurfing* and *warmshowers*. Both sites offer lodging and food for wayward cyclers. *Warmshowers* have a database of 60,000 people who offer a bed and lodging. *Couchsurfing* is similar. A profile is filled out and then people can open their home to travelers. Lauren and Jay are staying with their first couchsurfing host:

We connect to the internet and message Desmond, who has kindly agreed to put us up for a night. He's the first Couchsurfing host on our route since basically Cape Town, and we're thrilled to have some human connection. . . . Desmond's still at work, he tells us, but his mother and nephew are home and we're welcome to head over and settle in. We meet Lidia, Vandro, and Rocky, their gargantuan canine, at the gate.[16]

Their hosts give Jay and Lauren a bedroom, and after some showers allow them to wash their clothes. "We stopped at the market before reaching the house and loaded up on heaps of groceries, so we offer to make dinner for Lidia, Vandro, and Desmond, who's on his way home. Desmond arrives to a pair of strangers huddled over his stove . . . the next morning, after expressing our gratitude to the family for a lovely, relaxing stay, we depart."

While staying with the family, Jay uploads blog posts he has been writing on the road.

"We've been on the road a little longer than a month and it's been a tough one . . . we've been challenged physically, mentally, and emotionally. We've put ourselves through more isolation, desolation, rough roads, hard days, arduous climbs and stubborn headwinds thane we bargained for . . . at times we've been bored, frustrated, hopeless." Then he extends the blog post with an explanation that will be quoted extensively in the media. "But this is why we're traveling. Not to cycle fast but to cycle slow. Not be given things but to be given hope, confirmation that the oft maligned batch of humans that occupy this planet are largely good and kind."[17]

The Simply Cycling blog will be attacked when it is quoted in the *New York Times*, NPR, and other media outlets. Many of the comments are so dripping with vitriol, they would have to be scrubbed from the site later. The argument if evil exists in the world, ignited online by their deaths in Tajikistan, begins here with a simple blog post. One of Jay's posts on his blog is written in the third person, describing their emergence from the desert from the viewpoint of three Namibian women. It is a rare view of how Jay perceives others see them:

Three Namibian women sit peacefully in the sparing midday shade of a gnarled acacia tree. They watch two figures bump along the rough road on matching bicycles. Their rims are covered in dust, tires sending pebbles flying. Their faces are red. Their shirts are streaked with the salty residue of sweat. Their heads are down . . . the cyclists are stuck in the sand, deep sand . . . they lean forward and gnash the pedals through the muck . . . a front tire lifts out of the sand, finally finding purchase on the terra firms of black tar. . . . The people under the tree watch the people on the bicycles cross from gravel to asphalt . . . from a month of arduous, self-inflicted slogging through the sand to a coming month of pleasant coasting along the bitumen."[18]

Lauren's Instagram post is a picture of their bikes on a dirt road. They are 7 miles from the border of Namibia. They make connections with *couchsurfing* and stay with Linda, who has recently retired and globe-trots from one house-sitting gig to another. "Several times per year she will snag a great housesitting gig somewhere in the world, grab an airline ticket for next to nothing to get there and spend a few weeks with a free place to stay."[19] They stay in the house with a pool for a week. Seventeen days camping in the desert and the bush, then sleeping in the lap of luxury, resets their mood and their bodies. They leave and say goodbye to Linda and her cocker spaniel that travels with her.

They are on paved roads in Namibia, and it brings back the joys of cycling. But it is 100 degrees on the road. "Gusts of hot air surge from the east, slowing our progress."[20] A scrap of metal lodges in Jay's rear tire and punctures the tube. Jay unloads his heavy panniers that carry their tent, sleeping, bags, food, water, clothes. He flips the bike over and starts to work.

> As I work, sweat drips from my forehead, shoulders and arms. Flies flock to them for water and salt. They land on my face, my lips, and nose. Sand sticks to everything and it's near impossible to keep the gritty soil away from the tire and the fresh tube. I'm frustrated and I handle the tire levers aggressively as I work to reseat the firm tube in the tire's walls.[21]

The hardest part is getting the tire back on the rim, and Jay punctures the tube with the plastic wedges. "A whoosh of air escapes from the new tube, now useless with a wide gash torn into its side."[22] Jay has to repeat the process all over again. Finally, they continue, but are stopped by four policemen at a foot-and-mouth stop to fight the spread of cattle-born disease. The policemen ask them where they are sleeping and warn of elephants and lions. They insist they sleep in the police compound checkpoint. Jay's front tire is losing air again, so they agree to stay in the compound.

Namibia has a stable parliamentary democracy, but poverty remains significant. Forty percent of the population live in multidimensional poverty, and 400,000 people lives in shacks, hovels, or informal housing. Income disparity is the highest in the world. The country's name comes from the Namib Desert, the oldest in the world. Nama translates to "vast place." Lauren and Jay are thankful to be on a paved Nambian highway but there is danger. Biking deaths in America have been on the rise for the last decade. In 1977, bike deaths had fallen from a high of 1,000 in 1975 to about 950. A low of 640 was reached in 2003, but then started to climb in 2010 and are almost now back to 1,000 a year. I have had my own near misses over the twenty years I have biked. I have fallen in front of cars, trucks, and even a motorized crane. In 2024, biking became politicized along with everything else. The assumption is a biker is urban and takes up valuable space on a two-lane highway. I have been flipped off, yelled at, and pushed off the road by cars and trucks that have come so close that their mirrors nick my shoulder. The favorite trick of truckers is to blast sooty exhaust as they pass. A famous architect from Chicago, Helmut Jahn, was killed in 2021 on the route that I take every day. He crossed into a two lane and apparently didn't see the cars and was instantly killed.

So biking with cars is a known risk. The trick is to ride as far to the side of the painted highway borderline as possible. In the digital age with people texting, talking, responding to emails, watching favorite shows while driving, a cyclist needs to hear what is coming. But the worst is when someone attempts to pass and suddenly a two-ton armored missile is barreling down on the cyclist. Unfortunately, road rage for bikers has also become a phenomenon. I saw a man jump out of a car after a cyclist yelled at him. The man stopped his car in the middle of the highway and ran toward the older cyclist and threatened him.

When Lauren and Jay returned to paved highways after traveling on gravel roads for a thousand kilometers, their experience was marred by the people zooming by at 100 kilometers an hour. After several near misses, a driver attempts to pass and darts into their lane. "We're hardly ten kilometers into our ride when a white sedan emerges from behind a large oncoming truck," Jay writes.

The sedan pulls into our lane, aiming to pass the truck. We are in this lane so at the moment a passing maneuver is not possible. We assume the driver in the white sedan recognizes this, but apparently, he does not. He picks up speed roaring toward us. With no shoulder to bail onto, we swung into the far left of the lane at the last moment. He races on, very narrowly missing us. He beeps his horn. The trucker blares his horn in return. We shout profanities, but of course he doesn't hear us.

It is a near miss for Jay and Lauren, but there will be more. The unexpected has always been the biggest danger in cycling.

Notes

1   Simplycycling.org #4 Loeriesfontein, July 30, 2017.
2   Ibid.
3   Ibid.
4   Ibid.

5   Ibid.
6   Ibid.
7   Lauren Geoghegan Instagram, August 13, 2017.
8   Simplycycling.org #6 Namibia Gochas, August 20, 2017.
9   Instagram Lauren Geoghegan, August 16, 2017.
10 Ibid.
11 Simplycycling.org #6 Koes, August 20, 2017.
12 Instagram Lauren Geoghegan, July 23, 2017.
13 Simplycycling.org #6 Koes, August 20, 2017.
14 Ibid.
15 Ibid.
16 Simplycycling.org #7, September 4, 2017.
17 Ibid.
18 Ibid.
19 Simplycycling.org #8, September 22, 2017.
20 Ibid.
21 Ibid.
22 Ibid.

5
MILES FROM NOWHERE

1977

Forty years before Jay and Lauren decided to bike around the world, another couple did the same thing. In 1977, Larry and Barb Savage quit their jobs to bike around the world on a two-year journey on heavy Schwinn bikes. It began during a conversation over dinner one night, that easily could have been Jay and Lauren, when Larry turned to Barb:

> Ever notice how often people say, "I wish I'd done something really exciting and challenging when I was younger, because now I'm too old and don't have much to look back on?" . . . Well, pretty soon we're going to have enough money to make a down payment on a house. But once we do that we'll be tied down to the monthly payments. And then again, if we don't buy but instead spend our money on something else, like traveling, we might find ourselves priced out of the market by the time we return.

Barb nodded and Larry went on:

> But on the other hand, we're both in good physical shape right now, and who knows what'll happen in the next ten years. One of us might get injured, and then we wouldn't be able to bicycle across America like you've been talking about lately. And as for seeing the rest of the world, the way things are going, who knows how much of it will still be around years from now.

It did not go well with bear attacks, storms, road rage incidents, and near-death accidents. But their motivation was much the same as Jay and Lauren. Barb Savage later wrote in her book:

I'd developed the traditional welfare worker burnout syndrome losing my ability to cope or care about the mountains of paperwork and reams of every changing government regulation. Larry felt walled in, sitting at a desk every day designing and redesigning computers. Were we to spend the bulk of our lives toiling at unfulfilling jobs inside sterile office buildings we wondered.

The computer programmer and the social worker felt it was time to go on their trip while they were young. They went through the same preparation as Jay and Lauren:

As the last few months before our departure crept up on us there were passports to renew, money to be deposited in a bank account in our names and my parents' names (so they could wire us funds throughout the trip), travelers' checks to buy, and shots to flinch under. When we explained our plans to the nurse at the immunization center in Santa Barbara, she pulled out handfuls of tiny bottles of liquid for typhoid, typhus, tetanus, diphtheria, and smallpox shots.

On May 15, 1978, they packed their panniers to the brim but would eventually scale down to a "a couple of pairs of shorts, a few T shirts, one pair of long pants, a sweat shirt, rain jacket, down jacket, some socks and underwear." Not the Jay Austin list of electronics and high-tech biking gear. They caught a train north to Saun Luis Obiso, a city 100 miles north of Santa Barbara with a plan to bike across the United States first. Cold driving rain for the first five days of their trip soaked their "sweat shirts, shorts, wool knee socks and rain jackets." They spent miserable cold nights in their small tent and quickly ran out of food. Larry found a store and stocked up with "a two days supply of peanut butter, two loaves of bread, and oranges for lunches and snacks . . . macaroni and cheese, six eggs and a box of granola for breakfast."

During another storm with rain so fierce and cold they could barely steer down a small two-lane highway, they were confronted with a bear. Barbara later wrote in her book, "I heard a faint rustling sound, I turned my head to the right toward the shoulder of the road where I thought the noise came from and there thirty feet away and charging straight for us, was a gigantic black bear." Barbara screamed, and the bear reversed itself and disappeared into the woods. In Idaho, while going to a creek to bathe in, "a sudden noise at my feet halted me. . . . I knew it was a rattlesnake." Barbara ran back to the road and all the way to camp. In Florida, the couple almost dies on a bridge when caught between two dump trucks and a Winnebago RV. The bikes Larry and Barbara are on are Schwinn ten-speed bikes, not built for the loaded-down panniers they have clamped the frame front and back. On the bridge of dump trucks, Barbara and Larry navigate among the trucks until they become trapped.

"On one of the bridges, two of the trucks bore down on us from the rear, one behind the other, while a big RV approached from the opposite direction." At the last minute, the dump truck tried to pass Barbara and Larry by pulling into the oncoming lane. The truck driver had calculated wrong and pulled alongside Barbara but realized he had to swing back into her lane or hit the RV.

> As he came up beside me I was watching the Winnebago. . . . The rumbling of two dump trucks, one beside me and one behind me was deafening. I felt my knees and feet start to go weak then they began shaking so much I could hardly push my pedals. I sucked in a deep breath . . . as I first glimpsed it out of the corner of my left eye, the dump truck turned into me. I hit my brakes and watched in horror as eight tons of steel dove into the space I would have been occupying.

Larry and Barb were forced off the bridge and into the sand, where they both flipped over their handlebars. Barb's writing style veers between slapstick and a mellow sort of do-your-own-thing. Though the laid-back 1970s is betrayed in a road rage incident that followed the near accident with the dump trucks. Even the road rage seems a bit like a bad sitcom. Larry is bumped off the road by a driver who strikes his left rear pannier in Florida. With jagged gashes in his right arm and thigh, Larry sees a van pull over. The driver jumps out.

"Hey. I'm the guy you shook your fist at on the last bridge back down the road," he shouted.

"Oh so you're the idiot who nearly killed us back there," Larry shot back. "Haven't you noticed the no passing signs in front of the all the bridges."

A very civil debate then rages on the side of the road with 1970s biking attitudes on display.

> Don't go telling me how to drive. You bikers are so egotistical, you expect all the cars and trucks on the road to bow to you. Well roads are for cars. Cars have the right of way at all times and you bikers should get off the road whenever us drivers need room.

This is not a blog but a book written months, if not years, after the face-to-face. The dialogue is strangely melodramatic. One cannot blame Barb for filling in the blanks before the digital age allowed real-time transcription. Finally, the debate club winds down as Larry takes it up a notch:

> So what did you want us to do back there? Get off the bridge? Which means jump into the ocean so you could pass illegally without bothering about us!"

Larry hollers into the mans face. But no sooner had the words left Larrys lips than the man threw his fist into the side of Larrys head and sent him reeling back on to the ground next to his crashed bicycle.

When a sheriff stops, all is forgiven and Barb and Larry pedal on. The incident is suspect, but it is also of its time. No one is packing. No one is pressing charges and later suing for damages. In Morocco, they are attacked by a crowd of teenage boys who want cigarettes and then grab whatever they can. In Spain, after leaving the town of Rota, they bike for three hours battling the wind. Spain, they find, is littered with trash and garbage and the streams are polluted. The world is just beginning to discover the word "pollution." When they pull off the road to eat lunch, a fight breaks out.

> The next thing we knew, the two of us were standing beside our bikes screaming about being sick of traveling, sick of the trash and dirt, sick of the Spaniards whistling at me and sick of each other. "When I get to Sevilla, I'm flying home! I've had it! I'm through! The end! I'm going home!" I shouted. "And I never want to see you again, ever."
>
> "Fine. The feelings mutual. We're through!"

In his anger, Larry grabbed up "my bike" and tossed it into a ditch. Again one can excuse Barb for the bad movie script. This is a time when the romcom *The Goodbye Girl* was in the theaters, and Barb is relying on memory. Barb takes off in a fit of rage but Larry follows, and they reconcile. They end up in their sleeping bags that night, and all is forgiven. But just when the book seems to be a hopeless rendition of the world, before Madonna but after the Beatles, a through line develops and Lauren is suddenly there.

Barb's parents fly into Spain and spend time with the couple. When they leave, Barb is gripped by a feeling she didn't want. "Larry and I said goodbye to Mom and Dad. We wouldn't see them again until we returned home to California sometime next year and that moment seemed very far away right then." Lauren Geoghegan's parents would visit Lauren and Jay in Kyrgyzstan for seven days, where her mother had a premonition about Lauren continuing on to Tajikistan.

When Barb sees her parents off on June 23, 1979, a second feeling swept over her. "A strange sensation grabbed me as I watched my parents move through the airport; I was worried that maybe I might never again lay eyes on Dad's shiny bald head or Mom's tiny five foot frame." During an interview, Lauren's childhood friend Kendall later told me, "When Lauren decided to go on this trip, I was most concerned about how worried her mother was going to be . . . she had a very ominous feeling."

Barb in her book *Miles from Nowhere* ruminates on the eerie feeling she had watching her parents leave. "The old worries were coming back now, being struck and killed by an automobile, murdered by bandits, bit by a poisonous snake, or stricken by some incurable fatal disease . . . as I watched them disappear into the jet, I wondered if I would ever see them again, and I felt very alone."

Larry and Barb continue on to Egypt, where Muslims yelled, "We love Jimmy Carter." Then Larry and Barb are hit by a truck and survive. In Nepal and Bangkok, another fight breaks out as Barb want to return home. Larry is given the stage this time. "All you talked about was how being sick made you tired of traveling and want to go home. I'm sick of traveling with you anyway. I have it. This is it! We're through traveling together so lets split up the money right now . . . and I'm going on by myself." They reconciled and went on to India, where Barb had severe dysentery but made it through the rest of the trip, returning home on April 19, 1980. They had been gone just one month short of two years.

When they returned, Barb wrote a book, *Miles from Nowhere*, detailing their journey. It is doubtful Jay or Lauren knew of the social worker and computer programmer who veered to embrace a life of adventure in 1977 If they had read Barb's book, they might have recognized an earlier version of themselves. *Miles from Nowhere* would become a classic of adventure literature. A week before publication in 1983, Barb Savage was struck by a car and killed while she was cycling close to her home, in California. She died on July 17, 1983, shortly before the publication of *Miles from Nowhere*, a tragedy that would be mirrored forty years later by another couple cycling around the world.

6
BOTSWANA

AUGUST 2017

Jay and Lauren ride on into Botswana, which proves to be flat, arid, wild, and hot. The Kalahari Desert makes up 70 percent of the country, and drought is a constant problem. Botswana was ranked in 2023 as a flawed democracy. Homosexualism was outlawed up until 2019. Diamond mines provide 40 percent of all government revenues. Lauren and Jay park their bikes at the border and post a selfie that will be emblematic of their trip and picked up by the media. Their heads are together in front of the Botswana border sign. Jay has on a baseball cap, and Lauren is wearing her glasses. Jay has a stubble of a beard, and they look like two people who just biked a desert and a treacherous highway, but their smiles say they are doing it. Yes, we are.

There are no fences in Botswana, and animals wander and cross the road. But there is something else. Rotting carcasses line the side of the road:

> A horses skeleton picked clean. A pile of bones; skull, ribs, femurs. Husks of flesh and hair baked to leather under the unrelenting sun. A commotion of vultures swarming the roadside ahead, they scatter, the smell of putrefied meat, the smell of death . . . birds, dead hornbills, dead owls . . . dead jackals, dead donkeys, dead lizards. The rusted still of an old car, upturned and left to rot. The landscape speaks of desolation.[1]

They camp on the side of the road the first night in Botswana and make dinner in the Kalahari Desert. Jay posts on Instagram:

> Cooking in the desert can be tough. First you need to find a place to light a stove amidst endless fields of super-dry, super-flammable grasses. Then you need to make something that requires almost no water to cook and

creates almost no mess to be cleaned. That food, of course, must keep well in a black, vinyl pannier jostling in the sun for days on end. Ideally, you also manage to have everything cooked, eaten, and cleaned within that one magic hour of the afternoon where it's still light out but not blazing hot. Our staples to date include boiled potatoes, powdered soup, instant noodles, oatmeal, and when times are particularly dire, peanut butter sandwiches. We have not had very good luck with spaghetti.[2]

They are woken when a herd of cattle surround their tent in the middle of the night. Jay writes, "A stocky bull with big horns approaches. I shout for them to keep moving."[3] The bull is just a few meters away. Jay has read somewhere that sound is your best weapon with wild animals. He claps loudly. *We mean you no trouble*; the bull turns away with a huff and the others follow. Jay returns to the tent. Planning. Execution. Solve the problem. All his life Jay Austin has been the man who plans.

A few days later, after biking the highways of Botswana, he posts on his blog:

I can't really say enough great things about the people of Botswana. As we enter elephant/lion country, bush camping becomes more dangerous, and as we continue to get beaten down by 95F+ temperatures and violent headwinds, they've gone out of their way to keep us safe and encouraged. They've kept us apprised of recent elephant sightings on the road ahead, stopped their cars to offer us ice water, invited us to pitch camp in a fenced-off police compound, and allowed us to grab some shade, sleep, and shelter, free of charge.[4]

The next day they stopped at a gas station to refill water bottles. Some men outside the station ask Jay where they are headed. They ask him where they are from. They ask how long they have been biking. Jay answers all their questions. Jay's mother in an interview six years later would lament not making her son more wary of the world. In less than a year, on the last day of his life, a man will approach Jay at a gas station and ask the same questions. His mother wished he had not answered any of them.

The next day Jay and Lauren come across a herd of elephants. An elephant's brain weighs twelve pounds and has as many neurons as the human brain. They mourn their dead, take revenge on animals and humans, and understand complex subsonic rumblings from other elephants miles away. Elephants have been known to gore, crush, snap the backbones of their handlers. Trophy hunting of elephants is outlawed in the Nxai Pan National Park, but cyclists like Lauren and Jay can see the massive creatures up close.

BOTSWANA

In the town of Greta, they stay at a campground and buy a two-liter bottle of Coke and a bag of flavored maize snacks. In long-distance cycling, the body has been depleted of carbohydrates. Cereal. Bread. Chips. Pasta. Peanut butter. Burgers. Fries. The sugar of the Coke is like crack to the addict and makes lowered glucose levels crave more. The salt and carbohydrate load of the Flavor Maize Snack starts a cycle of one handful followed by another. Jay writes in his blog later:

> We suddenly filled our bodies with substances that could hardly be called food. By the time I walk from the pool to the tent I'm stumbling. My limbs feel weak, head heavy, sweat suddenly coating my skin. . . . I lie on the tent floor and begin eating everything within my reach. I make a bowl of cold oats and shove it into my mouth. I eat slices of plan bread. I have a half sleeve of Oreos I'd been saving for the ride tomorrow. . . . Lauren arrives in a similar condition. Lacking the energy to blow up her sleeping pad, she rests on the hard ground . . . we arrive at a consensus, blame the Flavored Maize Snack.[5]

They pitch their tent in a campground called Elephant Sands. When Jay goes to pay the fee for two nights, the owner asks him if he is one of the cyclists. He says he is. "Well then, you don't owe us anything. We think what you guys are doing is crazy and awesome and we won't accept your money." Jay writes in his blog later, "Biking around the world is like getting smacked in the face with the sheer force of human generosity and we're just getting used to people doing wonderful things for us as we travel."[6]

The next day they bike down the road and are confronted with a bull elephant eating leaves on the side of the road. Jay and Lauren stop to discuss their options. They could wait for a vehicle and ask the driver to act as a shield as they pass the elephant. The second option is to pass the elephant as fast as possible. A charging elephant can run 25 miles an hour. Biking speeds on thin-wheel road bikes under ideal conditions range in the 20 to 40 miles per hour range. The hybrid design of Jay and Lauren's bikes with fat knobby tires are built for endurance, strength, but not speed. The bikes are loaded down and are on a sandy road. Ten miles an hour is generous under these conditions.

They wait in the dusty 95-degree heat. Gusts of dry wind sting their eyes. A big truck coming toward them settles the issue. They would use the truck to block the elephant when they pass by. Jay and Lauren start pedaling their loaded-down bikes. The hardest part of biking is just getting going. Once you get started, then the cadence or the rate of pedaling is everything. Cadence builds upon itself. The faster a bike goes, the faster is the rate of cadence. Jay and Lauren's cadence is slow to start. By the time they reach the elephant, the truck has passed by, but they are committed.

"I eye the elephant in my periphery, watching us. It is no longer chewing. We pedal quickly. Don't make eye contact. . . . Don't look!" Jay writes in his blog. "The elephant seems distressed. It is having a fit, twisting its head back and forth and flapping its ears. I pedal faster." The elephant shakes his head, then bolts from the tree and begins a loping gate toward Jay and Lauren. They both look back in horror and realize the 10,000-pound creature is chasing them. Jay turns around again. "He is moving! He is running! He is charging toward us!" "Go! Go!"[7] Lauren's eyes widen as she pushes down her pedals, but the loaded bikes fight against speed. The elephant is charging down the roadside in a dusty gallop and closes the gap to 100 meters.

An elephant can gallop 25 miles an hour. Jay and Lauren can't even go 10 miles an hour. Jay knows what they are up against. "On our loaded bicycles pedaling into a headwind, we do about twenty kilometers at best." The elephant gallops full speed toward the two creatures on flashing metal as they pedal frantically. Fear-induced adrenaline gives extra speed, but it is not enough. "We have a head start though it is dwindling quickly," Jay writes. "The road is empty, just two small humans on leg powered steel triangles and one very large, very fast, very mean elephant rushing after them."

They can hear the thundering of the elephant now who means to crush them. Thoughts of abandoning the bikes and running flit through their minds. The slow bikes are no match for the raging creature coming ever closer. Jay pedals harder and harder, keeping himself between Lauren and the elephant. He looks back again, and the distance has suddenly grown. Mercifully, the elephant is slowing down. He slowly stops, dust kicking up all around, then heads back toward the tree. Jay writes later. "If this elephant had decided we were worth his time a few seconds earlier he certainly would have caught us and mauled us already." While slightly comic, Lauren and Jay were lucky to get away. Later, when they pulled up to a gas station and told the proprietor about their harrowing chase, he nodded slowly. "He most certainly would have killed you."[8] He then tells them that a Chinese tourist was killed the day before by an elephant.

They refill their water bottles and pedal on in the ninety-five-plus heat. That night they camp in an elephant-proof courtyard. An Instagram post later on sums up where they stayed in Botswana:

1. The elephant proof courtyard of a police station on the Botswana Zambia border, 2 the front yard of a gas station 3 Underneath a remote cell tower with the two lovely folks who keep it running. 4 at a marvelous campground visited by dozens of wild elephants 5 the home of a man and his family who offered us dinner, warm baths, and a spare room after knowing us for all of thirty seconds.[9]

Jay posts again on Instagram on August 27, 2017, "The roads are gorgeously smooth . . . there are also fewer fences so camping in the bush is much easier."[10] They pedal on to get to Zambia before Lauren's birthday. There are no more elephants. Just dead carcasses along the side of the highway. The cars continue to zoom by dangerously close "They blare their horns and speed past us at 120 kilometers per hour," Jay writes in his blog. "They swerve around us recklessly and push us back into the shoulder." He puts a red plastic bag on a stick to keep the cars away, but a truck "nearly runs me over and catches the edge of the stick. It snaps off and flies ten meters down the highway."[11]

Notes

1. Ibid.
2. Instagram Jay Austin, August 17, 2017.
3. Simplycycling.org #7, September 4, 2017.
4. Instagram Jay Austin, September 12, 2017.
5. Ibid.
6. Simplycycling.org, #9, October 2, 2017.
7. Ibid.
8. Ibid.
9. Ibid.
10. Jay Austin Instagram, August 27, 2017.
11. Simplycycling.org #9, October 2, 2017.

7
THE UNDER FIVE GANG
2015

Jay Austin was born in Brooklyn, New York. He would later claim to be a New Yorker, citing it in his blog, but he only spent two years in Brooklyn before moving to an upper-middle-class neighborhood 60 miles from New York, Manalapan, New Jersey. Jay was smart enough where he never had to do homework. He was not good at sports but his mother, Jea, took him to the library frequently where he would take out the limit, nine books. He was only seven when a contentious divorce split the famiy. The problems in the marriage had surfaced early. Jay and his sister, Jude, would take refuge in each other and would talk long into the night. Hours after going to bed, they arranged their blankets and pillows in the doorway so they could sleep next to each other. In an email, Jude wrote, "I remember Jay always going above and beyond. He would come home from elementary school with a large stack of books after challenging his classmates that he could read the most pages over the holidays."[1] Jude later changed her name and moved to a commune where she lived in a converted bus. Her partner converted the bus into a rolling home. There are articles showcasing the bus converted into a very livable rolling tiny house. The articles and websites harken to the hippies of the late 1960s, people working together in tandem with the land away from the bourgeois world. The pictures on the website detailing life in the commune show an outdoorsy couple who seem to have found nirvana. Jude's quotes sound like they could have come from Jay Austin: "What we found was a place that allowed us to learn and grow in whatever ways we chose, to develop meaningful connections with the land and the people that we share our lives with and to be a part of something greater than ourselves."[2]

Jay's worldview was rooted in Manalapan, New Jersey, where after the divorce he endured an economically challenged childhood in an upper-middle-class enclave. The commuter town of swimming pools and white-collar workers was the world he peered into from a keyhole in his modest home. His mother Jea Santovasco later said, "We did all the free things, went to park and museums and I showed them how to appreciate nature." Jea had to take work as a secretary but managed to take her kids to beaches, art exhibits, and apple orchards on her off days. On nice days, the family liked to climb to the top of a hill at a nearby park and spread out a picnic lunch. "You don't get happiness from money," Jea told her son. "You get it from being outdoors and appreciating the sunrises." One day Jay showed his mother his whole plan for his life written down in a notebook. After Jay had gone to work for HUD, his mother remarked, "He told me he was able to bowl in the basement of the White House. He really got a kick out of that. But he had it all planned out as a little boy, he showed me on paper how he was going to live his life and did it . . . he was driven even as a little boy."

His sister Judes memories of Jay are of a sister who admires her older brother. Smart. Precocious. She recounts when Jay taped the periodic table of elements up above his bed to memorize just for fun: "When given the opportunity to choose a bonus word for weekly spelling tests in elementary school, he would always choose the longest word he could find in the dictionary (while most kids would choose something easy)."[3] She points to Jay's Tiny House "the Matchbox" as the inspiration for living in the school bus with her partner in the commune. The parallels between Jay and Jude are uncanny. Both changed their names. Both eschewed a traditional life for a life off the grid. Jude chose to live in a commune far away from the vagaries of the suburb her family struggled to survive in. Jay chose to pursue a minimalist lifestyle, quit his Washington job, and bike around the world. In unpublished blog posts in Jay's phone returned to Jude by the FBI, two years after the attack, Jay wrote:

> So, this is the big adventure . . . this is one person's feeble attempt to live a life so absolutely free that my very existence is an act of rebellion. It's an attempt to carry myself, and a tent and a stove and a few other things, across the world, and to rely on the kindness of others, and to provide kindness to others, along the way. To travel not as a means, but as an end. To test this hypothesis of happiness in simplicity, to tie together everything I've learned within and between each adventure of my scattered, searching little life. The practicalities are more mundane, sure. There's nothing extraordinary about this adventure. Others have done it before, and many will do it after. It's something that will neither save the world nor bring an end to man's ever-oppressed and ever-oppressive nature. It's just the very first time where I feel I'll be doing exactly what I want to do exactly how I want to do it, to live a life unapologetically on my terms.[4]

THE UNDER FIVE GANG

As a boy Jay talked of becoming an astronaut. After Jay went to work at the Department of Housing and Urban Development (HUD) he began to question his education, his work, and the basic ethos of American life. He later wrote:

> I never did become an astronaut. I went to college to learn Liberal Arts. I went to graduate school to learn more about those Liberal Arts. It wasn't all that liberating learning about the arts. It came with tens of thousands of dollars of debt. My diploma and my first student loan bill arrived in the mail on the very same day.[5]

Jay had been at HUD less than five years along with Jenn Cribbs, an erudite woman with a continuous smile. She is now an organizational transformation consultant who lives in Brooklyn. "We were known as the *under-five gang* We weren't just there to be bureaucrats but to make the world a better place and Jay could do in weeks what other people took months," she explained. "He was going two hundred and forty miles an hour and he didn't see obstacles only solutions."[6] When standing desks became an issue, Jay furnished reams of research showing the benefits of standing desks:

> His whole thing was I am here because of a mission, and you are going to stand in my way because of a desk? I would get emails at 3 AM from Jay and they told him to quit working at night and his response was, I'm not billing anyone so if I want to work at night I will work at night. Jay didn't care about a fight; he didn't care about the temperature in the room. He came out swinging. Everything was mission driven with him at HUD and his mission was to change the world.[7]

Jenn is leaning back on her couch. There is a quality of wonder when she talks of Jay during his time at HUD. "There was a push to hire people who understood what Obama was doing in Chicago. Jay always came in shorts. Never wore a suit and the higher ups at HUD just accepted it the way they accepted his sabbaticals, working from home, everything. Because he was that good."[8] On April 21, 2015, an article appeared in *The Washington Post* about a twenty-five-year-old named Jay Austin, who had just come to work for the Department of Housing and Urban Development. Jay is looking at the camera with a well-clipped beard and short, receding brown hair. His custom powder-blue open shirt and Dior dark blue sport coat speak of a new type of bureaucrat, younger, progressive, the new millennial man. The headline, *Jay Austin Leading the way toward government innovation and transparency, one vote at a time,*"[9] paints Jay as bringing HUD into the twenty-first century.

"After Austin arrived in 2010, he started transforming the internal feedback tool into an agency wide idea board open to all."[10] The bearded millennial, all of twenty-three, was bringing innovation and light into the dusty Department of Housing and Urban Development. The laudatory article also paints Jay as a man of the streets. "Austin grew up in a pretty poor neighborhood and spent most of his years in foster care. It made him realize that 'not all spaces were created equal and that some were better than others.' I came to HUD hoping do my small part to correct that inequality—to create safe sustainable spaces for anyone who needs one."[11]

HIs mother Jea would later deny Jay was ever in foster care. Abby Miller, who also worked with Jay at HUD during this time and now works for a nonprofit, recalled, "When Jay arrived you talked to him five minutes and you understood he was very smart on several layers."[12] One of his first ideas was *Switchboard*, a website for people to weigh in on the agency's five-year strategic plan. But Jay transformed it into a feedback tool open to all. He is quoted in the article. "Anyone can submit an idea," said Austin, program manager in HUDS Office of Strategic Planning and Management and the main "Switchboard, operator." Jay was quoted again, saying, "we wanted to create something that allowed us to sell Switchboard as a connection to government. The idea that you can plug in and pitch ideas and concerns directly to HUD employees and leadership was important to us."[13] Jay followed this up with, "Government should be transparent, open and at all times reachable . . . that's what Switchboard aims to do."[14]

Jay took on parental leave polices as well. "If he saw there was a better solution then he drove for it," Abby continued. "He was the unstoppable force, and he would just blast people out of the way."[15] In the article, Jay is acknowledged as leader of the Switchboard movement, where if an idea gets more than 200 votes, it goes to HUD's deputy secretary. If it passes muster, Jay turns it into reality, working "on communications, branding, outreach and logistics." It's a lot of collecting people in a room, explaining what and who we need, and making it happen, "said Austin whose online signature is Jay."[16]

Switchboard continued to evolve at HUD, and Jay noticed people asking for help with foreclosures or getting housing. Jay added a new HUD service. "There are people in immediate need, and we really didn't have an effective way to deal with that." He added a ticketing function that made sure each request was responded to within forty-eight hours. "We're trying to give HUD a human face and voice."[17] Meanwhile Jay recreated his own job. The jacket and tie were no longer seen. He began coming to work all the time in shorts and a T-shirt. He wore sandals. He had a standing desk. He rode his bike to work every day and opted to work at home. He suggested HUD subsidize bike share memberships for employees to promote healthy commuting. He began taking extended vacations for his trips to Europe and Africa. He thrived as the renegade, and his supervisors loved him.

"He's a good agitator and does a great job stirring the pot," Henry Hensley, director of the Office of Strategic Planning and Management said in the article.

Jay is then quoted, "I came to HUD hoping to do my small part to correct that inequality—to create safe, sustainable spaces for anyone who needs one."[18] Abby Miller, in our interview, shook her head and smirked. "Jay tussled with the union at HUD. One time the president of the union came to his desk, and they got into a bad verbal altercation and Jay shouted at him, *you are nothing but a petty fucking tyrant!*" She paused. "The rage came when people told him no. He came into my office after the confrontation with the union and he was shaking he was so mad."[19]

When I asked about the trip around the world, Miller shook her head. "That was Jay. He was a romantic. I think it was stupid to go into Tajikistan, but Jay saw no boundaries."[20] At HUD, Jay continued pushing boundaries by taking more and longer vacations, refusing to play the game in any way. "He had agency after he had been at HUD a few years and the moment he could have a predictable life he didn't want a predictable life," Jenn Cribbs recalled.

So, he went off on a scooter trip across the country. I think Jay liked who he was on those trips more and more and I think that was why he changed his name. I think his attitude was my name was given to me. I want a name I choose, and that old name belonged to something that had nothing to do with him.

Jenn paused.

I think these risky trips is one way Jay survived . . . he was used to danger, so for him doing dangerous things was no big deal. Also, something happens to us in nature, something opens up and I think he was addicted to that, something like the eternal. So, if you can afford the nice thing, like going on a trip, you go, because you might not be able to afford it again.

Jenn pauses again. "I think Jay was more interested in the experience than worrying about the danger."

His boss, Henry Hensley could only say good things. "He's also good at connecting with people, particularly millennials . . . he is really changing the culture of HUD from one of a traditional government agency to one of a Silicon Valley tech startup . . . he wants to make HUD attractive to younger generation and he's done a remarkable job."[21] Jenn Cribbs picked up something else beyond the polished bureaucrat named Jay Austin. "He had scars," she said quietly. "I think his childhood was hard and he told me that it was a counselor who told him how he could pull out of all that. He put him on an accelerated track at high school and then lined him up for college. He saw something in him early on and then Jay had a path." Jenn paused. "He was so young. What . . . twenty-three and he already had his masters and now he was making good money at HUD . . . and I remember thinking this kid has been going like this for years . . . just nonstop." [22]

Jay continued to implement change at HUD while going on longer sabbaticals. Jenn shook her head and smiled. "No one stopped him, and I told him I wanted to go on a long vacation, and he just said, well did you ask? You just have to make a case for what you want."[23] Jay had made a case for coming into work in shorts and sandals, working from home, going on extended leave, riding his bike to work. "He was one hundred percent self-sufficient and then he met Lauren, and I think she changed him," Jenn said slowly. "Suddenly he saw something outside of himself."[24]

Before Lauren, Jay had spent lots of time and traveled with Abilene Miller. When I asked Abby if she and Jay were romantically involved, she laughed. "I was queer then. He knew it. But he dated another woman at HUD, Melanie who came up to me and said he wanted to be with me. Maybe he did. I don't know. I remember they went to China together and then had a bad breakup. Very different from Lauren." Abby paused. "Jay was never going to have anyone's foot on his neck for long. I didn't expect him to stay at HUD. He was not going to do what most people in the US do." Abby paused again:

> I remember one of our last fights was when I saw this guy riding down the street with a boombox. An old man playing sixties music. I told Jay that was going to be him in the way he was headed. He was so offended. Not because I said he was going to end up homeless, but I had dared to put the man on the bicycle in a box.[25]

Jenn Cribbs saw Jay and Abby more like a brother and sister. "They had both gone through difficult childhoods and knew how to show up for each other. They knew what lines not to cross." When I asked about the trip around the world, Jenn leaned back and crossed her arms:

> I knew Jay when he took his scooter across the country, and he survived being behind semis in rainstorm on mountains. So, when he said he was going to bike around the world I thought ok, that is still in his brand. But I also thought he was at the point where he didn't like the person who he was at HUD. That person was always fighting with the unions. I mean there were huge shifts at HUD, telework, paternity and maternity leave and the old guard just didn't like all this change, and they didn't like the technological changes. I think he got tired of having to accommodate to that power. I think he liked the person who was out there in nature, on his scooter, on his bike, camping in the wild, and increasingly disliking that person with the sword who had to fight.[26]

Jay's metamorphosis after the scooter trip across the country is evident in a blog post:

> I felt things. I felt freedom I could never hope to describe, limitless liberation that awakened the adventurer, the child, the vagabond within me. I lost myself to the spirit of the traveler; I felt my very being subsumed my something greater. I was born anew and born better, a new self within me conceived in the bayou and birthed in the canyons and baptized in the great Pacific, reared and raised by the rivers and roads of the West, nurtured and nourished by the never-ending nature of our neighbor to the north. I did things. I walked and I hiked, I climbed and I fell, I got lost and I got found. I slept in tents and I slept in hotels, in motels and hostels and public parks and parking garages and college faculty rooms, on couches of friends and on couches of perfect strangers. I met people. I met so many people, people who gave me faith in our collective future, people who gave me faith that what I was doing was about more than just me.

Jenn kept up with Jay through email, but on the trip she had no communication from him. "I was getting on a plane when Abby called me. She just started weeping and somehow, I knew it was about Jay. She said to me . . . 'they killed him.' I did not see that coming."

Abby Miller leans back in her chair and looks at the camera. She is silent and then shakes her head, speaking in a low voice. "Jay saw no boundaries. He was the unstoppable force . . . but in Tajikistan," she looked up, "He hit the immovable object."[27]

Notes

1. Email from Jude Delatela.
2. Email from Jude Delatela.
3. Ibid.
4. Ibid.
5. Ibid.
6. Jenn Cribbs Interview by William Hazelgrove, August 19, 2024.
7. Ibid.
8. Ibid.
9. Jay Austin. Leading the way toward Government innovation, *Washington Post*, April 21, 2015.
10. Ibid.

11. Ibid.
12. Abby Miller Interview by William Hazelgrove, April 30, 2024.
13. Jay Austin. Leading the way Toward Government Innovation, *Washington Post*, April 21, 2015.
14. Ibid.
15. Abby Miller Interview by William Hazelgrove, March 21, 2024.
16. Jay Austin. Leading the way Toward Government Innovation, *Washington Post*, April 21, 2015.
17. Ibid.
18. Ibid.
19. Abby Miller Interview by William Hazelgrove, April 30, 2024.
20. Ibid.
21. Jay Austin. Leading the way Toward Government Innovation, *Washington Post*, April 21, 2015.
22. Jenn Cribbs Interview by William Hazelgrove, August 19, 2024.
23. Ibid.
24. Ibid.
25. Abby Miller Interview by William Hazelgrove, April 30, 2024.
26. Jenn Cribbs Interview with William Hazelgrove, August 19, 2024.
27. Abby Miller Interview by William Hazelgrove, August 19, 2024.

8
ZAMBIA
SEPTEMBER 2017

Jay was pushing the envelope on the highways of Zambia now. Zambia is a landlocked country that was known as Northern Rhodesia up until 1964, when the country became independent from the British. Zambia has a Presidential Republic and, like Botswana, the poverty rate is high at 47.9 percent. The highways of Zambia are much worse than the ones in Botswana. The two-lane road has a shoulder littered with rocks and broken glass and debris. The worst of it are the drivers. They speed past Jay and Lauren at 120 kilometers an hour and recklessly push them onto the shoulder. Oncoming vehicles pass each other, coming within inches of the cyclists.

They finally make it to the capital of Zambia, Lusaka. It is Lauren's twenty-ninth birthday, and the *warmshowers* hosts give Lauren a chocolate cake. Lauren posts a picture of the cake with candles on Instagram with two children helping her blow out the candles. "We enjoyed four full rest days in Lusaka," she writes.

> We spent it with a wonderful American expat family who welcomed us so warmly folding us into their lives and routine and with them we shared yummy home cooked meals. Garden yoga, a night on the town, playtime in the yard and they helped me celebrate my birthday on the very first night we arrived with a chocolate cake made by the kids.[1]

On September 27, Jay posts on Instagram:

> Happy birthday to the best partner in travel and life and love a person could ask for. In the past few months alone, this woman has led me across four countries and four thousand kilometers of dirt and desert, outrun a charging elephant on a bicycle, inspired and amazed me on the regular, and warmed

the hearts of just about everyone we've met along the way. (Plus, she still manages to look good at 6AM after five straight days without a shower.) Looking forward to celebrating the day with some great people in Lusaka, and another year of adventures to come.[2]

They explore the falls around Malawi to the East of Zambia, and Lauren posts a celebration picture of herself by the rushing water. She is tan and lean from biking. "From Cape Town to Victoria Falls by bicycle. Powered by our bodies! Powered by lots of peanut butter sandwiches, salt and vinegar chips, biscuits, boiled potatoes, oatmeal and spaghetti . . . powered by human kindness. So much human kindness. Near and far."[3]

Lauren and Jay continue into the mountains and bike to higher elevations, 7,500 feet in 115 kilometers. Lauren posts on Instagram: "I pedaled the final revolutions to the highest point, tired, but still going strong, my eyes welled with tears of accomplishment and awe. I hadn't walked the bike once. I could not have done it four months ago. It was a beautiful ride."[4]

They have cycled 500 kilometers in five days, and they are on an arduous stretch made more difficult by headwinds. They are riding on dirt paths, and Jay is in front. The heat is stifling, and Jay glides down the path going 20 kilometers an hour.

> I gather speed. Twenty, thirty, forty kilometers per hour. At the very bottom of the hill, dirt meets tar. The road is once again paved, and I hurtle toward its smooth, glinting blackness. . . . It is the foundation for a new strip of pavement to be laid. It is the subfloor, and I am careening toward the edge of the hardwood. Blunt, sudden. Tall. Too tall.[5]

Bike long enough and you will have a crash. It is inevitable. You are balancing on two thin wheels with balance and gravity keeping you upright. If gravity or balance gets slightly out of kilter, then the rider will meet the road. Jay posts:

> My front tire hits this edge, maybe a foot high, and my bike goes airborne. It and I fly forward onto the pavement still upright for the moment. There's enough time to know I'm crashing but not enough time to stop myself from crashing. . . . I am lying on my right side at the bottom of a long hill with a burning sensation running through my skin. . . . I am bleeding at my foot, my knee, my hip, my shoulder, my upper back, my bicep and my elbow. I'm missing patches of skin, and these wounds are covered in dirt.[6]

Jay's bike is damaged. His front rim is bent and is rubbing against the front disc brake. He finds a place in the shade. Lauren pitches the tent, and they pull out the first aid kit and begin dressing the wounds. "Sweat runs into my lesions, the salt stings. Clods of dirt are fused to my skin. We are low on water with which to wash. I pull out our bundle of bandages and realize that their size is better suited to paper cuts."[7]

Jay lays down in the tent, but the heat makes it unbearable, and they begin to cycle again. He doesn't wear a shirt and lets the air and the sun heal him. Lauren posts a picture of Jay's scraped and bruised body on Instagram and describes the heat they had to deal with:

> The climbs were tough and the heat could be brutal . . . one night I woke up with difficulty breathing from local charcoal production . . . one afternoon Jay took a bad fall off the bicycle . . . our precious drinking water went from tepid to HOT in the midday sun . . . we tried to wait out the worst of the midday heat under a tree our sweaty bodies sticking to the nylon tent . . . we waited for the evening to bring relief only to spend some nights sticking to our sleeping pads.[8]

They stay at the home of Libby and Brian through *Warmshowers*. Lauren posts on Instagram. "We've cycled over 4800 kilometers (more than 3000 miles now) through South Africa, Namibia, Botswana, Zambia, and Malawi since July. It feels good!"[9] They are taken out for an Indian dinner and driven around the town to complete errands. Brian and Libby leave for the weekend and give the two cyclists the keys to their home, where they luxuriate in making pancakes, having popcorn, watching movies, using the internet connection, and drinking Brian's homebrew beer. "And for the moment," Jay writes, "That's actually really nice."[10]

After five days, Jay and Lauren pack up to leave but are invited to join their hosts at a beach house on Lake Malawi. Lake Malawi is served by a vintage 1949 ferry built in Scotland, the MV Ilawa. Jay and Lauren have to get their bikes and themselves on the ferry to get to the South end of the lake. The ferry is unreliable, and there is no dock. People reach the ferry by lifeboat, and then a ladder is climbed to get on board. They wait at a campground for two days before they hear the horn echoing through the bay.

Jay posts later:

> Lauren has gotten the bikes together and we hastily push them out onto the sand. It's about a kilometer to where the ferry "docks," which is to say the point where one should stand to most directly wade out to the lifeboats that will carry them the rest of the way to the ferry. . . . A few men offer to carry our bikes and bags out to the lifeboat . . . so we agree on two-hundred kwacha each (down from an initial 1,500) for them to carry the bikes while we do our best to keep the bags dry.[11]

They get into the second round of lifeboats with forty-five other passengers and heave their bikes up into the ferry. Lauren posts a picture to Instagram showing their crowded lifeboat. "The boarding process involved wading into the water and with some assistance hoisting our bags, our bicycles, and ourselves from the lifeboat into the ferry."[12] They set off with a stunning inky sunset over the mountains and sleep on the hard planks of the ferry. During the night, their bicycle lights are stolen. Jay later writes:

> I thought about how safe we've felt these past four months. . . . How often we've left our bikes unlocked outside of markets without trouble. How literally nothing has gone missing. I trusted they'd be just fine below deck until morning, and I went back to sleep. From this point forward, we're going to feel a little more nervous, wary. It's a little thing, these lights. Physically, financially, it's trivial. But emotionally, it leaves me a little less trusting of the people around me, and I don't like that feeling.[13]

They arrive past midnight at Monkey Bay and pitch camp. Jay's back is hurting, and the heat and humidity had taken their toll on Lauren. On Friday, they meet Sarah, Cassidy, and their kids at a resort hotel. The heat is oppressive, and beer and Tostitos are served. Jay doesn't feel well:

> The tortilla chips which I've regularly dreamed about during our months on the road seem oddly unappetizing. I finish the one beer and feel a little funny, like maybe I've drank too much. I slide down in my seat and watch the people around me talk to each other, and it feels confusing and tiring, like there's just too much going on. I turn my head, and everything takes a moment to refocus.[14]

Jay lies down in a darkened room in the air conditioning and tells Lauren it is just "too little sleep, too little water." Cassidy is a doctor and checks on him and wants him to get an immediate test for Malaria. The tiny pregnant mosquito that pierces skin with a six-pronged mouthpiece and finds blood is the culprit of anyone infected with malaria. The anticoagulant the mosquito injects is the carrier of the parasite that will cause all the problems. Malaria describes a wide range of mosquito-borne illnesses. But the parasite plasmodium falciparum is the agent of malaria. Most of the parasites will be destroyed by the immune system, but a few make it to the liver and within eleven days will regenerate into eukaryotes of hundreds of thousands. And then they attack, and the patient feels violently ill.

Jay writes in his blog:

> I spend Friday night, shaking and sweating and unable to regulate my body's temperature. The air conditioner is on full blast and I'm mildly aware that the

room cannot be more than 20C, but it feels like a sauna. I feel like I might vomit but do not vomit. A few times during the night I rise to use the toilet and walking to the bathroom next door feels like a herculean effort. I toss and turn and feel an ache in my bones.[15]

He and Lauren were both carrying Marone, which they had taken as a malaria preventive. Cassidy and Sarah have packed the malaria drug Coartern, and Jay starts a three-day dose. He feels better but then retreats to the bedroom, exhausted. Lauren posts on Instagram, "Since Monday we've been resting in Cape Maclear as Jay continues to recover from Malaria and I fight off persisting unnamed stomach issues."[16] The months of biking in foreign countries, wild camping, and eating different foods has been a slow drain on their health. For now, all they can do is rest and heal.

Notes

1. Lauren Geoghegan Instagram Post, October 15, 2017.
2. Jay Austin Instagram Post, September 27, 2017.
3. Lauren Geoghegan Instagram Post, September 21, 2017.
4. Ibid., November 12, 2017.
5. Simplycycling.org #11, October 26, 2017.
6. Ibid.
7. Ibid.
8. Ibid.
9. Ibid.
10. Simplycycling.org #12, October 31, 2017.
11. Simplycycling.org #13, November 10, 2017.
12. Ibid.
13. Ibid.
14. Ibid.
15. Ibid.
16. Lauren Geoghegan Instagram Post.

9

THE GEORGETOWN GANG

2025

Georgetown today is a series of slanting streets, gray stones, brown stones, and red brick townhomes with the black railings dropping to the sultry streets. The cicadas whine from ivy-covered porches that drop to sidewalks stained with chlorophyll with kitschy coffee shops, bars, and restaurants that service Washington's young professionals and the undergraduates from Georgetown University. Graduates from all over the country land in Georgetown to take their place in the backyard of raw power.

Tiffany Del Rio was in the graduate program at Georgetown with Jay. She is a not for profit leader and now lives in Alexandria VA. She has two children that are playing in the other room while we talk during our zoom interview. She pulls back her blond-streaked hair and positions a sandwich by her.

> Jay . . . so he read this book on running that said the way to run was to run barefoot and so he wanted to run across the Brooklyn bridge . . . everyone told him you can't do it, so of course he did it. I would run into him in Chinatown or Foggy Bottom, and he would be running barefoot in these tiny shorts. He didn't see much of his family during those years and so we spent a lot of holidays together . . . thanksgiving, Christmas.

When Tiffany met Lauren, she was impressed. "I knew they were in love when she stayed over at his Tiny House with a bucket for a toilet and no heat. I am not a fan of the bucket."[1] She pauses, and shakes her head:

> So, this one time Jay wanted to go skydiving for his birthday. So, this was his idea, and I went with him, and while we were up in the plane getting ready to jump, he began shaking all over. I put my hand on his leg and told him we

were going to be fine, but it was *his trip* . . . and here I was the one telling him we would be fine when I was scared to death too.[2]

Tiffany has the unmistakable accent of an urbanite from New York or Los Angeles. She speaks in a rapid fire stream of consciousness. "I mean we are talking about a guy who stood in a sandbox at work in his bare feet and set up checkerboards at peoples desk so people could play games at work." Tiffany is walking around with her computer while talking offscreen to her two boys. Our zoom conversation is late for a working mother, but we have been talking for an hour, and she laughs as she talks about Jay puking at a birthday party and then just continuing the conversation with her. They had both come to Georgetown and entered the graduate program at the same time. Tiffany lands at a table. "He told me he used to ditch school and take the train into New York and walk around all day as a kid. . . . I mean we are talking about a guy who would leave his cellphone home and use it as a landline and would work from a rock-climbing gym."

"Two things that happened sum Jay up," she recalled, taking a bite of a sandwich, licking her finger. She turns to her husband, "I'm talking to the author." Then she turns back:

> One time we went tubing at Harpers Ferry and the woman who was running the tubing place told us all to stay on the left side because of the current. Jay of course ignored this and disappeared, going down the other side. We freaked out and my husband had to go after them and when we caught up with the Jay and Lauren, they were just floating along eating a bag of chips. My husband had to walk all the way back. . . . another time we were all going to a ballgame and this woman from California was going with our group. And she put in the group chat that she didn't want anyone posting about anything but the game and not what people are eating. Jay immediately posted he was eating sushi and went on and on about how great sushi was.

Tiffany shrugged. "That was Jay, always pushing the envelope."[3,4]

She picks up the laptop and starts walking again. "Let's see he went through his sunscreen phase where he wouldn't wear sunscreen and got really burnt. Then the barefoot phase where he injured his feet running on the Brooklyn bridge. Then he taped off his apartment when he started thinking about the Tiny House thing and living in this small area of his apartment." [5] Tiffany lands at a desk and says something to her kids and then adjusts the camera. "When he ended up on the cover of The Washington Post magazine for the Tiny House thing he wanted to buy the email address Jay Austin." I ask her a question, and she pauses. "Why he changed his name, I'm not sure . . . but I think he wanted to get rid of his past. He told me once he had worked at McDonalds, and he would add the items up in his head and give change before the cash register could. I mean who does that?"[6]

Tiffany drinks her iced tea and eats like a mother who is doing three things at once. Talking to an author, watching her kids, and occasionally talking to her husband. We have had to reschedule several times, and now it is 10 at night, Eastern time. "When I saw them in Spain with Molly, Lauren said it had been really tough. There were some money issues." Tiffany pauses. "Jay was really excited about doing this Pamir highway I remember that." She pauses. "Like I said, he was always pushing the envelope."

Molly Scalise was the first to respond to my requests for interviews. She has long blond hair, and there are pictures of her dancing with Jay at a wedding. In the Georgetown University service dedicating the memorial bench for Lauren Geoghegan, she sang *So Far Away*, by Carol King. With long blond hair and a disarming smile, there is a girl-next-door quality to her. She is in a band and works as the deputy director of Communications. In the photos of Lauren in Georgetown, Molly is in almost every picture. She had lived with Lauren in a group house in Georgetown and was among her closest friends. In the house were Molly Scalise, Erin Howell, Lisa Koav, Lynn Massingale, and Lauren. They had met freshman year when Lauren was majoring in government with a minor in Spanish and Arabic.

I started out by asking about Jay's minimalism and how Lauren fit into that.

"She was very curious about the world but had maximalist tendencies. She liked to go out dancing and go to concerts."[7] Molly paused:

> I remember the day they left; Jay was all packed but Lauren was not. She was super organized but could not pack to save her life. It was a group effort, and we had to pack up all her stuff and get her out of the house and I remember it was raining and they took the metro to the airport with their bikes in these big cardboard boxes.[8]

Molly paused again:

> They must have been so tired by the time they reached the airport. I wondered how she would do on this trip. I mean Lauren was very sociable. Her favorite drinks were margaritas and daiquiris . . . we'd go dancing. She would suggest doing things outside of the Georgetown comfort zone, find poetry readings, green concerts . . . go on long walks around the city and walk for miles and stop in different coffee shop.

Molly shrugs:

Now she was going on this trip around the world. I do think she was torn on the trip. Initially she said she would go for a year and if she liked it, she would stick it out. I think part of her wanted to come home, maybe move to the West coast, and have a family. When I saw Lauren in Spain on the trip, she said, "Oh, Molly, it's been really hard."[9]

Molly leans back from the computer. She had been interviewed after the attack by several networks with the moniker *Friend of Lauren and Jay* and had been instrumental in helping me get interviews with other friends of Jay and Lauren. It has been six years since the tragedy, and we talk about Lauren's doubts about the trip. "I would get WhatsApp messages from her saying how she was homesick and missed hanging in DC and that it was hard with all these difficult bike rides. She said she wasn't sure she wanted to be on this long trip." Molly paused again. "I think there were great highs, but really low lows. Jay was a vegan, so Lauren adopted that too, but she was a meat eater and had a real sweet tooth. She was a strong personality and so was Jay and I know there were arguments. When I went to visit them in Spain, I brought her favorite candies . . . sour candies." Molly paused. "She was thinner and very muscular from all that biking."[10]

Molly drinks from a water bottle and leans closer into the computer.

"When her parents went over in Kosovo. I think that was a turning point. They really wanted her to come home, but I think Lauren wanted to stick it out for at least a year." She pauses. "I don't think she wanted to disappoint Jay and go home."[11]

There is a picture of Ryan Koronowski and Jay eating at an Ethiopian restaurant in 2013. They are both looking at the camera with wine glasses visible. They look like two friends solving the problems of the world. Jay has on a warm-up jacket, and Ryan is in a white T-shirt. This was eleven years ago. Ryan now works as a political consultant and has a five-year-old son. His wife Brook worked with Jay at HUD. We reschedule several times. My research on Ryan has turned up the article: "Two Bikers Killed by ISIS Militants a World Away: They Were My Friends."[12] The article was written on August 10, 2018, a few weeks after the tragedy.

Ryan is an elfin man with short, black receding hair. He looks how a political consultant might be cast in a movie. He has a slight smile as he sits back from his computer and gives short answers to my questions. He doesn't know the man who emailed him looking for information on an old friend. At the think tank he does political research which leads to my first question. "Yes, we talked politics. Lots of times late into the night. He was very undoctrinaire. Always took the other side. He interned for the Obama Administration, and I think he came into HUD as a Presidential fellow."[13] In his article, he remembers

> eating Ethiopian food with Jay late into the night and debating whether people should legitimize a broken political system by voting or a broken economic system by using currency. Listening to music at Jays tiny home before not so tiny bonfires . . . offering to have Jays mail sent to our address because he was legally homeless even with his gorgeous tiny home.[14]

The tone of the article is mournful. His friends had died two weeks before, and he explains motivations in the article for taking the trip:

> Jay and Lauren understood their trip to be an example for others. They believed in the fundamental goodness of people. They valued connection in an era when differences aren't always valued. They lived the life they longed to see more of in the world; for people to be kinder, more generous more adventurous. The worlds not as unknowable, scary or foreign as it might seem, they say. There are people you like just waiting to meet you.[15]

The day before Jay and Lauren left, there was a brunch with Ryan and his wife Brook. "We listened to their last-minute plans to lighten their touring loads and debated whether they'd need a solar charger to go along with the big batteries they bought to charge their electronic devices. Lauren loved playing with our daughter, Jocelyn," Ryan says sitting back from his computer. "I had used these portable solar chargers and I told them they should try those instead of lugging batteries."[16] They told Lauren and Jay about their recent trip to Barcelona biking around with a toddler and

> advised what tweaks might allow their commuter bikes to be touring bikes . . . we knew then that we were saying goodbye for a few years, but the internet allowed us to keep close tabs on Jay and Lauren and they were just as invested in keeping tabs on us—how our jobs were going, where our daughter was going to daycare.[17]

In the article, Ryan describes Lauren "as radiant and giving and had a way of stopping whatever social autopilot was running the conversation to pause and ask you what was really going on. How you were actually doing." At one point there was nothing more to say. "We knew then we were saying goodbye for a few years."[18]

My impression of Ryan was that he was the type of friend who would go out for a beer on a moment's notice. He talked about meeting Jay at a bar, The *Saloon*, and playing board games and how Jay didn't want to vote to support a system that was doing wrong things. He talked about Jay reducing his belongings to 100 things, living in a taped-off square in his apartment, and he believed Jay would have gone on the trip even if Lauren had not gone with him. He said Jay had thoughts of spending time on an uninhabited island to "simply exist for a reboot, a needed detox from a society of big wants and little attentions."[19]

Ryan concludes the article by saying, "you would have liked Jay and Lauren, if you'd had a chance to know them. If you are worried as I am, about how the world sees America these days, they were just the people you'd want as our ambassadors, compassionate, curious, humble and giving."[20] In our conversation, Ryan trails off and is quiet. "I think he never saw himself having a family, but that changed when he met Lauren." He paused again and looked at the camera in the same far away, slightly sad way he had begun the conversation. "Jay was a guy . . . Jay was a guy who wanted to push things just to see what was there."[21]

Notes

1. Interview with Tiffany Del Rio by William Hazelgrove, March 16, 2024.
2. Ibid.
3. Ibid.
4. Ibid.
5. Ibid.
6. Ibid.
7. Ibid.
8. Molly Scalise Interview by William Hazelgrove, March 12, 2024.
9. Interview with Molly Scalise by William Hazelgrove, March 12, 2024.
10. Ibid.
11. Ibid.
12. Koronowski, Ryan, Two Bikers Killed by ISIS Militants A World Away, Were My Friends, WBUR, August 10, 2018.
13. Interview with Ryan Koronowski by William Hazelgrove, May 6, 2017.
14. Koronowski, Ryan, Two Bikers Killed by ISIS Militants A World Away, Were My Friends, WBUR, August 10, 2018.
15. Ibid.
16. Interview with Ryan Koronowski by William Hazelgrove, May 6, 2017.
17. Ibid.
18. Koronowski, Ryan, Two Bikers Killed by ISIS Militants, A World Away Were My Friends, WBUR, August 10, 2018.
19. Ibid.
20. Ibid.
21. Interview with Ryan Koronowski by William Hazelgrove, May 6, 2017.

10
TANZANIA
NOVEMBER 2017

Getting back on the bike is everything. Biking heals the body. Talk to any cyclist, and they will tell you this is true. Jay recovers from his malaria and gets back on the bike. But it is too soon. And immediately feels sick again. He goes back to bed. After three weeks, the malaria won't let him go. The second time is better. One pedal, then another, then another. Biking after an illness is like that. Just make the trip. Tomorrow will be further. Baby steps. The bike heals the body. I have proved this over and over with my own cycling. Everything is put right, and Jay is now back in the saddle.

On October 25, 2017, Jay posted on Instagram:

Almost a week after falling ill with malaria, I'm feeling thankful for a number of things. First, finally being able to stand and walk and eat and feel (mostly) human again. Second, to have weathered the very worst of it with relative advantages: a caring companion, good friends (including a doctor), shelter, air conditioning, clean water, and ready access to quality treatment. Third, for the amazing people we're staying with now, who came to pick us and our bikes up from the petrol pump where I was stuck vomiting after I made the mistake of thinking I was well enough to cycle again.[1]

Jay recovers after several weeks, and they pass through Tanzania. Lauren's knee begins acting up from the nonstop biking. She posts on Instagram next to a sign from Mukami National Park:

We had to adjust our plans when knee pain and stiffness became too much to bear . . . not wanting to injure myself further and prolong the inevitable recovery period, we decided to rest a few days outside of the park . . . after several days . . . we cycled through Mikuni and saw Zebras, giraffes, impala and warthog, wild beast and Buffalo . . . we've been really fortunate with minimal physical injuries and setbacks on the trip so far.[2]

They arrive in the town of Mbeya and look for a place to camp as a storm begins. Jay posts on Instagram again on November 15:

So last week we arrived just as it was getting dark. We couldn't locate the campground we were planning to stay at, and I was standing next to a driveway as Lauren walked down a gravel road to see if it was over there. A woman pulled into the driveway and asked if we were okay. I said we were, that we were just looking for this campground. Well, if it doesn't work out, she said, you're more than welcome to camp in my yard. . . . You know, she said, you're free to use my guesthouse if it'd be more comfortable than your tent.[3]

Jay and Lauren end up staying four days. Jay posts again: "As the world seems to move ever closer to distrust and animosity, it's important to remember (and nice to be reminded) that on the whole, people are good and kind and always willing to help."[4] They decide to stay in the city of Dar for two weeks with another *warmshowers* host on the coast of the Indian Ocean. Lauren and Jay celebrate Thanksgiving in a lodge restaurant and spend days on the beach. Jay posts on his blog:

Every year, on the fourth Thursday of November, we Americans celebrate a holiday called Thanksgiving. It's a strange tradition . . . in which we show our appreciation for what we have by killing a quarter-billion turkeys, eating to the point of discomfort, queueing up outside shopping malls to buy electronics at reduced rates, and otherwise yearning for that which we do *not* have. But anyway. Stripped of all its cultural and historical baggage, it's nice to have a day predicated on giving thanks. . . . Our present life, a life of waking up and riding bicycles and seeing new places, is not without its challenges. But it is a life of our choosing, and for that we are tremendously grateful. We're thankful to be in a position, physically and financially and politically and practically, to be able to travel the world in this fashion. We're privileged to enjoy a freedom of movement some do not have. We're privileged to enjoy it together. These past five months cycling across Africa has been a mostly lovely, mostly joyous adventure, and we're thankful to be here living it. To be here at all.[5]

A picture is posted on Jay's Instagram of Lauren and Jay with their backs to the camera looking at the ocean. They sit in the sand with the cobalt sea washing in on a foamy surf. Lauren's curly hair is blown back over her shoulders. Jay has sand on his back. They both have green wristbands on. They are in their swimsuits and look like lovers who have just found a spot of paradise. The sky is a brilliant blue with wisps of clouds. It is a perfect day for two people who have left the world for the adventure of their lives. And for the moment, that is enough.

On December 6, Jay posted on Instagram: "Five months and 5,500+ kilometers later, the first chapter of our ride around the world draws to a close. It's been amazing and rewarding and so very memorable, and we're really sad to be leaving east Africa behind. But we're also plenty excited for the adventures ahead (starting tomorrow!). In the meantime, we're off to see about some pyramids."[6]

This is the first indication they are changing their plans. Jay was always loose about their exact route and holding out the option of flying when necessary. It would take six months to cross the rest of Africa and that put them in Europe and Asia at the wrong time. Jay cited the heat of the summer months, and dirt roads made impassable by summer rains, and Lauren's knee injury. So, they would fly to Morocco, and, on the way, they would stop over in Egypt for several days.

Jay lists in his blog other reasons that have more to do with safety:

Post-election security concerns in Kenya, rock-throwing children in Ethiopia, an uncertain and undoubtedly expensive visa application in Sudan, the nuisance of a required military escort along a substantial section of the Nile in Egypt. The absence of a trans-Mediterranean ferry from Cairo and thus the need for a flight out of eastern Africa anyway.[7]

Lauren posts another picture on Instagram on the beach, and they have both lost weight from cycling nonstop for five months:

Five months ago we boarded a plane for Cape Town to spend some time traveling the world by bicycle . . . our hearts full of the memories we made on and off the bicycles in southern and eastern Africa. . . . I'm excited for the next leg of this adventure, but I'm also already missing life as we knew it these past five months.[8]

Lauren has another post with a map showing their progress so far: "We've cycled 5500 kilometers through South Africa, Namibia, Botswana, Zambia, Malawi and Tanzania since mid-July."[9]

They pack their bikes into cardboard boxes and fly out of Africa and arrive in Egypt on December 7. Their bikes remain stored for Morocco in the airport while they briefly take in the sites. Jay takes a picture of a camel when a voice calls from behind: "A man some twenty meters away hurries over. Hand outstretched, palm upward to the darkening sky. 'You pay,' he calls before he even reaches me. 'Uhm, *la shukran*,' I reply. *No thank you*. 'You take a picture of my camel. You owe me money.'"[10]

Jay is tired. It's been a long day. They were up at dawn for the flight. Jay and the man argue face-to-face. The man grabs Jay by the shoulder. "You pay me! How much?" Jay turns around, "but the hand curls into a claw and tightens around my jacket. My voice rises a little and it's enough to scare his grip loose. I pull away and walk west, heavy steps in the coarse sand. The man is left muttering something begrudging about Americans or tourists or whomever to his camel."[11]

They leave Egypt and take another plane to Morocco. The bikes are retrieved, and there is a fast-motion video of Lauren and Jay reassembling their bikes at the airport. Putting a bike together from the wheels to the brakes to the gears to the seat would be hard enough in a garage, but doing it in an airport is amazing. "It takes us about an hour to properly disassemble and pack our bikes and gear into two large cardboard containers, and perhaps even less time to put them back together," Jay writes. "It requires just a few items (a multi-tool featuring three or four hex keys, a pump to reinflate the tires, and for us, a special little instrument to lock in our wheels) and about four square meters of floor space, preferably flat . . . forty minutes later, our bicycles are ready to roll."[12]

They head out into the heat of Morocco. They are befriended by a family who serves them dinner and offers an extra room. Jay writes of the friendship of strangers they had met along the way:

> We have been on the road for almost half a year and many of those nights—maybe *most* of those nights—we have not known where we'd be resting our heads twenty minutes before the sky turned to ink. And yet it has worked out. . . . *Every single time*. Some nights we have found ourselves pitching a tent in dense, prickly brush, and some nights we have found ourselves, well before the stars have woken, eating roasted ground nuts around a small fire with some new friend we've only just met.[13]

They reach the town of Tajine and camp in mud and rain, and once again a man offers his home and food. In a post that would be widely quoted later in many articles, Jay writes:

> You watch the news, and you read the papers, and you're led to believe that the world is a big, scary place. People, the narrative goes, are not to be trusted. People are bad. People are evil. People are axe murderers and

monsters and worse. I don't buy it. Evil is a make-believe concept we've invented to deal with the complexities of fellow humans holding values and beliefs and perspectives different than our own . . . the Badness exists, sure, but even that's quite rare. By and large, humans are kind. Self-interested sometimes, myopic sometimes, but kind. Generous and wonderful and kind. No greater revelation has come from our journey than this.[14]

In another home, they are offered a bowl of olives and orange slices and then a loaf of warm bread. Lauren posts on Instagram, summing up their trip so far:

We cycled nearly 6200 kilometers through Southern, Eastern and Northern Africa . . . we touched the Indian and Atlantic oceans in South Africa, returned to the Indian ocean in Tanzania, reunited with the Atlantic in in Morocco and finally met the Mediterranean. . . . There are places and people we want to visit again, and many places we did not make it to on this trip . . . the world is so big, yet moments of intimate and meaningful connection make it feel that much smaller. And more beautiful.[15]

They continue on. A man follows them in Morocco and offers a place to stay for a price. They decline his offer, but the man does not give up. "Cheap. Very cheap. You won't find a better price." Jay tells him to go away. "Ok . . . no hotel. Hashish? You want some hashish?" "No, I don't want any hashish . . . leave us alone." Jay shakes off the man as another descends and demands to shake Jay's hand. He refuses, and the man becomes belligerent: "What, do you not trust me? Is it because I am Moroccan? What have I done to offend you? Why do you not shake my hand? Is it because my skin is not like yours?" Jay turns around and scowls, "No, I say, *it's because you're going to try to sell me something*." He points an angry finger in my direction, "You Americans! I do not want to shake your hand, then, anyway. You have a mean face. A very mean face!"[16]

They bike on and head for Spain. On December 23, 2017, Jay uploads another Instagram post: "I'm saddened that our six-month trip bike ride through Africa, southern, eastern, northern has finally come to an end . . . there's plenty more to look forward to in Europe, Asia, Australia, and South America."[17]

This is the first mention of Australia. Their route as always is a work in progress. Jay and Lauren find themselves in a traffic jam at the border with Spain. The town of Ceuta is crowded with people and cars. The bumper-to-bumper traffic stretches for miles. They breathe in the lead heavy exhaust roiling in the sun. The cars honk; men swear at one another. They realize they are in the wrong lane. They are on the sidewalk, west of the southbound traffic, and want to cross traffic to the northbound lane. They wait for a gap to open between the cars. The cars are literally inches apart. They wait and wait, and finally a space opens between an SUV and a sedan. Lauren walks quickly and manages to pass between two cars with her bike. Jay follows.

Dealing with cars is always dangerous. The trick is to make eye contact with the driver and make sure he or she sees you. In intersections or lines of cars, this is critical. Jay waves his arm at the man driving. "I look at the driver in the southbound lane, signal that I'm just cutting through to turn left as well, and scoot in between his SUV and the car ahead." Jay moves forward with his bike. Blue exhaust from the car in front blinds him momentarily, and his eyes water. He is now between the two cars when the SUV suddenly pushes forward, pinning Jay and his bike between the bumpers. "I'm almost clear of the lane when he begins to run me over. Slowly, very slowly. His front bumper makes contact with my pannier. He inches forward, trapping my bike between his SUV and the bumper of the car in front of him. I'm pushed sideways. I begin hitting the hood of his truck."[18]

Jay shouts and bangs on the hood with his fist as the man stares at him, "not with malice nor anger. With indifference. Blankness."[19] Being hit by a car on a bike is a surreal experience. The sheer mass and power of the one-ton machine makes it into a death match with the cyclist bound to lose. Jay screams as his bike and his body are compressed between the cars. The man presses down on his accelerator. Jay's bike is levered under the bumper, and he goes down with it. Lauren screams hysterically. Jay is being run over in plain sight.

Notes

1. Jay Austin Instagram Post, October 25, 2017.
2. Lauren Geoghegan Instagram, November 30, 2017.
3. Jay Austin Instagram Post, November 15, 2017.
4. Ibid.
5. Simplycycling.org.
6. Jay Austin Instagram Post, November 23, 2017.
7. Simplycycling.org, March 23, 2018.
8. Lauren Geoghegan Instagram, December 6, 2017.
9. Ibid.
10. Simplycycling.org, March 23, 2018, #19.
11. Ibid.
12. Ibid., #20, March 27, 2018.
13. Ibid.

14 Ibid., #22, March 5, 2018.
15 Lauren Geoghegan Instagram Post, January 7, 2018.
16 Simplycycling.org, #22, March 5, 2018.
17 Jay Austin Instagram Post, December 23, 2017.
18 Simplycycling.org, #22, March 5, 2018.
19 Ibid.

11
THE TINY HOUSE
2012

There would seem to be two sides to Jay Austin. One side was the misanthropic minimalistic nonvoting vegan wanderer who didn't care about the trappings of the world and who quit his job to go around the world on a bike. This person has more in common with the wanderer, Chris McCandless, of *Into the Wild*, who saw salvation in a life apart from the world. But there was another side, a person who liked the spotlight. In our media-centric age, media coverage is the final badge of success.

Jay's highpoint was his picture on the cover of *The Washington Post Magazine* that came out July 25, 2015. Jay is featured in full color in front of his 143 square foot Tiny House dressed in hip millennial garb with a striped open sweatshirt and tennis shoes. The article interviews several people who have built Tiny Houses, and Jay is the final interview where he reveals his house cost 50,000 to build and he had just returned from a five-week trip to India. At this point in his life, the twenty-six-year-old Jay Austin is the progressive millennial looking to find a better way to live who frequently takes unpaid leave from his job at HUD.

In the interviews about his Tiny House (the matchbox), Jay comes across as a media personality. Well spoken. Looking directly at the camera. Very at ease. There are over twenty hits on Google citing documentaries, articles, films, podcasts when *Jay Austin Tiny House* is searched, but the Tiny House movement did not start with Jay. Shotgun shacks built around the late nineteenth century and through the Great Depression were the original Tiny Houses. Blue-collar families built these small homes in many Southern cities. In comparison, the original size of an average home grew from 1,780 square feet in 1978 to 2,479 square feet in 2007 and then 2,662 square feet in 2013. The 143-square-foot home Jay Austin built was a throwback to when people could not afford basic housing. *Walden* by Henry David Thoreau is considered an early influence on the

Tiny House movement followed by Loyd Kahn, who wrote *Shelter* in 1973, and Lester Walker, author of *Tiny Houses* in 1997, followed by Sarah Susanka in the book *The Not So Big House* in 1997.

The Great Recession of 2007 gave Tiny Houses a boost, but they were only 1 percent of all real estate transactions. A "Tiny House" became the answer for people looking to go off the grid or live a minimalist lifestyle. Cue the man living in a taped-off area of 100 square feet of his apartment, getting his belongings down to 100 items. In the interviews, Jay explains his motivations for moving from his Washington apartment into a 143 square foot home: "My primary reason for building this home is that I want to live simply. I want to limit my distractions and pursue my passions and devote my time to what really matters: kindness, leisure, friendship, companionship. Living in a structure that has just what's needed and nothing more."[1] In an article in *Dwell Magazine*, under the banner of *Washingtons Beautiful Illegal Tiny Houses*, Jay is quoted: "I got driven down the tiny house road because of affordability, simplicity, sustainability and then mobility."[2] In the article, his Tiny House is described as "stylish, well built, and includes all of life's necessities and some of its luxuries, a bathroom, a shower, a modest kitchen, office space, and a bedroom loft. There is even a hot tub outside, high ceilings, skylight, and wide windows give the small space a modern, uncluttered and open feel."[3] There are pictures of Jay in his hot tub outside with a drink in hand. In the embedded video, he comes across as a progressive Washingtonian looking to shake up the way people live.

On the Tiny House website, there is an interview of Jay published in the fall of 2015, where he laments his newfound Tiny House fame. "Since building my home . . . I'm known by friends and friends of friends and friends of friends of friends as *the tiny house guy* and it's hard to go even a day without someone asking me to tell so and so about my house."[4] In the article where Jay explains the benefits and the process of building a Tiny House, he comes across as the ambassador of the movement. There are Tiny House concerts and plays in the community, and Jay pitches the Tiny House movement as not just a different type of housing but a different way of living. There is a definite commune feel to Jay's vision. He finishes the article with a quote from Chris McCandless of *Into the Wild*:

> Make radical change in your lifestyle and begin to boldly do things which you may have previously never have thought of doing or been too hesitant to accept. So many people live within unhappy circumstances and yet will not take the initiative to change their situation because they are conditioned to a life of security, conformity and conservation . . . in reality nothing is more damaging to the adventurous spirit within a man than a secure future.[5]

THE TINY HOUSE

But there is another side of the Jay Austin Tiny House story.

Lee Para now lives in Mexico. Lee is an angular woman with a big smile who says she has lived in twenty-six different places in her life. Her home is bright and airy and doesn't look particularly small. She headed up the Tiny House project *Boneyard Studios* with Brian L and Jay Austin in 2012.

"I met Jay when he told me he wanted to build a Tiny home," she begins in our interview. "He thought he could just build one all by himself, but then he realized he needed help. I think I met Lauren the first time when she was making coffee on his porch and I could tell she had a deep inner knowing. Jay was moving toward community at that time."[6]

Lee had headed up the Boneyard Studios enclave, where they held concerts and seminars on building Tiny Homes. Boneyard Studios was to be the beginning of a utopic community built on minimalistic living. Our conversation is far-ranging, centering on the Tiny Home part of Austin's life. I asked about an article that detailed how the Tiny House movement and Boneyard Studios unraveled. Lee sighed then shook her head: "Brian bought the property that we built the houses on, and I was like what the fuck, we were supposed to do all this together and he just went and bought it."[7]

Jenn Cribbs, an associate at HUD, felt that Jay and Lee realized Brian wasn't committed to the utopic ideal of Tiny House living and was more interested in monetization of the movement. "Brian had the idea and Lee and Jay were grateful to be able to live there initially." The three friends organized what they felt was a groundbreaking Tiny House Community when Brian L bought the vacant lot they had put their homes on. At this time Jay was garnering media for his Tiny House, the cover story in the *Washington Post Magazine*, an NPR interview, and *Dwell Magazine*, while banking a healthy six-figure income at HUD. *Reason Magazine* would later lead with a headline, Jay Austin Killed in Tajikistan, Tiny House Innovator.[8] Another article led with a quote by one of his favorite philosophers, Albert Camus: "The only way to deal with an unfree world is to become absolutely free that your very existence is an act of rebellion."[9]

Lee brushes back her short brown hair and shakes her head. "All that media came later after his house was completed and the problems with Brian came after that. When I met Jay he was a year in and still didn't have any insulation, and he was using a bucket for a toilet,"[10] Jay started on his home in 2012, and it took him several years to complete. In 2014, Jay left his $1,200 a month apartment in DC and moved into the "Matchbox." Videos of Jay show him with a skullcap on with his bike inside of his house or in the hot tub behind his Tiny House. In one video, he is leaning on the tawny wooden kitchen counter inside his home. His quotes are paraphrased and headline the videos. "I got to drive down the tiny house road because of affordability, simplicity, sustainability and then mobility."[11] A fast-action video shows Jay and others building his house from a pile of lumber to a square box and then slowly home. He speaks as a prophet of the new way of living.

> I've always been something of a minimalist but living small cemented it as a foundation of my identity. I love the freedom it offers not just the freedom from a mortgage or a big stationary home, or just the freedom from the water grid or the power grid, but the freedom from consuming, from always looking to buy and buy.[12]

In another long-ranging interview, Jay describes the process of building a Tiny House:

> I started building the house in the summer of 2012. Pleased with the initial month of progress, I put in the 30-days' notice for my old place and got ready to move into my finished tiny house. Of course, progress stalled while waiting for interior materials, and I ended up moving into a simple plywood box—no insulation, no electricity, no running water or plumbing or shower. It was a rough few months of camping, something like watching industrialization fast-forward as modern amenities returned to my life one by one. Still, it took almost a year to get a truly working shower, and many more months after that before I really considered the house "complete."[13]

It would seem Jay had stumbled on a better way to live in a "simple home that is ecofriendly and sustainable using features such as rainwater catchment, solar panels, and Shou Sugi Ban siding."[14] But the article "What Happened to the Tiny Home Commune Boneyard Studios" tells a different side of minimalist living. The Tiny House Community featured on *Fox 5*, *Dwell*, *The Washington Post*, and *Washington City Paper* had disappeared. Lee Para, Brian, and Jay had gone their separate ways by 2015, but not before drama spilled into the media. Jay and Lee published a letter on the website of Boneyard accusing Brian of acting erratically and causing Boneyard to fail. Jay wrote on the blog: "We knew that one person holding the title to our communal property could impact decision making but we trusted that three adults could communicate and come to consensus on most things."[15]

This began a public brawl over Boneyard Studios. The letter detailed further that Brian had "cancelled plans for a public water system, seizing the communal garden and trapping tenants inside their homes by padlocking the gates . . . entering Paras tiny home in the middle of the night without permission."[16] Lee Para reacted to all this by getting a restraining order on Brian, whom she had been dating. "We dated for a few months . . . then he began stalking me." Brian called the police on Jay for trespassing after he didn't pay rent for six months and

THE TINY HOUSE

didn't leave after stating he would twice in writing. Jay described the lot in one of the videos: "When we arrived at the lot on Evarts Street, it was an abandoned alley with crumbling concrete. It was nothing that anyone would ever want to spend an evening on. We wanted to create a space that would be welcoming to others, and where people would want to come see events."[17]

Brian said Boneyard failed because of city zoning and endless construction. He bought the lot for $29,000.00 and then upgraded it with another $85,000. "I received not one dollar from Lee and Jay for any of the tens of thousands of dollars I spent on bringing in electricity, putting up fencing, clearing out concrete and putting in gardens and countless other improvements,"[18] he said in a statement to *Curbed DC*. Brian demanded Austin and Para vacate, and had Austin's home ticketed and called the police again, calling Jay an intruder. Jay was fined $500 for illegally parking on private party. In another statement to *Curbed DC*, Brian said, "Lee and Jay seemed to believe they were entitled to ownership of the property after making minimal payments to partly cover utilities insurance payments and a fraction of the interest I was paying on the personal loans to underwrite the project."[19]

Eventually Lee and Jay relocated their Tiny Houses after Brian claimed that "private conversations were recorded, personal emails were intercepted and deleted, and various threats were made by Para and Austin to go to the press to slander him."[20] Lee said that what they wanted was a proper thirty-day notice from Brian, which they never received.

Lee Para leans forward and sips her tea in her tiled white kitchen. A single green cactus plant is on the kitchen table. We have been talking for almost an hour. "Jay and I kept in contact after everything blew up and then I heard Jay quit his job and somewhere he told me about this trip he was taking with Lauren around the world." Jay and Lee talked several times on the phone during his trip. "He did talk about going to California after the trip and said he would work again. He talked about kids. He said he might have stopped in Africa if it wasn't for Lauren, and it was because of Lauren they got invited into all sorts of homes. I know her parents didn't want her to go," she recalled faintly. "I think she was going to fly back and take a break after they reached that one town in Tajikistan."

Lee was quiet, breathed deeply. "Then I heard you know . . . about the attack." She leans back and speaks quietly, directly to the camera. "I will say this. . . . Jay lived his life the way he wanted to."[21]

Notes

1 The Jay Austin Simply Be Kind Foundation, Jay and Tiny House Living, Fall 2015.
2 Washington's Beautiful Illegal Tiny Houses.

3   Ibid.
4   The Jay Austin Simply Be Kind Foundation, Jay and Tiny House Living, Fall 2015.
5   Ibid.
6   Lee Para Interview by William Hazelgrove, March 26, 2024.
7   Ibid.
8   *Reason Magazine* Jay Austin Killed in Tajikistan Tiny House Innovator.
9   The Jay Austin Simply Be Kind Foundation, Jay and Tiny House Living, Fall 2015.
10 Lee Para Interview by William Hazelgrove, March 26, 2024.
11 The Jay Austin Simply Be Kind Foundation, Jay and Tiny House Living, Fall 2015.
12 Ibid.
13 Ibid.
14 Ibid.
15 Article "What happened to the Tiny Home Commune Boneyard Studios."
16 Ibid.
17 The Jay Austin Simply Be Kind Foundation Jay and Tiny House Living, Fall 2015.
18 Article Curbed DC.
19 Ibid.
20 Ibid.
21 Lee Para Interview by William Hazelgrove, March 26, 2024.

PART II
EUROPE

12
SPAIN
DECEMBER 2017

The border crossing in Spain is loud, exhaust roiling in the sunshine, cars honking. The SUV is still moving forward as Jay and his bike are compressed between two bumpers. Lauren screams. Jay screams. The driver stares ahead blankly. Lauren shouts from the other side to stop. The man continues to drive forward. "His front bumper makes contact with my pannier. He inches forward, trapping my bike between his SUV and the bumper of the car in front of him,"[1] Jay writes later in his blog. "I'm pushed sideways. I begin hitting the hood of his truck to get his attention. I turn my head to make eye contact. To my surprise, he is looking right at me . . . *with indifference*. . . . I am occupying space where he wants his vehicle to be."[2]

Jay continues banging his fist on "his hood, his windshield, his mirror as Lauren shouts for him *to please stop his car*!"[3] Jay grips the handlebars, trying to pull his bike free. "All the while he watches me blankly."[4] He finally gets his bike free of the car and joins Lauren on the other side of the road as the driver closes the gap. The man ignores them and never turns. Shaken, Jay and Lauren continue into the border town of Ceuta and pause at a stoplight with their bikes. A woman making a left turn crashes into Jay's back wheel with her bumper. "I turn around startled. She shrugs, blankly, still inching forward and pushing me with her."[5] Jay once again drags his bike free.

Jay later addresses the man who had tried to run him over:

I started our last post by saying that I don't believe in the concept of evil. It would be easy to portray this man—the one actively running me over—as a deranged sociopath. Really though, the guy is probably just having a bad day. His bad day has probably been made worse by sitting in standstill traffic for the past two or four or ten hours. Driving a motorized vehicle does crazy things to our psyche. It dehumanizes us and the people around us. So, I get it . . . a little. I understand . . . why I'm being run over.[6]

Lauren and Jay can't find anywhere to camp in Ceuta and have tickets for the ferry in the morning. The police recommend they find a hotel. Jay posts:

> It is now dark. Lauren and I are standing outside the ferry terminal arguing with one another about what to do and why the hell we came to Europe in the first place. This is the first time in six months we have been truly at a loss for a safe place to sleep. Hotels are wildly out of our budget. If this is a harbinger of what Europe has to offer, we are in trouble.[7]

Africa was bucolic compared to Europe. Modern society doesn't make room for those who want to wild camp and bike around the world. Jay writes, "We are not happy with one another, not happy with our predicament . . . but here we are, like it or not, Europe."[8] The fights between Lauren and Jay quickly spill into money. There have been fights over buying some *Gummy Bears* that Lauren wanted and hotel rooms. Jay's ascetic budget-driven world conflicts with Lauren's more practical view. They need a hotel and should get one. To Jay, going off budget threatens the trip. Going off budget threatens the new life he has laid out for them. They finally find a place, but it is a bad omen for the European phase of their trip. Jay writes in his blog: "In the past five hours, I have been hit by two cars . . . we have wanted nothing more than a place to camp—one we'd gladly pay for—and we've been rejected by everyone we asked. The blaring of car horns is still ringing in my ears."[9]

They compromise and find a hotel room for the night. The next day Lauren and Jay realize that Christmas is approaching. The towns are festive with lights, and cheerful people scurry by the two weary, dirty, lonely travelers. It is a few days before the holiday as they wheel their bikes through Algeciras, Spain. The holidays are a time of family, and Lauren's Instagram post aches of loneliness.

> We arrived in Algeciras the Friday before Christmas. It was already dark when we arrived, and we didn't know where we would spend the night. Jay thought something would work out, but I wasn't so sure. The streets were filled with people dressed up for the holidays, smiling and celebrating with their families and friends. And there we were pushing out loaded bicycles through the narrow streets, looking far from festive in our cycling attire. I had a major pang of homesickness. I thought of how I might be spending this Friday night at home, surrounded by loved ones.[10]

It is three days before Christmas and Jay and Lauren have lost the shield of being travelers. In Spain, they are treated as vagrants. Jay writes:

> In Africa, we were two funny looking light skinned people on shiny bicycle . . . in Europe . . . we are two funny looking people on dirty bicycles skin bronzed by months in the sun. We are carrying all our belongings with us . . . our clothes are dusty, and we do not smell wonderful. In a crowded street of plush pea coats and pressed shirts and freshly cleaned faces, we stand out.[11]

Lauren and Jay are no longer two hip urbanites biking around the world, but vagrants. When they can't find somewhere to camp, Lauren approaches a well-dressed woman outside of a church. People are carrying colorful gifts into the church. "Is there by chance somewhere we could sleep on the church grounds? Inside, outside, whatever. We're traveling around the world by bicycle and just arrived in Europe and are having a hard time finding anywhere to camp."[12]

The woman turns away. Vagrants. They are no longer the exploring young couple, but a couple of homeless people. They trudge on with their bikes. They are in a foreign country, and it is Christmas. Lauren's memory of her mother baking her favorite cookies haunts her; the tree adorned with ornaments and gifts, her father and her mother in the same house she had grown up in in Glendale, California. Her best friend Kendall down the street. Going caroling around the neighborhood. This was Christmas. Christmas was not being on a bike in a foreign country.

Jay had no great use for holidays. He didn't like the commercialism, . The tree with gifts piled up around the bottom was not his reality, so being in Spain during the holidays was not the worst thing in the world. Still, he felt some of the same pangs as Lauren.

"You miss a lot when you go on a trip like this," Jay wrote later. "You miss the little things, dinners with friends, parties, game nights, casual lunches, picnics in the park. You miss the big things, weddings, engagement parties . . . and holidays too. You miss celebrating holidays with people who celebrate those same holidays. I'm not big on holidays for all the commercialization they been saddled with." But in the same blog post, Jay admits to "having no plans nor place to enjoy Christmas and New Years Eve here in Spain, we're feeling a little lonely. Unmoored. Homesick, maybe."[13]

They agree to look for fifteen more minutes for a place to camp and then find a cheap hotel. Lauren and Jay walk their bikes toward a church next to a park. "The park is filled with perhaps a hundred locals having what looks like the most joyous time imaginable," Jay writes.

> They are singing Christmas carols and drinking hot coca and eating pastries. They are surrounded by friends and family . . . we stop and look at the scene before us. It's like in every Christmas movie ever made where the protagonist hasn't made it home in time for Christmas . . . that is us right now. We are

the trope. We are the outsiders looking in, the lonely individuals with faces pressed up against the windowpane. We just want a family to celebrate the holidays with.[14]

Then a voice calls from inside the park.

"Hey . . . do you need any help?"[15]

Then, as if in a movie, Lauren and Jay are rescued by a man, Pablo, and his family. They are suddenly drinking hot chocolate and eating pastries, and Pablo offers the yard of his home for them to camp in. Then a new plan is hatched. They will leave their bicycles in a garage owned by brother Miguel and Pablo's aunt, and they will sleep in Pablo's house. It is the Christmas miracle, and Jay and Lauren stay three days. Lauren writes in her Instagram post later: "and then we met the most wonderful family, or rather two families, joined by marriage who took us in and not only invited us to spend Christmas with them, but insisted on it. We truly felt like part of their family and they ours. And we ended up spending Christmas surrounded by loved ones."[16]

In Lauren's Instagram picture, she and Jay are surrounded by five members of Pablo and Migel's family. In the picture they look like one big family. Jay has on a tight-fitting blue coat as do the members of the family. Lauren and Jay are beaming. Lauren's Instagram posts are generally more saccharine than Jay's blog, but in this one both views merged. They had been rescued from a lonely Christmas in a dingy hotel room or a cold tent. Instead, they enjoyed "food. Lots and lots of it. Salad and soup and pasta and bread and chocolate and cake and one million little tapas . . . coffee served at two in the morning . . . long lazy mornings. Hangovers."[17]

On the twenty-sixth of December, they thank their hosts and leave and head out into the rain. The temperature plummets, and Jay and Lauren begin to cycle in what will be a brutal winter in Spain. Biking can be wonderful and awful. It is an amazing high biking on a sunny day in 68 degrees through the countryside with the perfume of dew rising from the grass. But when the temperature dips and rain, sleet, or snow, comes along, biking turns into pure hell. The cold air scalds your lungs, your muscles don't heat up, your fingers and toes freeze, and you put your head down against the wind and push yourself to get where you are going. Winter biking is just not fun.

On January 15, 2018, Jay and Lauren are due to meet Tiffany, her husband, Justin, and Molly in Barcelona. They have to keep going and can't afford to wait out the weather. Lauren posts on Instagram: "we still had 800 kilometers to go with less than ideal weather forecasted until we reach the coast. And while greatly improved, we still were on the mend health wise."[18] The rain comes down harder as they are splashed by the cars on the highway. A police car pulls them over and tells them it is a bad highway for bikers. They camp in an old slaughterhouse and reach the town Ronda, and it gets even colder.

The low-pressure band of arctic air, *the polar vortex,* is dipping down, and Europe is in the grip of an unusually frigid winter. Jay develops a cough and sore throat. Lauren has pink eye. They ride through olive groves, and the next day Lauren has Jay's cold and Jay has pink eye. He writes in his blog: "I don't even have to open my eyes. I just know. I know because I can't open my eyes. My left one anyway. It's sealed shut in a thick layer of crusty mucus."[19]

Through *warmshowers* they arrive in Jaen and connect with a host, Eladio, and have a long meal with several bottles of wine and eat twelve grapes during the first twelve seconds of the new year, a Spanish tradition. Lauren coughs her way through the night, and they stay in Eladio's flat for almost a week to recover. Lauren gets medicine from a doctor. She posts on Instagram:

In Jaen we had an amazing host, Eladio. . . . We ended up staying in Jaen for five nights as we recovered from terrible colds and pinkeye (in all four eyes). It was pretty awful, and we were pretty miserable . . . we shared wonderful meals on the 31st and 1st. . . . Eladio was so kind and understanding through it all.[20]

They take off on January 5, but have stayed too long to make it to Barcelona in time. They must cycle through the mountains of Barcelona, and that will take weeks. Jay and Lauren take off anyway in the rain, and their gloves are immediately saturated. They are 25 miles from Linares and headed for the next mountain. Jay writes: "The sky ahead is even grayer than the sky behind. Water has gotten into our rain gear and we're trembling in the cold."[21]

They pull over to the side of the road and stare at each other.

Lauren turns and asks Jay a direct question: "What the hell are we doing . . . and why are we here?"[22]

They are on a mountain road in Spain in the night in the freezing rain and Lauren's question sounds more like a statement. *Why were they here? Why did she go on this trip with Jay? What is this really? What were they doing?* This has gone way beyond adventure into some sort of deranged outward-bound hell. But beyond the existential questions, the immediate problem is how to get to Barcelona in time to see their friends. They decide to take a train to Valencia and ride the rest of the way to Barcelona from there. They just need to get to a train station. But the rain is increasing, and they need to find shelter. In Jay's blog post, he catalogs the fight that predictably breaks out:

And so, you and your partner argue on the side of the road in the rain for fifteen minutes about in which direction the nearest cover is to be found. One of you (Lauren) shouts that there was an overpass ten kilometers back that was dry. The other (jay) contends that while they remember the overpass well and it was indeed dry underneath it, they're not going ten kilometers back down a hill for a little bit of cover when there's a full-fledged town just five kilometers up the hill. You bicker back and forth about knowns and unknowns, all the while getting wetter and colder. You continue up the hill a few hundred meters. One of you (Lauren) gets off the bike and demands the tent. One of you is going to wrap themselves in the rain fly and figure this all out dressed like a waterproof Halloween ghost on the side of the road. The other (Jay) says no way are they getting the presently dry tent soaking wet for just a minute or two of shelter . . . that thing will never dry in this weather. You bicker back and forth about who's going to carry the wet tent, all the while getting wetter and colder.[23]

One of you (Lauren) unpacks the tent and climbs under the rainfly and can barely operate her phone on account of all the condensation. Together you discover that there is no train station in Arquillos, which answers one question, but also that there are no Valencia-bound trains leaving Linares for days, which presents a half-dozen more. You discuss what to do, and you disagree about what to do, and your emotions are high and wild because this is no place to be having a thoughtful, rational discussion. You bicker back and forth about who's right and who's wrong. You're no longer getting wetter, because your clothes have now reached their saturation point. Now you're just getting colder. . . . A calm, happy couple traveling in a car passes a two-headed waterproof Halloween ghost on the side of the road and splashes water onto it. The calm, happy couple in the car, faces illuminated by the soft blue glow of a phone screen, appear to know just where they're going.[24]

Jay and Lauren finally reach Arquillos and find all cafes and stores closed on account of the holiday, "Happy Three Kings Day." Every Spaniard is home celebrating, and every store is closed until Monday. They find a gas station and are informed that no trains or buses are running, and no trucks are hauling freight, and so hitching will not work. They are frustrated at every turn. Lauren checks her phone and finds out that even if they made it to a bus station, all the tickets are sold out. Jay writes later, "we are shivering. The small shop in the gas station is not heated and were not exactly extended an invitation to hang around and dry off."[25]

They get back on their bikes and Jay gets rid of his wet gloves, gripping the handlebars with bare hands. Jay writes in his blog: "This is the worst. Of all our rough days on bikes these past six months, this is the worst . . . we just don't know what to do . . . the temperature is almost freezing and sure to hit freezing by sundown. Tomorrow will be colder and next day colder still."[26] They bike on and climb higher into the mountains. "Water sloshes in my shoes and my teeth are chattering. I can't feel my fingers and thus I cannot brake but that's fine because we are going up an endless hill."

Jay catches up with Lauren and hears a squeal from her bike. "Your bike isn't sounding so good," he says through shivers. "It isn't riding so good either," she says.[27]

They stop and inspect the bike; there's a lot of resistance to the front wheel but there is nothing they can do. It is dark, and their hands are too cold to take out tools from the pannier and work on the bike. They continue, and Lauren's tire goes flat. It is an awful feeling every cyclist has had. You are riding along miles from your home and suddenly the bike just slows, bumps, and you feel the road through your hands. You have a flat tire. "This is the worst," Lauren says in the cold darkness.

"This really is the worst," Jay agrees.[28]

Then it gets worse. The rain begins to turn into sleet and then wet soggy flakes of snow descend. The fat snowflakes look like cotton balls floating down through the darkness. It is a heavy blinding wet snow. Jay and Lauren stare at each other. They are in the middle of the night on a cold mountain road in Spain during a holiday when people are home and all the stores are closed. They have no choice but to pedal on with Lauren's rim creaking against the snowy cold pavement. They come to a stop again. The snow hisses around them. The wind blows. Their jackets, their hands, their feet are wet. The snow only comes down harder. The bike trip around the world has come to a halt. They are stranded in the middle of the night on the side of a mountain in Spain in a snowstorm. Lauren has snow streaming down her helmet, her cheeks blue from cold, shivering wildly. There is no high from traveling anymore. There is no greater meaning. They are lonely, cold, and miserable. Lauren turns to Jay. He is covered in snow, even his eyelashes brim with flakes. Her voice is not accusing, but it could be. Through chattering teeth, she asks the question:

"What do we do now?"[29]

Notes

1. Simplycycling.org, #22, March 5, 2018.
2. Ibid.
3. Ibid.
4. Simplycycling.Org, #23, April 10, 2018.

5   Ibid.
6   Ibid.
7   Ibid.
8   Ibid.
9   Ibid.
10 Lauren Geoghegan Instagram, January 7, 2018.
11 Ibid.
12 Ibid.
13 Ibid.
14 Ibid.
15 Ibid.
16 Lauren Geoghegan Instagram, January 7, 2018.
17 Simplycycling.Org, #23, April 10, 2018.
18 Lauren Geoghegan Instagram, January 25, 2018.
19 Simplycycling.org, #25, April 17, 2018.
20 Ibid.
21 Ibid., #26, April 19, 2018.
22 Ibid.
23 Ibid.
24 Ibid.
25 Ibid.
26 Ibid.
27 Ibid.
28 Ibid.
29 Ibid.

13
INTO THE WILD
1992

Jay Austin's favorite book was *Into the Wild*. Chris McCandless left his upper-middle-class life to go live off the land in Alaska. Like Jay, Chris found no solace in modern life. Chris wrote on the back cover of Thoreau's *Walden* that he left in the Yukon. "I am reborn. This is my dawn. Real life has just begun. Deliberate living. Conscious attention to the basics of life and constant attention to your immediate environment and its concerns, for example—a job, a task, a book, anything requiring efficient concentration . . . the great holiness of food, the vital heat."[1]

Chris had left his suburban upbringing after getting a degree at Emory University and abandoning his car, burning his money and identification, he disappeared off the grid. Jay's determination to go on a four-year journey around the world after quitting his job has the same echoes, and at times, Chris and Jay's fears, desires, and goals seem identical. Jay wrote in his blog,

> After spending a year or two or three cycling and camping and cooking our way around the world, living life on our terms, avoiding the glowing rectangles of the cube so far, doing what we want when we want, catching the lion's share of sunrises and sunsets the world has to offer and making memories—the kind to tell the grandkids. . . . I worry less about never being able to find a job again and more and more never wanting a job again.[2]

More echoes of Jay abound in the story of Chris McCandless, who graduated college and bid his parents farewell after the ceremony, then never saw them again. He gave away his college fund of $25,000 to charity, changed his name to Alexander Supertramp, and started a life on the road. When asked his name, he quickly gave it as Alex. When his body was found in an abandoned bus in the wilds of Alaska, there was a piece of wood engraved, *Jack London is King Alexander Supertramp May 1992.*

The young man who survived a childhood with an abusive father and had a secret yearning to be someone else, simply didn't exist anymore. He became the wanderer pilgrim, outdoorsman, explorer, Alexander Supertramp. He left Chris McCandless behind with the car in a dried up river bed, the money he burned in a small pile, the mail he had the post office hold so his parents wouldn't know he had taken to the road.

The young man at HUD did the same thing. After a life with a single mother struggling to make ends meet, he changed his name to Jay Austin. The new Jay Austin excelled and got his bachelor's degree from the University of Delaware in three years, a master's degree from Georgetown University in one year, and then interned for the Obama administration and bowled in the White House bowling alley. That Jay Austin worked for HUD and was in the papers and on television.

The book *Into the Wild*, by Jon Krakauer, became a smash bestseller and then a movie by Sean Penn. Undoubtedly, when the story of the young man who left his life behind to go into the Alaskan wilderness crossed Jay Austin's orbit, he ate it up. Chris McCandless roamed the American west for two years before his final trip into the wild. His exploration was a preparation for the ultimate Alaska adventure. Much like Jay's warm-up adventures, the Scooter Diaries, the Iceland biking trip with Lauren, a previous trip to Africa, and to India, these were all leading to the mother of all adventures, which for Jay was a bike trip around the world.

For Chis McCandless, it was going into the Alaskan wilderness with a sack of rice, a .22 rifle, and a few camping provisions. The two young men followed the same prophets, and Alex's journal sounds a lot at times like Jay's blog: "I wanted movement and not a calm course of existence. I wanted excitement and danger and the chance to sacrifice myself for my life. I felt in myself a superabundance of energy which found no outlet in our quiet life."[3] The quote from Tolstoy was highlighted in one of the books found with Chris McCandless's body and is certainly one that Jay Austin followed. Jay took a scooter across the country, while Alex took a canoe into Mexico. The Scooter Diaries is about a near miss with one catastrophe after another. Alex's canoe trip is much the same. Writing in the third person' which shows he is still trying to deal with the new persona of Alex Supertramp, he writes:

> Alex resumes quest for opening to the sea, but only becomes more confused, traveling in circles. Completely demoralized and frustrated he lays in his canoe at days end and weeps. But then by chance he comes upon Mexican duck hunting guides who can speak English . . . they drive him and his canoe in the bed of a pickup to the ocean. It is a miracle.[4]

Alex works harvesting wheat for a combine crew, and then for a short while he works at a McDonalds. All the time he goes under the name Alexander Supertramp. He joins old hippie communes, travels with other wanderers in campers, rides the rails in open boxcars. Alex goes to Mexico, and is almost arrested when he returns. He befriends an eighty-year-old man whom he stays with until he begins his greatest adventure. Both young men have read Jack London's tales of adventure in the Northland. Alex and Jay believe that the answers to life lie in nature. Jack London grew up in a household of poverty and abuse and became a wandering child at sixteen; he projected into the wilderness a utopic world that was his answer to the hell of humanity and bourgeois life. His writings point to a world where the great problems of life are reduced to survival. Young men since the early twentieth century have become lost in London's Edenic tales of answers found in the open world of the Great North. In tales like *To Build a Fire, Love of Life, and White Fang*, romantic imagery is merged with the mystical brutality of nature:

> Dark spruce forest frowned on either side of the frozen waterway. The trees had been stripped by a recent wind of their white covering of frost and they seemed to lean toward each other, black and ominous, in the fading light. A vast silence reigned over the land. The land itself was desolation, lifeless, without movement, so lone and cold that the spirit of it was not even that of sadness. There was a hint in it of laughter, but of a laughter more terrible than any sadness—a laughter that was mirthless as the smile of the Sphinx, a laughter cold as the frost and partaking of the grimness of infallibility. It was the masterful and incommunicable wisdom of eternity laughing at the futility of life and the effort of life. It was the Wild, the savage frozen hearted Northland Wild.[5]

When Christopher McCandless's body was found by two hunters in a bus skidded into the woods by loggers decades before, it set off a nationwide search to find out his true identity. In his writings are echoes of the naturalist John Muir, "But we little know until we have tried . . . how much of the uncontrollable there is in us, urging across glaciers and torrents and up dangerous heights, let the judgment forbid as it may."[6] In Jay Austin's Tiny House, on a plaque above his kitchen, is John Muir's famous quote, "The mountains are calling and I must go."[7] When Jon Krakauer covered McCandless's death for an article in *Outside Magazine*, he became fascinated with the story of the young man who threw away a promising career and life in American society to disappear off the grid and go into the wild. For Alexander Supertramp, his four-month odyssey into the Great North did not go well.

After holing up in the abandoned logging bus, he found it difficult to find game and began to exist on plant life and berries he could identify from a book he had with him. He finally kills a moose only to find he doesn't know how to clean the creature and extract the meat. "Maggots already. Smoking appears ineffective. Don't know, looks like disaster. I now wish I had never shot the moose. One of the great tragedies of my life."[8] After reading and reciting Thoreau, he writes in his journal. "I am reborn . . . positivism, the Unsurpassable Joy of the Life Aesthetic. Absolute truth and honesty. Reality. Independence."[9]

But for all his positivism, he had had enough. A picture Alexander Supertramp took of himself shows him with sunken cheeks and the tendons in his neck prominent. Existing on small game and berries had taken its toll. "Patch jeans, shave, organize pack" was found later written on a piece of birchbark. On July 2, he marked up Tolstoy's *Family Happiness* and highlighted several passages.

> He was right in saying that the only certain happiness in life is to live for others. . . . I have lived through much and now I think I found what is needed for happiness. A quiet secluded life in the country . . . then rest, nature, books, music, love for one's neighbors—such is my idea of happiness. And then, on top of all that, you for a mate and children, perhaps—what more can the heart of a man desire?[10]

Alexander Supertramp wanted to reconnect with people having found the solace of nature to be one of hardship, starving, and loneliness. But when he returned to the West bank of the Teklanika River, which had been frozen when he went into the wilderness, it had become a raging, freezing-cold river of white water. McCandless was not a good swimmer. Even a good swimmer couldn't have crossed the one-hundred-foot-wide channel. Sixty-seven days before, in April, he had simply walked across the river, but rain and snowmelt had changed the sleepy meandering river into a torrent. He was trapped in the wilderness and turned around to his campsite and the abandoned bus. With his ten pounds of rice mostly gone, Alexander Supertramp was looking at riding out a coming winter with what he could hunt or the berries and plant life he could forage.

The weather was favorable still and "the game seems to have been plentiful. In the last three weeks of July, he killed thirty-five squirrels, four spruce grouse, five jays and woodpeckers, and two frogs, all of which he supplemented with wild potatoes and rhubarb, various species of berries and large numbers of mushrooms."[11] But it wasn't enough. The meat from the small creatures was lean, and he was still burning more calories than he was taking in. In late July, two things happened. Alexander Supertramp had an epiphanic moment that coincided with a physical mistake that would kill him in less than three weeks.

On July 28, he read *Doctor Zhivago* and underlined several passages toward the end. "For a moment she rediscovered the purpose of her life. She was here on earth to grasp the meaning of its wild enchantment and to call each thing by its name right now or if this were not in her power to give birth out of love for life to successors who would do it in her place."[12]

Then McCandless wrote, "and so it turned out that only a life similar to the life of those around us, merging with it without a ripple, is genuine life and that an unshared happiness is not happiness . . . and this was most vexing of all . . . HAPPINESSS ONLY REAL WHEN SHARED."[13] It would seem Alexander Supertramp was turning back into the young man who wanted to go home. Two days later, in his journal he wrote, "EXTREMELY WEAK, FAULT OF POT. SEED. MUCH TROUBLE JUST TO STAND UP. STARVING. GREAT JEOPARDY."[14] What had happened in just a few days? He was caloric starved, but he was not sick. Jon Krakauer's hypothesis is that Chris McCandless was subsisting on wild potato plants called *H. Mackenzie*. A similar but toxic potato plant was *H. alpinum*. Krakauer deduced that McCandless ate the seeds of the plant that had a toxic mold which produced swainsomine, a virulent toxin that blocks the body from getting sustenance from food. Chris had put hundreds of the seeds in zplock bags, which induced the mold growth.

He was suddenly too weak to hike out and too weak to hunt. On August 2, there is a journal entry: "TERRIBLE WIND."[15] The temperature was dropping and daylight becoming shorter. Each night was more frigid. On August 5, McCandless wrote in his journal: "DAY 100 MADE IT! BUT IN WEAKEST CONDITION OF LIFE. DEATH LOOMS AS A SERIOUS THREAT. TOO WEAK TO WALK OUT. HAVE LITERALLY BECOME TRAPPED IN THE WILD—NO GAME."[16] On August 9, he notes that he shot at a bear and killed five squirrels. On August 11, he killed and ate one ptarmigan. On August 12, he managed to get out of the bus to look for berries. He writes a sign that will haunt the hikers who come across it nineteen days after his death: "SOS, I NEED YOUR HELP. I AM INJURED, NEAR DEATH AND TOO WEAK TO HIKE OUT OF HERE. I AM ALL ALONE. THIS IS NO JOKE. IN THE NAME OF GOD, PLEASE REMAIN TO SAVE ME. I AM OUT COLLECTING BERRIES CLOSE BY AND SHALL RETURN THIS EVENING. THANK YOU."[17]

Alexander Supertramp had vanished. He signed the cardboard, "CHRIS MCCANDLESS AUGUST?" Then he slowly starved to death. Not a good way to die. "The victim suffers muscle pain, heart disturbances, loss of hair, dizziness, shortness of breath, extreme sensitivity to cold, physical and mental exhaustion. The skin becomes discolored . . . a severe chemical imbalance develops in the brain, inducing convulsions and hallucinations." On August 12, a final entry, "BEAUTIFUL BLUEBERRIES." For the next five days, he ticks them off in his journal. He tears a final page from Louis Lamour memoir, *Education of a Wandering Man*. On the page is a quote of a poem by Robinson Jeffers, "Wise Men in Their Bad Hours."

Deaths a fierce meadowlark, . . .
And a few dead men's thoughts have the same tempter.[18]

Then, on the other side, Chris McCandless wrote a goodbye note: "I HAVE HAD A HAPPY LIFE AND THANK THE LORD. GOODBYE AND MAY GOD BLESS ALL."[19] He took a picture of himself with his sign. He is thin but he does not look unhappy. Then he crawled into his sleeping bag. Death came on August 18. His great adventure into the wild lasted 112 days. After his death came the comments, the slurs, the derogatory attacks that would also mark the deaths of Jay and Lauren: "Alex is a nut in my book . . . the author describes a man who has given away a small fortune, forsaken a loving family, abandoned his car, watch, and map and burned the last of his money." Another writer: "Krakauer is a kook if he doesn't think Chris Alexander Supertramp McCandless was a kook. . . . McCandless had already gone over the edge and just happened to hit bottom in Alaska."[20]

The parallels between Jay Austin and Chris McCandless are even in death. But one great difference is that Jay Austin was a methodical planner who anticipated many scenarios. He had worked for seven years and prepared for his trip extensively. A final letter written to Jon Krakauer came from an Inupiat village on the Kobuk River north of the Arctic Circle. The writer prefaced his letter by saying he had knocked off most of a bottle of Seagram's and it was 1:00 a.m.

> Over the past 15 years, I've run into several McCandless types out in the country. Same story, idealistic, energetic young guys who overestimated themselves, underestimated the country, and ended up in trouble. McCandless was hardly unique, there's quite a few of these guys hanging around the state, so much alike that they're almost a collective cliché. The only difference is that McCandless ended up dead, with the story of his dumbaassedness splashed across the media. . . . McCandless is finally just a pale 20th century burlesque of London's protagonist (To Build A Fire) who freezes because he ignores advice and commits big time hubris.[21]

If Jay Austin had read the drunken writer's musings in the Yukon, he might have written him off as another person who didn't understand what he was trying to do. But on the mountain road in Spain, in the snowstorm in the year 2018, Jay would have been forced to recognize the man *"who freezes because he ignores advice and commits big time hubris."*[22]

Notes

1. Krakauer Jon, Into the Wild, Anchor Books, NY, 1997.
2. Simplycycling.org, January 10, 2017.
3. Krakauer Jon, Into the Wild Anchor Books, NY, 1997.
4. Ibid.
5. London, Jack White Fang.
6. Muir, John.
7. Ibid.
8. Krakauer Jon, Into the Wild, Anchor Books, NY, 1997.
9. Ibid.
10. Ibid.
11. Ibid.
12. Ibid.
13. Ibid.
14. Ibid.
15. Ibid.
16. Ibid.
17. Ibid.
18. Ibid.
19. Ibid.
20. Ibid.
21. Ibid.
22. Ibid.

14
VALENCIA, SPAIN
JANUARY 2018

The snow is coming down heavier on the side of the dark mountain. The wind is blowing the tent fly they have over their heads in the middle of the night in the middle of nowhere. Lauren and Jay's trip around the world in the snowstorm with a flat tire has moved from arduous to dangerous. They could freeze if something didn't change fast. Jay's Instagram post is bleak:

> Huddled under our tent fly on the side of the road, I looked for train tickets out of the mountains on my damp phone and found nothing available in a hundred-kilometer radius for days and days. With nothing else to do, we got back on the bikes and pedaled. Lauren's front tire started to go flat as well. Her rear brake wasn't working and her front brake then started to make some pretty awful noises. Our fingers were too stiff and numb to do anything about it. And then it started to snow.[1]

Winter biking in snow. Your tires slip around. You fall. The snow is blinding. It is when I turn around on my bike. But Jay and Lauren cannot turn around and head for home. They are on a mountain road in a snowstorm during a Spanish holiday where no one is on the road. When they hear a car, they jump off their bikes, and wave their thumbs. No one stops. Jay writes in his blog: "Utterly hopeless, wet, and cold, we did all we could do. We pedal on. Broken bike. Frozen fingers. What else can we do? We pedal and I listen to the rumble of an engine behind us. Its loud enough I look back. It's a truck."[2]

Mountain biking is a whole different beast from road biking. Mountain biking is all about low gears and fat tires and bikes built like small tanks. When riding a road bike, the momentum builds very fast, and you put your head down and thin tires with little friction increase your speed while you shoot up a to a cool 30 miles an hour on straight flat roads. In mountain biking, you are the engine that has to keep pushing all the time. Mountain biking is herculean. But for Ricardo, he is used to the man strength required to power up the side of a mountain. He drives his white van to find the thin biking roads that snake up the mountain that he can ride up and down, taking air when he can, losing it sometimes, but then getting back on the bike and continuing in the endless pursuit of the adrenaline ride. Tonight, he is headed home when the weather changed in the mountains with his bike in the back of his van. He sees two cyclists on the side of the road, waving to him. They look distressed, snow covered, and he can tell right away they are from another country.

Ricardo passes them and knows what it is like in a snowstorm on a bike. It has happened to him many times. Cyclists are a club with unwritten rules. One is that you always help a cyclist in distress. Ricardo pulls the van over and grabs a couple of towels out of the back and opens the door, running toward the two frozen people. Jay posts on Instagram: "Just as we hit the pits of despair, a smiling couple in a big white van pulled to the side of the road and hopped out."[3] Riccardo and his girlfriend Paqui take them to their home and give them warm tea and leftover cake from Three Kings Day. They are in the pueblo of Santisteban. Jay and Lauren learn a bus is leaving that night from Valencia. Ricardo insists he drives them to the bus leaving in an hour. After a harrowing drive on the dark snow-covered mountain highways, they arrive at 8:45, and there is no bus. Thirty minutes later, the bus arrives, and the driver refuses to take their bikes, and then says if they can take off the wheels, he will take them.

Jay and Lauren struggle to get the wheels off and stow the bikes. The bus driver demands cash, of which they have none. Ricardo puts a hundred euro note in Lauren's hands and tells her to send it back to him when they can. Jay and Lauren get on the bus. Jay writes about these acts of kindness later:

> We live in a world where people will bring other people into their homes, feed them, and drive them up and down a snowy mountain in the depths of a winter's night. We live in a world where people will hand strangers they only just met one hundred euros . . . mostly we live in a world where how you live is dictated largely by how you trust. If you do not trust others, if you believe human nature to be something dark and rotten, you close yourself off to a whole lot.[4]

They get to Valencia and stay with another *warmshowers* hosts. Tony and Vicki are bicycle travelers who had been traveling from Europe to India the year before when Vicki became pregnant. Morning sickness in a tent was not pleasant. Up to now Jay hasn't embraced the idea of having a family, stating there are too many children in the world already. Now there seems to be a sea change in his blog post as he considers a future with children:

> Vicki and Tony are lovely. We meet their daughter. She, they tell us is the happy reason their bike journey came to an end . . . she is small and shy and adorable. Vicki and Tony are really cool parents. Like parents we might hope to be some day. They ride around Valencia with little Elena strapped in a kids seat on the back of Tonys bike. They're young and energetic and amazing cooks.[5]

They help fix Lauren's bike and send them on their way to Barcelona to meet their Georgetown friends, Molly, Tiffany, and Justin. It has been six months since they have seen anyone they know. Justin has work in Spain, and his wife Tiffany comes along for the reunion. Molly Scalise is added in later, and it becomes a reunion of old friends. Jay and Lauren book a hostel for three nights and carry their bikes up long, skinny stairs. Molly arrives, and they hug. It is a narcotic to see their old Georgetown friend after six months. The good tidings flood back in as the three friends walk around the Gothic Quarter, eat tapas, and start a collection of empty wine bottles in their room. Lauren's Instagram posts are happy and positive: "And with the help of an incredibly kind couple, Ricardo and Paqui, who stopped their white van (while it was hailing) to pick us up on the side of the road and take us to their home in the next town. . . . later that day we took a night bus to Valencia. Things really turned around for us."[6]

But when Molly sees her old roommate and friend from Georgetown, she hears a different story. "She looked really fit and she had lost weight, but she said she wasn't sure she wanted to be on the trip and wanted to go back," Molly recalled in an interview six years later. "I remember her saying, 'Oh Molly, its' been really hard' . . . that she was so tired and freezing. I didn't know if she wanted me to encourage her to keep going or not. . . . I think after the Spain experience, the cold, the snow, she had enough. And I think Jay was a very strong personality and so was Lauren and when things went wrong . . . they butted heads."[7]

Lauren posts a picture on Instagram of the three friends in winter coats in Spain. It looks cold. Tiffany and Justin arrive, and they stay at a hotel a few kilometers away. Molly and Tiffany bring supplies. Electronics, a new cooking pan, a windscreen for their stove. They take a walking tour of Barcelona and then Tiffany, Molly, and Lauren go shopping. "I knew they had been on this tiny budget Jay set up," Tiffany related later. "I mean Lauren loved to eat and we stop and get some breakfast and I ask her if she wants another cinnamon roll and Lauren stares at the menu and then says no. I knew she wanted it so I bought it for her."[8] Tiffany pulls back her hair and leans toward her computer. Her son is playing in the other room, and she is watching him while talking to me:

Lauren was out of money. She didn't have big savings like Jay, and they were using his money now. I mean, I know Jay was trading bitcoin and crypto on the trip and now he was the keeper of the purse. Lauren had some money come in from her parents and she bought some earrings and shoes and told us Jay mustn't know, and asked if we could take them home.[9]

There is something incongruous about the minimalist monk trading bitcoin through his phone while going around the world. Chris McCandless of *Into the Wild* burned his money and existed on rice and berries and plants at different times. Thoreau eschewed money. Jack Kerouac never had any. Jay's bank account balance is not known at this point, but he has alluded to banking his six-figure income ever since he moved into the Tiny House. Fights over buying power bars, candy, and staying in hotels have broken out. The minimalist can be brutal for the woman with the man who had set their daily expenditures at $23 a day. "I remember Lauren bought this scarf while we were in Spain," Molly recalls:

And it was a beautiful scarf. Lauren loved colorful clothing, but she said, don't show it to Jay and hide it from him. Another time at a dinner, Lauren wanted another cocktail, and they ended up in a fight. Jay didn't want to spend the money; he just didn't care about big dinners and clothes and things like that. He saw food as for subsistence and clothes in the utilitarian sense.[10]

In the Instagram picture of Molly, Lauren, and Jay, Jay is in the middle of the two women who are smiling for the camera. They spend six days together, and then it is time for Molly, Justin, and Tiffany to leave.

"It is Saturday, and, in the morning, our three dear friends are headed to the airport," Jay writes in his blog. "By evening they'll be back in their beds in America, a return journey that for us may take another three years." And then a prophetic eerie sentence. "We don't know when we'll next see them again. We don't know when well see anyone again."[11] This could be read several ways, but there is the unmistakable taint of fatalism. The assumption they will be biking for three more years seems crazy when after six months Lauren has hit the wall. Tiffany later said that Lauren told her, "That it had been really tough." She still wants to continue on, she tells her, but there have been close calls and sicknesses; malaria, flu, gastric issues; Jay almost being crushed between two cars; the woman who hit his bike; the elephant that chased them; stuck on the side of a mountain in a snowstorm. To push out three more years and then to follow with the line, "We don't know when we'll next see anyone again," which could easily be read as, "We don't know if we will ever see anyone again."[12]

The man who had walked away from his former life seems to have a different agenda. Jay Austin seems more on a journey quest than someone biking around the world who will return to their old life. A man planning to be on the road for almost four years has little intention of returning to anything resembling his former life. The question is, what intention does Jay Austin have? The man, who was only two years away from getting all his student loans forgiven if he had stayed at HUD and postponed his trip, finishes his blog post: "We say goodbye to Tiffany and Justin and later to Molly. Our friends fly west, across the Atlantic, toward the Americas. We turn east. Toward Asia."[13]

Lauren and Jay wave goodbye to their friends. It's hard to know if Tiffany, Molly, or Justin ever brought up the terrorist attack in New York just four months before. Why would they? But the mowing down of cyclists by an Islamic radical with a truck was front-page news.

Notes

1. Jay Austin Instagram Post, January 8, 2018.
2. Ibid.
3. Ibid.
4. Simplycycling.org, #27, April 24, 2018.
5. Ibid.
6. Lauren Geoghegan Instagram Post, January 25, 2018.
7. Molly Scalise Interview by William Hazelgrove, March 12, 2024.
8. Tiffany Del Rio Interview by William Hazelgrove, March 16, 2024.
9. Ibid.
10. Molly Scalise Interview by William Hazelgrove, March 12, 2024.
11. Simplycycling.org, #28, April 26, 2018.
12. Ibid.
13. Ibid.

15
THE NEW YORK BICYCLE MURDERS

2017

On Halloween October 31, 2017, a slight Mideastern man with a scraggly black beard rented a pickup truck at a Home Depot in Passaic New Jersey. He drove off in the white truck toward New York, and at 2:43 p.m. crossed the George Washington Bridge and entered lower Manhattan, and then drove South down the West Side Highway. At Houston Street near Pier 40, he swerved onto the Hudson River Greenway, a bike lane that runs along the Hudson River and Hudson River Park and West Street and is full of cyclists pedaling up and down Manhattan.

Sayfullo Habibullaevic Saipov pressed down on the accelerator of the truck and began swerving his pickup truck as he crushed one cyclist after another. After driving a full mile down the bike path, the truck crashed into a school bus, where Sayfullo jumped out with a paintball gun and a pellet gun. He shouted out, *God is Great God is Great*, and then Officer Ryan Nash shot him in the abdomen, and he was taken into custody. A bloody trail of twisted bikes and bodies lay on the bike path. Eight cyclists died, and seven lay injured.

This is three months after Jay Austin and Lauren Geoghegan began their biking trip around the world. The story of the ISIS-radicalized Sayfullo Saipov was splashed all over the front pages of the newspapers. By this time, Jay and Lauren were in Africa crossing deserts and being chased by elephants. Jay and Lauren didn't read the articles about Sayfullo, who was born in Tashkent, Uzbekistan, on February 8, 1988, and had graduated from college and studied at the Tashkent Financial Institute until 2009 as an accountant. He entered the United States with a Diversity Immigrant Visa and moved to Stow, Ohio, and then Tampa, Florida, and Patterson, New Jersey. In Patterson, he had a brief six-month stint as an Uber driver and acquired a commercial truck license. He lost jobs because of a bad temper and was interviewed by the FBI in 2015 for communications with suspected terrorists.

Jay and Lauren knew the history of the Mideast. Undoubtedly, in the hot dusty deserts and savannahs of Africa, they gave little thought to the history that produced the radicalized Sayfullo. Those policies could be traced back to the Sykes Picot Agreement that pulled the rug out from Lawrence of Arabia and the Arabs in 1917 and gave power to Britain and France over their land. Then the United States sponsored coup in Iran in 1953. While President Dwight Eisenhower swung his golf club in the postwar lassitude of the 1950s, agents from Britain and the United States organized a coup in Iran to put in Mohammad Reza Shah as ruler and puppet. Britain had long been pumping oil out of Iran and became indignant when President Turman suggested they should pay Iran for the oil. The agents of Britain could get nowhere with the man who ended the Second World War by dropping two atomic bombs on Japan.

But Eisenhower was not the hands-on man that Truman was. He let his advisors handle the Iran problem, and his advisors were pro-British and Eisenhower was pro-golf. The coup was engineered, and the United States pumped in one billion dollars in the decade after. The Shah was a brutal dictator and hated by the Iranian people. Even up to the Truman administration, the United States was seen as a friend of the Arabs, while the British were viewed as the hated colonialists. But after the coup, the United States became Satan. The Shah spent lavishly on his family and palace and on arms. The people of Iran were destitute, imprisoned, and tortured. Dissent was dealt with brutally. When the inevitable overthrow came in 1979, President Jimmy Carter gave the Shah asylum in the United States. The radicals who had suffered under the Shah's tyrannical rule flew into a rage and stormed the US Embassy, taking fifty-two American hostages for fourteen months.

The hostage crisis was the boiling cauldron of hate between Iran and the United States and allowed the radical clerics not only to enforce their extreme Islamic beliefs at home but also to export terror aboard.

> With their devotion to radical Islam and their eagerness to embrace even the most horrific kinds of violence, Iran's revolutionary leaders became heroes to fanatics in many countries . . . they began financing and arming of Hamas, Hezbollah and other Mid East factions . . . among those who were inspired by their example were Afghans who founded the Taliban, led it to power in Kabul and gave Osama Bin Laden the base from which he launched devastating terror attacks.[1]

The code name for the coup of 1953 in Iran was Operation Ajax, and it is not hard to draw a line between "the Shahs oppressive regime and the Islamic Revolution to the fireballs that engulfed the World Trade Center in New York."[2] The United States justified the coup as a way to stop Soviet expansion into the Middle East, but oil was the real catalyst, and a friendly regime was needed to pump out the crude oil under the deserts that Lawrence of Arabia had pounded across forty years before.

Saipov was found to be self-radicalized and said he had killed the cyclists on the bike path in the name of the Islamic State of Iraq and ISIL. He said he was motivated to carry out the attack after watching a video of Abu Bakr al-Baghdadi. Investigators found ISIL videos on his computer and other devices. In a famous photo of the time, Saipov requested to have the ISIL flag displayed in his hospital room and said, "he felt good about what he had done."[3] On May 17, 2023, he was sentenced to eight consecutive life terms without parole plus two concurrent life terms plus 260 years. During the trial, he said that "thousands and thousands of Muslims are dying all over the world, why should he be judged for the death of eight people."[4] The terror attack on cyclists in New York would resonate with Hussein Abdusamadov. The radicalized drifter with a mission to commit jihad had recently returned from Russia to the old Soviet-aligned country of Tajikistan. A country that two American cyclists were steadily pedaling toward.

Notes

1   Kinzer, Stephen, All the Shah's Men, Wiley, NY, 2003.
2   Ibid.
3   *New York Times*.
4   Ibid.

16
FRANCE
FEBRUARY 2018

Lauren and Jay reach Southern France in a rainstorm that continues for days. Lauren posts on Instagram, "in many ways moving from Spain to France was an easy adjustment. On the language front it was a challenge. Our ability to communicate and connect hindered by our nonexistent French."[1] In Marseilles, Lauren goes to a hospital for a clogged ear. They had visited an emergency clinic, but both ears are sealed with wax. At the hospital the doctors clear the blockage, and they cycle on using *warmshowers* and *couchsurfing* to find hosts to stay with. Lauren and Jay bike past towering mountains and cliffs and Jay posts a picture that the *New York Times* will later feature with headline, *A Dream Ended on a Mountain Road: The Cyclists and the ISIS Militants*.[2] In the picture, Jay has on a baseball cap and Lauren's hair is tied up with a bandana. The sea is in the background and they are leaning together and kissing on top of a cliff. There is an iconic quality to the picture taken halfway through their trip that the media will pick up on.

Lauren and Jay push on to the seaside hamlet of Cassis. In his blog, Jay describes the people they stay with using *warmshowers* and what is expected of them. "Sometimes it is okay. Sometimes it is not. Sometimes people are a good fit and sometimes people are not a good fit and sometimes people are available and sometimes people are not available. Sometimes hosts approve guests' requests, and sometimes they say 'sorry, find somewhere else.'"[3]

Jay writes:

> But the key here, what sets these communities apart from a commercial endeavor like Airbnb, is that they are fundamentally non-transactional. That is, guests do not pay money to hosts. Staying with a host is a lot like staying with a friend or family member. You don't pay for your stay; you just act kind

and decent. You don't come back at three in the morning, loud from the bar, and sleep until noon. You don't leave dirty dishes in the sink. You don't go see the sights, then retreat to your room and flip through your phone like you might do if you're staying in an Airbnb or hotel. You pay for your stay with time and with care. And in return you get not just a safe place to sleep, but a really special and intimate experience with someone whom you would probably never otherwise meet.[4]

They leave Cassis and "had a short super steep climb," Lauren posts. "With the steep grade we pushed our loaded bicycles all the way up." They continue biking through France and stay with many different hosts "who kindly welcomed us into their warm homes, generously offered us a shower and a bed and yummy food and freely shared their great company in Narbonne, Montpellier, Miramas, Les Pennes, Mirabeau, Cassis, LeParadet, Hyeres, and Nice."[5] They enter Italy. The weather has changed, and cycling is quickly becoming impossible. The polar vortex of freezing temperatures with arctic wind and snow is coming to the Southern Europe and the mountains of Northern Italy. "It is colder in Europe than at the North Pole . . . the polar vortex is upon us,"[6] Jay writes as they bike across Italy.

They can't camp, and Italy is too expensive to wait out the cold. They decide to take a train to the other side of the country and stay with a friend of Lauren's mother. "We decided to make alternate plans to avoid biking and camping in the polar vortex conditions and to take a train to Trieste where we had an open invitation from a family friend. . . . Instead of crossing the top of Italy by bicycle over weeks, we would cross by train over hours,"[7] Lauren posts on Instagram.

They bike to Ventimiglia, but the train isn't leaving until the next morning. They stay in a McDonalds until it closes at midnight and then wait in the train station through the night. They sleep on the cold, hard marble floor. It is 2:00 a.m. when Jay sees a man approaching. The man asks them for an apple out of their food jugs.

"Hey, give me that apple," he demands.

"No," we say. "Get your own apple."

"Oh, come on. I just want one apple."

The man reaches toward the jug of food strapped to the fork of Jay's bike.

"Get your hands away from our bikes,"[8] Jay growls from the cold floor with his jacket zipped up to his nose. The man finally leaves. Lauren posts a picture on Instagram of her on the marble station floor next to her bike. She has on a purple winter coat with her hood up and a scarf wrapped around her face. Her hands are in her pockets, and she is lying on the inflatable mat they used for the tent. The bikes are locked together with a kryptonite lock. The station looks deserted. She writes, "We passed the 12 hours in between at McDonalds (open

FRANCE

until midnight and with Wi-Fi) and the train station, where we settled in along this wall until it was time to board. Traveling the world by bicycle has been full of many wonderful experiences but for us, it also includes many moments like this."[9]

The train rumbles in at 5:00 a.m., and the conductor refuses to let them on with their bikes.

"It's a tense moment," Jay later writes.

I rush to the platform to meet Lauren, and we run with our bikes alongside the slowing train. *Carriage 5, Carriage 5.* We scan the numbers on the side of each train car. There it is. We hurry toward it. A man in a Trenitalia uniform stops us and asks where we're going. *Carriage 5, kind sir.* With the bikes? Why yes. Here's our bike supplement. *But bikes are not allowed on this train*, he says. *But your website says bikes are allowed on this train.*[10]

The train screeches to a halt. He winces and relents.

The second train they board is crowded, and two police officers ask if they have permission to board the train with their bikes. Jay shows them the ticket with the bike supplement. "Right, that's fine, but you need permission from the conductor to bring the bikes on."[11] Jay goes off to search but can't find the conductor. They ride the ninety minutes squeezed into a corner of the train with their bikes. The third train is the international train, and bikes aren't allowed but Jay finds an exception on the website.

"Our train is delayed, so I take the time to ask around the station. *Yes, hello, can I verify that when this train pulls up and bodies rush toward it, us and our bikes won't be denied?* I wind up at a ticket window with a woman who speaks only marginally more English than I speak Italian."

"This international train. No bicycle on an international train."

"Right, but the website. I slide my phone underneath the thick, scratched glass and ask her to read the page I've downloaded. The website's banner matches the one on her shirt."

She looks at it. "Website is wrong. No bicycle on international train."[12]

They board the train anyway and are hassled by the conductors, but they allow Jay and Lauren to stay on their bikes. Lauren posts. "We arrived in Trieste before the worst of the polar vortex hit. We were picked up at the train station by my mother's dear friend, Myrna and her son Francisco."[13] Jay and Lauren stay in Muggia for two weeks with Myrna. Jay fixes his wheel rim that has fractured. Lauren posts on Instagram, "Waiting out the storm and waiting for better cycling. . . . Enjoying the company and generous hospitality of Myrna and her immediate family and enjoying indoor rest and relaxation, sheltered from the cold and the elements."[14]

They leave Myrna and her son on March 8. They had planned to cycle 1,000 kilometers across Italy but ended up cycling only 25. They cross the Italy-Slovenia border and bike to Croatia and get caught in a snowstorm as dark descends. They can find nowhere to camp, and the temperature plummets. Lauren posts on Instagram.

> Now our sweat has cooled and begun to sap heat from our bodies. Now we are few kilometers into Croatia and suddenly smacked with the acknowledgment that we've maybe arrived a little too early in the year. Our first day on the bikes since leaving France two weeks ago has been neither fun nor easy. Our leg muscles have atrophied during our fortnight of sloth in Muggia, and now there are hills.

Lauren posts a photo on Instagram of her bike on its side at the bottom of a hill.

> We started the day in high spirits but by our second hour "back on the road" our smiles were gone and our water snack break at a village bus stop had turned into a fight (a great place for a fight . . .) it was pretty awful. And we were still unhappy with each other when we began the first of the day's steep climbs. The hill may not look steep, but it was. . . . I was completely demoralized, letting my bike fall with a thud to its side and carrying my panniers to the top to lighten the overall bicycle load.[15]

Traveling with anyone is a challenge. Biking and wild camping with a significant other across the world is a daunting challenge. The logistics are a constant headache that invariably leads to arguments. Jay admits in his blog post:

> We have been bickering all day, out of step with one another and our old routine. It has been hot, and then cold, and now very cold. And here we are, atop a mountain pass. On the edge of the Alps. In winter. It is late. Earlier we were cycling across the Slovenian lowlands and huffing up ancient, crumbling goat trails and climbing toward a mountain pass on the Slovenian Croatian border, going downhill from the pass for the better part of an hour. Trying to get beneath the snow line. Trying to find somewhere dry to camp. Our fingers are numb, and our spirits deflated. We stop every now and then to inspect a patch of forest and find them all to be unsuitable for one reason or another. Mud. Ice. Thornbushes. We descend further.[16]

They coast into a town in the dark with their lights piercing the snowy darkness. They ask a German woman if they can camp in her yard. *Nein*, she responds and then opens the door to her home where they are offered lodging and fed. "The woman tosses some wood into the furnace and feeling returns to our fingertips." They leave in the morning after sleeping very well and "wish goodbye to our benefactor as best we can which is say mostly smiles and hands pressed to our hearts."[17] They stop off in Rijeka with another *couchsurfing* host where they stay for three days. They continue to Croatia where Lauren's shifter cable snaps. They set up camp and replace the cable. Croatia is barren and cold and winter has swooped down once again. For now, they have had enough. Jay writes in his blog:

> We're cold and we're tired. . . . we've been in Europe since December and it is now March and not once have we actually *had* a place of our own, set of keys and kitchen and all. We've been the recipients of a great deal of generosity—heaps of it, surely—but we're feeling a little untethered, and could use a little stability for a moment or two, a place to unpack our things. A place where we can leave dirty dishes in the sink until morning and not feel guilty. A place to dry out our tent, perpetually soaked, that isn't a gas station parking lot, my really fantastic now-former colleagues had the very kind thought to send us off with an Airbnb gift card for just such an occasion.[18]

They book a flat on the Croatian coast for a week and "shower and wash our clothes and go to the grocery and buy normal people quantities of foodstuffs and make piles of pancakes and walk around Splits old town and otherwise do very little."[19] They decide to book another Airbnb for two weeks. Jay writes of a domesticity that surprises him.

> We do precisely the opposite of what most people do when they're on vacation. We stay at home and cook. We sleep late. We sit on the couch and read books and lie in bed and watch movies and catch up on emails . . . we're enjoying this, this simple bout of domesticity. We're enjoying the kitchen and the bed and the shower and the many other small luxuries we go without most days: an electric kettle, a mirror, chairs.[20]

There is a picture posted on Instagram of Lauren in bed reading her kindle luxuriating in clean white sheets. She writes, "We decided to take some time off the bicycles to enjoy the comforts and pleasure of stationary domestic life on our own. We rented an apartment in Split and then another in Markasa and we had the apartments and the time all to ourselves. Every cupboard and every hour. For a total of 3.5 weeks. It was bliss."[21] The question I put in every interview was would Lauren and Jay had stayed together. The answers are varied as the people. But there is nothing more intimate, challenging, or difficult than traveling together to shake out the truth of a relationship. The iconoclastic Jay Austin seemed to be taking a back seat to someone else now. "Lauren always wanted a family,"[22] Kendall, her childhood friend, told me emphatically. Jay was still a question mark with the gruff answer of there are too many children in the world already, but the question mark seemed to be changing into an ellipsis. Another Instagram picture is of a pancake Jay made for Lauren in the perfect shape of a heart. They are like any couple, nesting and enjoying time in their home and the company of each other.

Notes

1. Lauren Geoghegan Instagram, March 3, 2018.
2. New York Times, A Dream Ended on A Mountain Road.
3. Simplycycling.org, #30, May 3, 2018.
4. Ibid.
5. Lauren Geoghegan Instagram.
6. Simplycycling.org, #32, May 11, 2018.
7. Lauren Geoghegan Instagram, April 6, 2018.
8. Simplycycling, org, #32, March 20, 2018.
9. Lauren Geoghegan Instagram, April 6, 2018.
10. Simplycycling.org, #32, May 11, 2018.
11. Ibid.
12. Ibid.
13. Lauren Geoghegan Instagram Post.
14. Ibid., May 18, 2018.
15. Laureen Geoghegan Instagram Post, May 25, 2018.
16. Simplycycling.org, #33, May 30, 2018.
17. Ibid.
18. Ibid.
19. Ibid.
20. Ibid.
21. Lauren Geoghegan Instagram, June 22, 2018.
22. Interview with Kendall O'Connor, May 6, 2024.

17

THE ADVENTURES OF HUCKLEBERRY FINN

1871

Where does the wanderlust come from?

In the late nineteenth century, a new term was coined, "neurasthenia," or nervous disease. It was a catchall for the strange maladies afflicting Americans who found themselves working in factories and offices. Cancer, heart disease, diabetes, and mental illness became rampant. The antidote was given by a showman named Buffalo Bill. He toured the east with his Wild West show and championed the real men who were out West on the frontier. Americans were meant to be out laboring under Gods light, not cooped up in offices.

Jay Austin's proclamation that he didn't want to spend thirty years In front of a computer, retire, then die ten years later resonates with the sufferers of neurasthenia that today we call *stress*. The restless quality of Americans, which F. Scott Fitzgerald defined as "that resourcefulness of movement that is so peculiarly American,"[1] is what permeates the American character with a duality that we are in the moment, but not quite satisfied with the moment. Clearly, there is something better over the next hill, so we quit our jobs, go for our dreams, or, like Jay and Lauren, take a bike trip around the world. It is one of our cherished cultural beliefs to risk all on an unknown outcome. Our national DNA began with an article in a Terra Haute newspaper in 1883 that advised restless souls to "Go West young Man."[2] Go gamble all you know on an uncertain outcome. The cowboy. The pioneer. The explorer. The entrepreneur. These are regarded as the high-water marks of our collective aspiration. Horatio Algeir stories abound. Rags to riches are celebrated every day in our movies, television, newspapers, and talk shows. And always in the story is the high-risk, high-reward ratio. And it is not about money, it is about finding a new identity in the great unknown which for Americans in the nineteenth century was the wilderness.

And our cultural literary heritage has one early explorer who runs away to find himself much like Jay Austin. Ernest Hemingway called *The Adventures of Huckleberry Finn* the first American novel. The story of a poor boy along the Mississippi might not at first glance have anything to do with Jay Austin or Lauren Geoghegan, but this American obsession with breaking away from a traditional life has deep roots in our history and literature. Thirty years before the Civil War, a poor boy with a drunken abusive father, who beats him and threatens him, escapes down the Mississippi with a runaway slave, Jim. But what was he escaping from? Twain put his finger on the pulse of America at the time, the distrust of authority, the stultifying quality of bourgeois life, and he put it all in the boy who was afraid Widow Douglas would "civilize me but it was rough living in the house all the time considering how dismal regular and decent the widow was in all her ways; and so when I couldn't stand it anymore; I lit out. I got into my old rags and my sugar hogshead again and was free and satisfied"[3]

Is this so different from the conformity Jay Austin rails against 147 years later? "Pretty soon I wanted to smoke and asked the widow to let me. But she wouldn't. She said it was a mean practice and wasn't clean and I must try not to do it anymore. That is just the way with some people. They get down on a thing when they don't know nothing about it."[4] Huckleberry Finn not only rejects gentile life, but he rejects the notion of heaven and hell as well. "She told me about the bad place, and I said I wished I was there . . . she said it was wicked to say what I said, said she wouldn't say it for the whole world, she was going to live as to go the good place."[5]

And so, Huckleberry Finn runs away for good, running toward existential freedom.

In 1840 the United States was largely unsettled, but people were wrestling with a vanishing frontier even then. Huckleberry Finn sees freedom in the woods and later on the Mississippi river. The salvation Jay Austin craves in leaving his life is the same salvation a twelve-year-old boy in Hannibal Missouri pines for while locked up in his aunt's house.

"I set down in a chair by the window and tried to think of something cheerful, but it wasn't no use. I felt so lonesome, I wished I was dead. The stars were shining and the leaves rustled in the woods ever so mournful and I heard an owl away off, who whooing about somebody that was dead and a whippoorwill and a dog crying about somebody that was going to die, and the wind was trying to whisper something to me and I couldn't make out what it was."[6]

Twain lets Eden creep into his tale of a boy finding his moral compass as he makes a tour of the border states along the Mississippi before the Civil War. And his deliverance is always in nature:

> "Pretty soon I heard a twig snap down in the dark amongst the trees something was a stirring. I set still and listened. Directly I could just barely hear a meow down there. That was good I say. Says I meow meow as soft as I could and then I put out the light and scrambled out the window onto the shed. Then I slipped to the ground and crawled in among the trees and sure enough there was Tom Sawyer waiting for me."[7]

And so, Huckleberry Finn escapes on his own bike trip around the world, floating down the Mississippi River with a runaway slave. And as Huckleberry runs away toward the Mississippi and his grand adventure, he is already parted from that civilized life of the town. "We looked away down into the village and could see three or four lights twinkling where there was sick folks maybe and the stars over us was sparking ever so fine and down by the village was the river a whole mile broad and awful still and grand."[8] And what else is Huckleberry running from, but an abusive father. "Pap he hadn't been seen for more than a year and that was comfortable for me . . . he used to always whale me when he was sober and could get his hands on me, though I used to take to the woods most of the time when he was around."[9]

American boys and their fathers. It pops up again and again and again. Huckleberry Finn is marked by his cleverness and his perspective on his own life when he looks back. "The longer I went to school the easier it got to be. I was getting sort of used to the widow's ways . . . living in a house and sleeping in a bed pulled on me pretty tight . . . but before the cold weather I used to slide and out and sleep in the woods sometimes. . . . I liked the old ways best."[10] The "old ways" are the conflict at the heart of the American soul that is fundamentally a harkening to an agrarian past. After Huckleberry fakes his own death, he is essentially free to live life as he wants it on the Mississippi River. And so, his tour of America begins as Jay and Lauren's tour of the world begins. There is good and bad. When Jim and Huckleberry come across a drifting house, there is a dead man in a room who has come to a violent end. Jim tells him, "It's a dead man. Yes indeedy naked too. Hed been shot in the back. I reckon he ben [sic] dead two or three days. Come in Huck but down look at his face—its too gashly."[11]

And as they head north where Jim is hoping to be set free, there is a slow-growing undercurrent of danger. It is a tour of the human condition, and it mirrors Jay and Lauren's tour of Africa, Europe, and then Central Asia. There is good and bad, and nature is a redeeming constant.

"This second night we run between seven and eight hours, with a current that was making over four mile an hour. We catched fish and talked and we took a swim now and then . . . it was kind of solemn, drifting down the big still river laying on our backs looking up at the stars and we didn't even feel like talking loud and it warnt [sic] often that we laughed . . . every night we passed towns, some of them away up on black hillsides, nothing but just a shiny bed of lights."[12]

A snapshot of antebellum America through the eyes of a boy yes, but as with Jay and Lauren, nature is a constant balm. They come upon a steamship wreck with two men about to murder another man, and Huckleberry and Jim thwart the murder by taking the boat belonging to the men. Like the near disasters Lauren and Jay encounter on the highways with cars and people, a steamboat runs over Huck and Jim's raft:

"She was a big one and she was coming in a hurry too looking like a black cloud with rows of glow worms around it, but all of a sudden she bulged out big and scary with a long row of wide open furnace doors shining like red hot teeth and her monstrous bows and guards handing right over us . . . as Jim went overboard one side and I on the other, she came smashing straight through the raft. I dived and I aimed to find the bottom too for a thirty-foot wheel had to go over me."[13]

Violence and deception are a constant in Twain's America, but also acts of kindness as Huck receives food from an old woman and money from two men who think his family is infected with smallpox. The violence of his father is never far behind as he becomes involved in a feud between two families, and a boy who has befriended him is gunned down. The boys jumped for the river, both of them hurt, and as they swam down the current, the men ran along the bank shooting at them and singing out, "'Kill them Kill them!' It made me so sick I almost fell out of the tree."[14] After covering the dead body of his friend Buck, Huckleberry makes his way back to the raft. "I was powerful glad to get away from the feuds and so was Jim to get away from the swamp. We said there weren't no home like a raft after all. Other places do seem so cramped up and smothery but a raft don't. You feel mighty free and easy and comfortable on a raft."[15]

One could certainly hear Jay and Lauren saying the same about cycling, which allows them to leave good and bad situations. Huckleberry's descriptions on the raft certainly echoes Jay and Lauren's descriptions.

"Sometimes we'd have that whole river all to ourselves for the longest time. Yonder was the banks and the islands, across the water; and maybe a spark—which was a candle in a cabin window and sometimes on the water you could see a spark or two—on a raft or a scow, you know and maybe you could hear a fiddle or a song coming over one of them crafts. It's lovely to live on a raft."[16]

The difference between Huckleberry Finn and Jay and Lauren is that the Mississippi River was there in 1840 to float Huck and Jim away from the carnage of humankind. Jay and Lauren have no magic carpet flowing out under the wide American night to take them away. They have loaded-down bikes that must be pedaled or pushed through countries as foreign and violent as the antebellum South.

Notes

1. Fitzgerald, F. Scott, The Great Gatsby, Scribners, NY, 1925.
2. Terre Haute newspaper.
3. Twain, Mark, The Adventures of Huckleberry Finn London, Collectors Library, 1885.
4. Ibid.
5. Ibid.
6. Ibid.
7. Ibid.
8. Ibid.
9. Ibid.
10. Ibid.
11. Ibid.
12. Ibid.
13. Ibid.
14. Ibid.
15. Ibid.
16. Ibid.

Photo 1 Jay and Lauren early in the trip reached Botswana Africa, 2018. *"Photos,"* *Simply Cycling [blog], posted by Jude Della Terra, 2021. https://www.simplycycling.org/blog/2021/5/29/ne41g4kll4eeu4rkm2mfoc0v0xknv2.*

Photo 2 Jay and Laruen crossing the deserts of Africa. *"Photos,"* *Simply Cycling [blog], posted by Jude Della Terra, 2021. https://www.simplycycling.org/blog/2021/5/29/ne41g4kll4eeu4rkm2mfoc0v0xknv2.*

Photo 3 Jay and Lauren on a highway in Spain. *"Photos," Simply Cycling [blog], posted by Jude Della Terra, 2021. https://www.simplycycling.org/blog/2021/5/29/ne41g4kll4eeu4rkm2mfoc0v0xknv2.*

Photo 4 Jay and Lauren on the Cliffs of France. *"Photos," Simply Cycling [blog], posted by Jude Della Terra, 2021. https://www.simplycycling.org/blog/2021/5/29/ne41g4kll4eeu4rkm2mfoc0v0xknv2.*

Photo 5 Wild camping along the highways was often difficult in Europe with many areas fenced off. *"Photos," Simply Cycling [blog], posted by Jude Della Terra, 2021. https://www.simplycycling.org/blog/2021/5/29/ne41g4kll4eeu4rkm2mfoc0v0xknv2.*

Photo 6 A stopover in Egypt on their way to Europe. They had to fly several times to make it to the Pamirs Mountains before the winter. Austin, Jay. *"#19 (Dar es Salaam, Tanzania - Cairo, Egypt." Simply Cycling [blog], 2018. https://www.simplycycling.org/blog/2018/3/3/19-dar-tanzania-cairo-egypt?rq=egypt.*

Photo 7 Jay and Lauren facing the Pamir Mountains known as The Roof of the World in Tajikistan. *"Photos," Simply Cycling [blog], posted by Jude Della Terra, 2021. https://www.simplycycling.org/blog/2021/5/29/ne41g4kll4eeu4rkm2mfoc0v0xknv2.*

Photo 8 Lauren riding along the Roof of the World in the Pamirs. *"Photos," Simply Cycling [blog], posted by Jude Della Terra, 2021. https://www.simplycycling.org/blog /2021/5/29/ne41g4kll4eeu4rkm2mfoc0v0xknv2.*

Photo 9 The summit of the Pamir Mountains Jay reached alone. *"Photos,"* Simply Cycling [blog], posted by Jude Della Terra, 2021. https://www.simplycycling.org/photos.

Photo 10 Lauren takes an old ambulance after falling ill in the Pamir Mountains. *"Photos,"* Simply Cycling [blog], posted by Jude Della Terra, 2021. https://www.simplycycling.org/photos.

Photo 11 Jay and Lauren and other cyclists camping on the day before the fatal attack where they were interviewed by a local television station. *"Photos," Simply Cycling [blog], posted by Jude Della Terra, 2021. https://www.simplycycling.org/blog/2021/5/29/ne4 1g4kll4eeu4rkm2mfoc0v0xknv2.*

Photo 12 Jay and Lauren with the other cyclists on the day of the attack in Tajikistan. *"Photos," Simply Cycling [blog], posted by Jude Della Terra, 2021. https://www .simplycycling.org/blog/2021/5/29/ne41g4kll4eeu4rkm2mfoc0v0xknv2.*

18
CROATIA AND MONTENEGRO
APRIL 2018

Lauren is not Jay. She is not running from anything, nor is she seeking anything. She is taking a great adventure with the man she loves and is open to experience. But even in her carefully worded Instagram posts, there is loneliness. A yearning to be home and to see her family again. Three days before Christmas, she posted: "I got a little teary on the bicycle. . . . I was homesick for family and friend and for home itself (both in California and Washington DC) especially during this holiday time. And some days are just harder than others to get back on the bicycle and pedal."[1] And now four months later, they have pedaled to Croatia and rented an apartment in Muo. Lauren and Jay rent a car outside the Tivat airport. Jay writes: "We open the doors of a crisp white sedan and climb inside. I'm handed the keys. I twist them in the ignition and an engine roars to life. I put the car into gear and drive for the first time in almost a year."[2]

Not driving for any amount of time brings renewed shock at the sheer amount of technology in a car. When I was working on my first novel, I went to an island off the tip of Wisconsin in Door County. Washington Island on Lake Michigan is a study in isolation with mail brought in still by seaplane and a ferry. It was winter, and I took a ferry to this cottage, and then for a week I saw no one and worked on my book. After nine days, I got in my car and drove to the ferry. I was in shock. The stereo sounded amazing. The speed of the car was amazing. The lit-up dashboard looked space age.

Lauren and Jay had been biking just short of a year, and the smell and the sounds and the sight of a new car was like entering a past life. Lauren can barely contain her excitement as they park the car in the airport and go inside. Those memories of her mother's tamales and special Christmas cookies. The smell of a barbecue and cut grass. The thousand moments of childhood crowd in. They walk in the quiet, cool airport and wait and watch as a plane lands. The baggage truck goes out to the airplane and people disembark, emerging from the long corridor into the waiting area. Lauren steps forward. It has been a year since she saw her parents, and it is impossible to believe that they have just emerged from the tunnel of the boarding passage. The visit that always seemed so far away is here. And they walk back into her life. There is that bond there. Mother and daughter. The love of life of good food and clothes and the quiet understanding between a mother and daughter that men will never understand.

Lauren posts on Instagram: "I eagerly awaited their arrival after ten months apart. My eyes glued to the sliding doors, scanning for their familiar faces . . . and then they emerged! With those smiles and hugs and kisses I love so much! We were overjoyed to see each other and to have twelve days together."[3]

Her parents have flown into Southern Croatia to spend a week with their daughter and Jay. They drive back to Montenegro to the apartment. Jay writes in his blog:

> We drive back to our rental on the shores of Muo, a beautiful little home very literally a stone's throw from the water. We catch up and choose rooms and unpack . . . a pile of bags and boxes onto the table, deliveries, and spare supplies from America we'd asked if they wouldn't mind bringing. Following the shipments kindly brought over by Tiffany, Justin, and Molly, it's like third Christmas for us. A few new pieces of clothing, some bike parts, a new phone to replace my broken one, and heaps of only-at-Trader-Joe's snacks for Lauren. We rifle through them like kids on Christmas morning. We're excited for the stuff, sure, but mostly we're excited to spend the next twelve or so days with her parents.

It is like another Christmas for Jay and Lauren. Another twelve days of kitchen access and sleeping in beds. Jay writes in his blog: "we spend long leisurely mornings at home, sipping tea and eating breakfast and talking and watching massive cruise ships maneuver themselves in and out of the docks."[4] They play board games and explore Montenegro. Lauren posts a selfie of them on Instagram. They are all smiles but between the dinners and the good times is a quiet campaign to get Lauren to come home "Her mother always had an ominous feeling about the trip, about Tajikistan," Kendall O'Connor said later. "Come home. You can always go back later."[5]

They tour the parks and forests. "Big pizzas and tasty risottos and some of the best mushrooms I've ever eaten. We put on a few pounds," Jay writes later. "I relish another few weeks of kitchen access making pancakes and baking rolls and garlic knots and bread."[6] Lauren's post on Instagram sums up the twelve-day visit:

Twelve days of our Muo-Kotor walks and cruise ship sightings in the Bay. Twelve days of sunshine. Twelve days of winding roads and bold drivers. Twelve days of washing machine cycles that puzzlingly ran for hours. Twelve days of IDEA grocery stores runs with Dad usually waiting outside. Twelve days of delicious meals (Thank you Mom and Dad) . . . twelve days of charming towns, historic city walls, and stunning landscapes. Twelve days of good mornings and good nights, accompanied by hugs and kisses. Twelve days of heart-to-heart talks and late night conversations (sometimes over Bolkus). . . . April turned to May and Jay celebrated another year around the sun. He turns twenty-nine.[7]

Lauren posts again on Instagram:

Celebrating Jays birthday today! Appreciating your intellect, wit, generosity, inventiveness, sensitivity, conscience, and love (among many other qualities). You have changed my life and changed me. And my life is richer and full of more adventures because of you. You do so much to keep us safe and smiling and our bicycles running smoothly and in the right direction. And you make sleeping in a tent night after night wherever we may be, feel like home. Happy happy birthday Jay. I love you![8]

It is a declaration. Kendall and Molly said Jay was Lauren's first sustained relationship. Her first lover perhaps. There is no way she is going home. "You have changed my life and changed me."[9] Could it be any clearer? The smiling girl in the photos has changed since she met Jay Austin. She has put her faith in the man who went skydiving with Tiffany and starts shaking in the plane while she comforts him. Is he always pushing the envelope? Will he know when to pull back with their daughter? These things are unsaid. Blame can be a cancer. Kim Postma later remembers the fear Lauren had. "She was afraid. She was scared."[10] She remembers staring across the river at Afghanistan and Lauren asking her if she was scared. Her mother is onto something, but it is too late.

The last night and the last day, Lauren stays close to her mother and father. Kendall asks me in her interview six years later: "Do you know what Lauren said to her mother? Do you know her last words? She said that she was afraid that she was never going to see her again. She said it as she hugged her."[11]

After twelve days, they return to the airport, which is once again quiet and empty. They go to the check-in counter and accompany Lauren's parents up to the security checkpoint. "We thank the two of them for a wonderful visit and they thank us for taking the time and we all hug goodbye. It's a sad moment, an inevitable one," Jay writes later. Another final hug between mother and daughter and father and daughter. "We all promise to see each other soon. None of us is sure where or when. But soon. They turn away, passports and boarding passes in hand. We wave and they wave back . . . and disappear into the terminal."[12]

Lauren posts on Instagram: "It was sad to say goodbye, but I was so grateful for my parents visit and our time together. Until next time."[13] At the end of her post is a heart.

Jay and Lauren resume biking and leave Montenegro in the pouring rain and enter Albania as the sun breaks through. "We tear across eastern Europe. Back in Africa and western Europe we'd cycle through maybe one country per month," Jay records in his blog. "Sometimes less than that. One state, one language, one currency. One passport stamp. Here, in the small, broken-up bits of Yugoslavia and its neighbors, we're ripping through countries every few days. Montenegro. Albania. Kosovo and Macedonia and Bulgaria. We're pushing ourselves hard and stopping little. We're gunning for Istanbul and making good progress."

They camp at an upscale campground and then in the morning head into the Accursed Mountains, but are stopped by a long, slow funeral procession in the middle of the street. "Several hundred Albanians walk sullenly behind a hearse. Heads bowed, outfitted in all black. The sky matches the mood. It is cloudy, then gray, then black. We wind through the mountains and begin to climb."[14] A storm breaks over the mountain with violent wind, rain, and lightning. Ominous blue bolts touch down around them as they continue to climb. "The diffused afternoon glow paints the mountains violet. A pretty sheen besides the suffering of torched thighs and numb fingertips." Some German cyclists wave them over and invite them to camp with them on the grass outside a tavern.

Jay and Lauren have a hearty meal and go into their tent. Already Lauren's parents' visit is becoming a memory. Jay posts: "By the time we return to Montenegro, Lauren's parents are some thirty thousand feet above us. By the time we return the car to Enterprise they are in Germany. By the time we're back on the bikes they're maybe in England, and by the time we pack up our tent the next morning, they're home in California."[15] The ominous feeling Lauren had leaving her mother has passed. Maybe things will work out. After all, they are young and healthy and not even thirty. Besides, other people have done things that some would call crazy and survived. Some might call quitting a job you loved at Georgetown University and going on a four-year bike trip around the world with your boyfriend crazy, but people have different reasons for going off the grid.

The question is, what were Lauren's?

Notes

1 Lauren Geoghegan Instagram Post.
2 Simplycycling.org, #34, June 1, 2018.

3   Lauren Geoghegan Instagram Post, June 26, 2018.
4   Simplycycling.org, #34, June 1, 2018.
5   Interview with Kendall O'Connor, May 6, 2024.
6   Ibid.
7   Lauren Geoghegan Instagram Post, June 27, 2018.
8   Lauren Geoghegan Instagram Post, May 1, 2018.
9   Ibid.
10 Interview with Kim Postma by William Hazelgrove, April 29, 2024.
11 Interview with Kendall O'Connor by William Hazelgrove, March 6, 2024.
12 Simplycycling.org, #35, June 7, 2018.
13 Lauren Geoghegan Instagram Post, June 27, 2018.
14 Simplycycling.org, #35, June 7, 2018.
15 Ibid.

19
WILD
1995

In 1995, a twenty-six-year-old divorced woman grieving over the cancer death of her mother while using heroin off and on, and estranged from her stepfather, sister, and brother, decided to hike the Pacific Crest Trail. Cheryl Stray had no wilderness experience. Her journey would begin in the Mojave Desert. From there she would hike through California, Oregon, to the Bridge of Gods into Washington. The Pacific Crest Trail is 2,653 miles long and ranges in elevations up to 13,000 feet. The trail was proposed in 1932 by Clinton C. Clarke as a path running from Mexico to Canada through the mountains of California, Oregon, and Washington. Planning went on through 1938 when groups under the banner of The Pacific Crest Trail System mapped out a route through the 2,000 miles of potential trails. In 1968, construction began under President Johnson and was finished in 1993.

If *Into the Wild* is a man's version of going off the grid, then certainly the 2012 memoir *Wild* of Cheryl Stray hiking the Pacific Crest Trail is a woman's. Like *Into the Wild*, the book would become an instant bestseller and would eventually be hailed as "a classic of wilderness writing and modern feminism."[1] A movie with Reese Witherspoon soon followed, which mirrored Sean Penn's interpretation of *Into the Wild*. Like many whose lives have unraveled, Cheryl Strange set off to find herself on the desolate and unforgiving Pacific Northwest Trail and then wrote about it in a funny, poignant, and at times disturbing memoir. She had no experience in the wilderness and with minimal planning set off down the Pacific Northwest Trail.

The morning she was to begin, she couldn't pick up her backpack from the floor of her hotel room. She took an inventory then of her pack:

a paci or fleece pants, a long sleeved thermal shirt, a thick fleece anorak with hood, two pair of gloves, a sun hat, a fleece hat and rain pants . . . a dry sack packed to the gills with food . . . a sleeping bag, and headlamp . . . water purifier, tiny collapsible stove, canister of gas, a little pink lighter . . . cooking pot nestled inside a larger cooking pot . . . sport sandals . . . a thermometer keychain, a tarp, insulated plastic mug . . . snakebite kit . . . Swiss army knife . . . binoculars . . . first aid kit . . . small bag of toiletries . . . a compass's . . . a book called *Staying Found, The Pacific Crest Trail Volume 1, AS I Lay Dying*, Adrienne Richs *The Adrienne Richs The Dream of a Common Language* . . . hairbrush . . . flashlight . . . metal candle lantern . . . a tent . . . two 32 ounce plastic bottles . . . a raincoat . . . .extra batteries . . . waterproof matches . . . Mylar blanket . . . bottle of iodine pills . . . two pens and three books . . . a full sized professional quality 35 millimeter Minolta x-700 camera with a separate attachable zoom lens.[2]

Cheryl shoved everything into her pack and tried to lift it on her shoulders. When she couldn't lift the pack, she sat down on the floor and scooted up next to the pack and slipped the straps over her shoulders. She was able to stand after crawling to a standing position and using an air conditioner as leverage to pull against.

The frame of the pack squeaked as I rose, it too straining from the tremendous weight. By the time I was standing—which is to say, hunching in a remotely upright position—I was holding the vented metal panel that I'd accidentally ripped loose from the cooling unit . . . my pack rose up like a mantle behind me, towering several inches above my head and gripped me like a vise all the way down to my tailbone.[3]

Cheryl opened the door and headed for the trail.

Her memoir ranges from flashbacks to her abusive father, to shooting heroin, to her failed marriage, her promiscuous lifestyle, to her time on the Pacific Northwest Trail. While she is hiking, she ruminates on what drove her to undertake the journey few could do as a "thru hiker," where the trial is completed end to end in a single trip. "I had to change, was the thought that drove me in those months of planning. Not into a different person, but back to the person I used to be—strong and responsible, clear eyed and driven, ethical and good. And the PCT would make me that way."[4]

Through hiking, the Pacific Northwest Trail takes most hikers six to eight months with an average completion rate of 14 percent. Hikers set up resupply spots in advance, which are usually post offices or towns where groceries and other supplies can be replenished. Thru-hiking requires a set amount of miles be completed each day with weather an omnipresent factor. Snow can stop the hiker in places like the Sierra Nevada and other passes. Most hikers need to cover 20 miles a day.

Cheryl set off in early June and entered the Pacific Northwest Trail at Tehachapi Pass off Highway 58, 12 miles west of the town of Mojave, California. She realizes quickly that the best she can do is 9 miles a day. On the eighth day, Cheryl had exhausted the food that required no cooking, but her stove no longer worked. She started down a jeep road looking for a town to get food and realized the condition she was in. "I could smell myself as I moved. . . . I hadn't bathed in over a week. My body was covered with dirt and blood, my hair dense with dust and dried sweat . . . my feet hurt inside and out, their flesh rubbed raw with blisters."[5]

She bumps into three men and takes a ride with a man named Frank, who has a gun in his truck. Cheryl during her trip will take risks on the trail and risks that are not on the trail. A dangerous heat waves descends when she reaches the Sierra Nevada Mountains. "By noon the heat was so merciless, and the trail so exposed to the sun I wondered honestly if I would survive. It was so hot the only way I could keep going was by stopping every ten minutes to rest for five when I would chug water from my bottle that was hot as tea."[6]

Cheryl Stray's childhood was one of struggle. Her father beat her mother continually and once pulled her down the sidewalk with her hair. When her mother finally left, she took up with men from motorcycle gangs. She started dating men with names "like Killer and Doobie and Motorcycle Dan . . . they would give us five-dollar bills to buy candy from the store so they could be alone in the apartment with mom."[7]

Her mother married a man just awarded $12,000 after falling off a roof. They bought land west of Duluth Minnesota. Cheryl grew up in a tarpaper shack with no running water. In parallels to Jay Austin's childhood, her mother stressed the beauty of nature. It was a life of isolation, poverty, and the beauty that could only be found in nature. The quixotic uncertain childhood haunted Cheryl in her marriage, and her life hovered in a constant state of chaos.

In the heat of the mountains, she questions why she had ever taken on the PCT. "Elsewhere people were having barbecues and days of ease, lounging by lakes and taking naps. They had access to ice cubes and lemonade and rooms whose temperature was seventy degrees. I knew those people. I loved those people. I hated them too. . . . I was going to quit. *Quit Quit Quit.*"[8] There are echoes of Lauren's questioning Instagram posts in Spain before and after Christmas. And then just when quitting seemed inevitable for Cheryl, she bumps into another hiker, Greg, who befriends her and helps her on her way. After he leaves, Cheryl realizes she has to stay the course. "I hiked in the heat of that day with a new determination. Inspired by Gregs faith in me, I didn't give quitting another thought."[9]

Wildlife for Lauren and Jay was a challenge, especially in Africa. The day Cheryl met Greg, she saw her first bear:

> I heard it first, an unmistakably muscular snort that stopped me in my tracks. When I looked up, I saw an animal as big as a refrigerator standing on all fours on the trail twenty feet away from me. The instant our eyes met; the same startled expression swept across both of our faces. "BEAR," I yelped and reached for my whistle the moment after he turned and ran.

Cheryl runs, singing one song after another to scare the bear. Shortly after seeing the bear, she almost steps on a rattlesnake:

> I shrieked when my eyes landed on the on the snake coiled up a few feet from me. If I'd been able to jump, I would have. . . . I scrambled away from the snake's small blunt head, yowling in terror. It was a good ten minutes I could work up the courage to step around it in a wide arc.[10]

Cheryl slowly reveals the backstory of her relationship with her husband, Paul. When he was twenty-one and she was nineteen, they married, but "we didn't think of ourselves as married people."[11] In a parallel to Jay and Lauren, they box up their bicycles and fly to Ireland, where they rent a flat in Galway, and then moved to Dublin, where they both got jobs in restaurants. Four months later, they moved to London and "walked the streets so destitute we searched for coins on the sidewalk."[12] They returned home, and with her mother's death, Cheryl's life began to unravel as she cheated on her husband with one man after another. Divorce soon followed.

When she meets a man named Matt, she reveals her reasons for hiking the trial. "It's been a hard time in my life, and I've sort of gotten off track. So, I . . . I thought it would help me to find my center, to come out here."[13] Jenn Cribbs, who worked with Jay at HUD, said she thought what drew Lauren to Jay: "she liked who she was when she was with Jay. She wanted to get to know the world and she liked the world Jay saw as being possible. Lauren was a woman who did what was expected . . . but here was this man proposing a life of the unexpected."[14]

Cheryl hikes on realizing the PCT had changed her concept of the world. "Alone wasn't a room anymore but the whole wide world. . . . I hadn't truly understood the worlds vastness."[15] And then the past crowds in on her again and her abusive father has returned. The unrequited love and terror haunted her as an adult:

> There was my father smashing our dinner plates full of food against the wall in a rage. There was my father choking my mother while straddling her chest

and banging her head against the wall . . . there was my father scooping my sister and me out of bed in the middle of the night when I was five to ask if we would leave with him while my mother stood by, bloodied and clutching my sleeping baby brother to her chest . . . once he threatened to throw my mother and her children naked into the street.[16]

Cheryl's mother would leave and then return, and her father would be back, sober and scrambling eggs.

On the PCT trail, Cheryl is rousted from a camping spot by a woman who demands money for staying on her property. She tries to reason with her, but has to leave in the middle of the night. During her hiking, Cheryl reveals she always saw herself as a writer. "Of all the things I'd done in my life, of all the versions of myself I'd live out, there was one that never changed: I was a writer."[17]

Further on the trail, she becomes severely dehydrated from the heat and uses iodine pills to purify dirty water. "The warm water tasted like iron and mud, and yet seldom have I ever consumed anything so amazing."[18] Toward the end of her hike, danger comes in the form of a sandy-haired man, who appears in the forest and leers at her. He leaves only to return later when she is setting up her tent. "I peeled off my sweaty clothes, pulled out my red fleece leggings and long-sleeved shirt and dressed in them. I laid out my tarp and was shaking my tent out of its bag when the sandy haired man reappeared . . . at the sight of him . . . I knew he'd come back for me."[19]

Cheryl tries to remain calm. "It was as if I'd finally come across a mountain lion . . . and not to incite him any fast motions."[20] She realizes the man had been watching her all along as she changed her clothes. "I like your pants," he said with a little smirk. "they look good on you. They show off your hips and legs." Cheryl realizes she might have to fight him off. "My mind went to the Swiss Army knife not too far away in the upper left side pocket of my pack . . . the not yet boiling water in the handleless pot on my little stove."[21]

The man refuses to leave when she orders him to. The danger has come out of nowhere. Up until now, nature has been her biggest adversary and her inspiration. But now there is something evil in the forest. The man leers across the fire, and Cheryl realizes that no one can help her. "I crossed my arms hard against my chest, acutely aware of the fact that I wasn't wearing a bra."[22] She thinks about grabbing the arrows from the man's pack and stabbing him in the throat.

"I think you better get going. It'll be getting dark soon."

"It's a free country," he said. "I'll go when I'm ready. I got a right you know."[23]

Eventually, the man leaves. "You be careful out there," the sandy-haired man said to me, pulling on his pack. "He lifted his Pepsi can in my direction. 'Here's to a young girl all alone in the woods.'"[24] When he leaves, Cheryl loses no time in packing up her camp and vanishing into the forest. "I walked and walked my mind shifting into a primal gear that was void of anything, but forward motion and I walked until walking became unbearable."[25] She walks all night to get away from the evil that has appeared.

Eventually, she finishes her hike, and has the answers she had been searching for.

> Thank you, I thought over and over again. Thank you. Not just for the long walk, but for everything the trail had taught me and everything I couldn't yet know, though I felt somehow contained within me . . . it was enough to trust that what I'd done was true. To understand its meaning without yet being able to say precisely what it was . . . to believe that I didn't need to reach with my bare hands anymore. To know that seeing the fish beneath the surface of the water was enough. That it was everything. It was my life, like all lives, mysterious and irrevocable and sacred. So very close, so very present, so very belonging to me. How wild it was, to let it be.[26]

Lauren does like who she is with Jay. The "wild" part of her is brought forth on their trips and unlocked. Like Cheryl, the trip around the world brings forth something that had laid dormant. "To know that seeing the fish beneath the water was enough."[27] The woman working in admissions at Georgetown had been let go for the woman who biked through deserts, mountains in snowstorms, wild camped all over Africa, and was chased by elephants. That new person chose to stay with Jay and not return with her parents.

Cheryl writes her book and reaps the rewards of a bestseller and a movie deal. *Wild* is a great narrative of survival, but in her book the scene with the sandy-haired man is different from the rest of her narrative. It is the strange interlude in a long-running wilderness memoir. The randomness of the possible violence is shocking. Suddenly there is danger in the forest, and Cheryl is at the mercy of the man watching her from the trees. Twenty-three years later, Lauren and Jay will be watched on their own journey, but they won't be given the chance to vanish into the forest. And to keep running.

Notes

1 Strayed, Cheryl Wild, Knopf, NY, 2012, Review.
2 Ibid., 39.
3 Ibid., 43.
4 Ibid.

5 Ibid., 70.
6 Ibid., 83.
7 Ibid., 14.
8 Ibid., 84.
9 Ibid.
10 Ibid.
11 Ibid.
12 Ibid.
13 Ibid.
14 Ibid.
15 Ibid.
16 Ibid.
17 Ibid.
18 Ibid.
19 Ibid.
20 Ibid.
21 Ibid.
22 Ibid.
23 Ibid.
24 Ibid.
25 Ibid.
26 Ibid.
27 Ibid.

20
ON THE ROAD TO KAZAKHSTAN

MAY 2018

Jay and Lauren tear across Eastern Europe enjoying the hospitality of Yugoslavia, where they are literally passing from one country to another every few days: Montenegro, Albania, Kosovo, Macedonia, Bulgaria. They bike hard and push for Istanbul, enjoying amazing hospitality and kindness along the way. They are warned that Albanians are dangerous by people who ask them where they are headed. The weather is not good. Jay posts on Instagram: "Our time in Albania was wet. Wet days, wet nights, thunderstorms the moment we entered the country and thunderstorms the moment we left. Cloudy, with little sunshine to dry out our sopping tent."[1] They find a rustic country where donkeys pull old men and women in wooden carts. They find a campground and take shelter from a furious storm.

Lauren and Jay catch a ferry to Northern Albania and then enter Kosovo, where people buy them drinks and food and want pictures taken with them. They buy bread at a bakery and are offered a room to stay in. No one lets them pay for anything. In a hailstorm, a man rushes out from a liquor store and invites them in until the storm passes. As Jay notes in an Instagram post: "the people are tremendously friendly and after American intervention in the late 90s (the Kosovo war) really really really love Americans."[2]

They enter Serbia after some trouble at the border and head for Macedonia. Jay later writes in his blog: "So we were about fifteen kilometers from the Macedonian border . . . when a police truck pulled up alongside of us and told us that the border had recently closed."[3] They have to go back and enter Serbia and then Macedonia. Jay is nervous about entering Serbia. "Kosovo's love of America is only matched by Serbia's loathing of America."[4]

But they have no choice and detour through Serbia. When they try and reenter, a construction crew blocks their way 12 kilometers from the border of Macedonia. Jay pleads with a man guiding dump trucks. "'Road closed,' he tersely informs. I point to the mountains in the distance, lost for words. 'Macedonia, right there.' He picks up a large pebble and points to the road. 'That's okay,' I exclaim. 'Really, we can ride on gravel. . . . *Fine*, he shrugs.'"[5]

They pedal out of Kosovo and into Macedonia. "We ride and watch the breeze ripple through the hills like wind on water. Lots of green. Dollops of red and purples and blue."[6] This is when biking becomes heavenly. When the weather and the landscape and health align, and the bikes suddenly feel light. A man rushes out of his car with his daughter and gives them energy drinks and canned peaches. They reach Greece and pedal onto into Turkey. Jay writes that the Turks are unbelievably friendly. At a gas station, they are handed bread and cups of Turkish tea. When they ask for a tap to fill their Nalgene's, they are given free bottles of water.

In Istanbul, they book an Airbnb and explore the city and pick up supplies. They eat well, and Jay catches up on his blog in a café. Jay notes he and Lauren usually spend all day together, and it's nice to have some solitude. In the café, he recounts the last month of riding in Europe and the limitations of blogging:

> I don't have the energy or the time to recount an entertaining half hour stuck at the Slovenian Croatian border in the back of a van with Myrna, Francesco and Sara when we discovered that not having an entry stamp into Europe (which wed been told back in Spain wouldn't be a problem) was most definitely a big problem . . . gloss over great swaths of Easter Europe in just a few paragraphs. I forget to detail a million beautiful little sights and sounds and serendipities . . . whole days and nights that have faded and muddied together. . . . I jam this heap of words together and call it a day.[7]

On the 29th of May, they disassemble their bikes and box them up and catch a five-hour flight to Kazakhstan. Jay looks out the right window of the plane and sees "immense snowcapped mountains. Mountains piggy backing mountains."[8] He is already thinking about biking the Pamir Highway. Jay explains cutting the trip short and skipping Turkey. "We're headed to a part of the world with roads over 15,400 feet and getting there too late in the year means these roads will be freezing and snowed in."[9] He finishes his final blog post in Istanbul with the John Muir quote: "The Mountains are Calling and We Must Go."[10]

They arrive in Kazakhstan as dawn breaks. It is 5:00 a.m., and neither of them have slept much. They wait for their bikes in the baggage claim. At 5:40 a.m., two brown boxes emerge. Jay and Lauren pull them off the conveyor and get to work assembling their bikes. Now there is another fast-motion video assembling of their bikes, but they are tired and several of Jay's spokes have broken. By 8:00 a.m., the panniers are back on, and the bikes are ready. They pedal out of the airport onto suburban streets. Jay and Lauren can see the snowy peaks of the mountains towering over the city. Kazak drivers go by and stare at the two people on their loaded-down bikes and shout out their windows.

"Otkuda! Where are you from?"

"America." They call back.

"America! Then why are you here?"[11]

It is not a good omen. They stand out in their brightly colored clothes and Lauren's fluorescent green riding vest. Their bikes stand out. Americans. Rich Americans by their bikes and equipment. Their physical presence stands out. Even though they have been on the road for almost a year, they are healthier than many in Eastern Europe. Their teeth are whiter, their muscles are firmer, their food and water are better, their faces are unlined. They have money, and they have a phone where Jay trades in crypto markets that people in Kosovo have never heard of. They are what they are. Well-educated, upper-middle-class Americans, who worked at well-paid jobs in the most powerful city in the world. Jay's Tiny House with its sleek amenities and the hot tub outside would be seen as a rich man's plaything. There is no blending in. They are not from Kazakhstan. Not by a long shot. They are from America. Then why are you here? As Jay prophetically writes in his blog after this exchange, "That's a good question."[12]

Then Jay answers the question:

The Pamir Mountains are among the highest in the world. They stand at their proudest in eastern Tajikistan, in the cold, windswept provinces of Gorno-Badakhshan, but from atop the Pamir plateau they leap across rivers and spill into neighboring Afghanistan and Kyrgyzstan and China, too big and unruly for borders to contain. The taller peaks pierce the sky at 24,000 feet; the mighty Kongur Tagh sits at a regal 25,095. The few navigable passes that have been artfully carved through these mountains—first by water, later by Russian engineers—still clock in above four thousand meters. Fifteen thousand feet.[13]

Their decision to fly reflects the goal of getting to the Pamirs before winter hits. Jay explains why the Pamir Mountains are special:

Central Asia is a battlefield of past wars. It's where capitalism came to blows with communism and where British imperialism drew swords with Russian expansion, but well before then, half a billion years before then, it's where the Himalayas crashed into the Tian Shan, where the Karakoram slammed into the Hindu Kush, where the Kunlun dug in against the Suleman. Whole rocky ranges charging headlong into battle. It has left its mark, this tectonic *melee*. A graveyard of granite. They call it the Pamir.[14]

So, their decision to fly to Kazakhstan was made under the shadow of the mountains and involved skipping all of Turkey to get to the Pamirs in July. With one flight they shave off three months from their trip. Jay laments the flight, saying that it "surrenders something . . . principles, maybe ego, our desire to get as far as we can with our own pedal power."[15] They tell themselves they will return to Turkey and bike it another time, but Lauren and Jay's decision to fly to Kazakhstan is a fateful one. Had they decided to stay the course and pedal across Turkey, and the Caucasus, and the Caspian, and reach the Pamirs in early fall, they would have never crossed paths with Hussein Abdusamadov.

Notes

1. Simplycycling.org, #36, June 22, 2018.
2. Ibid.
3. Ibid.
4. Ibid.
5. Ibid.
6. Ibid.
7. Ibid.
8. Simplycycling.org, #37, June 28, 2018.
9. Ibid.
10. Ibid.
11. Ibid.
12. Ibid.
13. Ibid.
14. Ibid.
15. Ibid.

PART III
CENTRAL ASIA

21
SELGA, KHATLONG PROVINCE
TAJIKISTAN, 1985

Hussein Nakhaudov didn't like his name either. Like Jay Austin, he felt the name didn't represent who he was, and it was slightly embarrassing. His surname in Tajik meant "pea." Born in 1985 in the village of Selga, in the Khatlong Province close to the Tajik Soviet Socialist Republics border with Afghanistan, he rejected his name and changed it to Hussein Abdusamadov. There was more power in his new name. He would need all the power he could get. Hussein's father died when he was three years old, and by the 1990s, the now-independent Tajikistan had descended into civil war after the disintegration of the Soviet Union. Hussein and his mother and two brothers settled in Dushanbe, a city of a half million people.

Abdusamadov at the age of ten went to the prestigious Presidential Lyceum boarding school that had ties to the government and very high academic standards. Hussein graduated, and in 2002 enrolled in the Tajik State University of Commerce in the international relations program. He excelled and was elected president of the Student government. All seemed bright for the promising student who looked like a young executive in a picture from his time at the university. But his mother noticed Hussein and her other son spending time with a local religious man, Nosirhoja Ubaidov, or as many knew him, Qori Nosir. He would later be identified as a recruiter for Islamic extremists. Hussein's mother blamed Nosir for her son dropping out of college in his third year.

"After he finished his third year at the university, my son told me, 'I want to have a gap year or change the focus of my studies. I'll go to Russia for work,'"[1] his mother later told RFE/RLS Tajik News Service. His mother soon realized he wasn't working in Russia. "One day he would call me (saying he was calling from

Russia), another time from Dubai, then from Kazakhstan."[2] When she confronted Hussein about not working in Russia, he responded by saying he needed to travel. Whenever he came to Dushanbe, he would be more secretive about his movements and his work. Still, like many young men in Tajikistan forced to work aboard in Russia or wherever they could find work, Hussein did not stand out.

Tajikistan like many eastern European satellites of the old Soviet Union had found its new independence unsettling with a civil war raging for five years. The landlocked country bordered by China to the east, Kyrgyzstan to the north, Uzbekistan to the west, and Afghanistan to the south emerged from the war with 100,000 dead and an authoritarian regime in 1997. Forty-nine percent of Tajik GDP is dependent on migrant work in Russia. Millions of Tajikistanis depend on the Russian Federation for income. Forty-seven percent of the population live on less than US$1.25 per day. The malnutrition rate in Tajikistan is 30 percent. In 2012, it was estimated that 680,152 people were living with food insecurity. It is a fertile breeding ground for the Islamic extremism exported from Afghanistan.

In 2010, Islamic militants escaped from a Tajikistan prison and murdered twenty-eight soldiers, further fanning the fear of the expansion of Islamic militarism. In 2015, Colonel Gulmurod Kohalimov of the special purpose police of the Interior Ministry defected to the Islamic State. Concern over the influence of Islamic Radicalism in Tajikistan, prompted Russia to send in troops. The Islamic Resistance Party with its 23,000 members fought against the government during the civil war and would eventually be outlawed in 1993 and then legalized in 1998 at the end of the war. It was later banned again in 2015 and viewed as a threat to President Emomali Rahmon's regime, which had been in power for seven terms. In 2021, Tajikistan would ask for assistance from the Collective Security Treaty Organization of ex-Soviet States to help with security issues regarding Afghanistan.

This was the country Hussein grew up in and the State Department deemed it safe in 2017 on their website; the same website that Lauren Geoghegan had checked and assured her mother it was safe. This was the country where the authorities were growing more suspicious about the man who changed his name to the more forceful Hussein Abdusamadov. After an interview with the police, his mother told them she would offer to visit him where he was living. "Well, it's not possible," he would respond. "There are a lot of guys there. I'll just call you and well meet up some place." His mother was later quoted by the police as saying, "he'd call me, and we meet up on the city streets. We'd talk. Each time I met him, I warned him that I knew he wasn't working."[3]

In a surveillance video, Hussein is seen receiving money sent from contacts in Russia. In other interviews with the media, Shodmonova said she thought he might be involved with crime. Tajikistan is a transit country for Afghan narcotics route for Russian and Western European markets. The heroin and opium confiscations in Tajikistan are the third highest in the world. Drug money corrupts government officials and gives young men like Hussein an alternative income than being a migrant worker in Russia. Still, Hussein assured his mother he would never be involved in something illegal.

When Hussein came to Dushanbe, he would only consent to meet on the crowded streets of the capital where she begged him for answers to his suspicious behavior. "Hussein you're my son. I'd like to sit and talk with you over a cup of tea," she recalled telling him. "You're behaving this way, what am I supposed to do? Tell me where you are staying so I can visit you."[4] He never would. In April 2018, authorities became suspicious enough of Hussein to summon Shodmonova to the Interior Ministry and told her, "they were seeking her son for his activities abroad."[5] His mother's neighbors reported that "the police had questioned relatives and knocked on the doors in Abdusamadov's old Dushanbe neighborhood looking for him." She saw Hussein one more time after being told her son was a wanted man. His mother begged him to turn himself in. Hussein no longer was telling her he was working in Russia. In their last conversation, he told Shodmonova that if he turned himself in, they would simply arrest him.

In an interview with a reporter from the New York Times for the series episode Collision, his mother claims Hussein was "a good boy. He received certificates and praise and studied with enthusiasm. He was my best and spoiled child." His mother said after he met the cleric Qori Nosir he dropped out of the university, and wouldn't come home. "He hasn't come home for fourteen years."

Hussein had been radicalized and was now looking for potential terrorist targets. "He left and I never saw him again. But he would call me and ask how I am," she told the Tajik police later. "He would call from payphone and from random people's homes." He would often hang up hurriedly. She told the police she was "disappointed for him being so weak that he fell under the influence and allowed others to change his ideas."[6]

In June 2018, she told the RFE/RL that she would try and get an address so they could arrest him. But Hussein would never call again, and Shodmonova could only wonder where her son was. Hussein was somewhere in Tajikistan, a loose cannon unmoored, a hunter looking for a target. He was another young man who changed his name and grew up without a father, raised by a mother in hard economic circumstances. A young man who leaves the conventional road to embrace a counter-ideology. Did Qori Nosir tell Hussein about the betrayal of the Sykes/Picot agreement of 1917, the coup in Iran in 1953? Or did the cleric simply point to something higher with his reward in heaven? Maybe it was simply finding the meaning that Hussein couldn't find in an elite school or the university or what would be a traditional career. The meaning Jay Austin couldn't find in his Georgetown degree, his government job, or conventional American life. It is hard to know, but they would soon find each other on a deserted highway on the Roof of the World.

Notes

1. Radio Free Europe. Tajik Cyclists Attacker Was Influenced By Others, https://www.youtube.com/watch?v=yC8e8b5XXIM&t=43s.
2. Ibid.
3. Ibid.
4. Ibid.
5. Ibid.
6. Ibid.

22
KAZAKHSTAN

JUNE 2018

Kazakhstan declared its independence from the Soviet Union in August 1991, but the shadow of those years as a vassal state is everywhere. "Kazakhstan heavily restricts freedom of assembly, speech, and religion": Human Rights Watch describes the government as authoritarian. Exile of prisoners and mass deportations by the Soviet Union to the country were carried out in the 1930s. The first nuclear bomb was set off near the town of Semipalatinsk. Hundreds more bomb tests were conducted by the Soviet Union in Kazakhstan, poisoning the country and the people. The pall of the Soviet years is felt in the drab landscape, decaying statues, and lax environmental regulations.

Jay and Lauren stay in a Holiday Inn in the former capital of Kazakhstan, Almaty, with points they have accumulated. They collapse into bed and later in the afternoon wash their clothes and repair the holes in their tent. Lauren brings back sushi platters, Indian food, and Chinese dishes for dinner. On the fifth day, they leave the hotel room and pedal out of Almaty's glamorous downtown and enter "a rotten hellscape." The air is sulfurous and "our lungs feel tight, and our nostrils burn and my eyes tearing. The pollution from diesel exhaust and burning piles of trash in the gutter makes the air unbreathable."[1]

They learn the Air Quality Index is 50 percent above what is hazardous to breathe. The air is so noxious that birds fall from the sky. "Dead birds in the gutter, men fighting in the streets,"[2] is how Jay sums it up. Two men fight in a gas station over the pump. Men are yelling at each other in the street, throwing punches. Giant potholes cause cars to swerve wildly as people drive from the right and left sides. Jay and Lauren are caught in a thunderstorm and get soaked.

They reach Kyrgyzstan and stay with an old friend from the Tiny House days. They stay one night and push on toward the Pamir Mountains. They head for the first pass, Too-Ashu, elevation 10,500 feet, and begin a long laborious slow climb. Biking up a mountain is hard enough. Biking up a mountain on a bike loaded down with fifty pounds of gear is even harder. Biking up a mountain that is 10,000 feet above sea level is almost impossible.

Biking requires oxygen and lots of it. On cool clear days when the sky is dark blue, the oxygen is rich and a cyclist can really fly. Fall in the Midwest is the best time for cycling. Conversely on warm humid days when the air is thick, it takes more effort to go the same distance. Lance Armstrong used blood infusions and testosterone to give himself an advantage in the Tour De France. That oxygen-rich blood was like rocket fuel while the other bikers were working with depleted oxygen stores. When there is not enough oxygen, the body goes into emergency mode and greedily distributes the oxygen between vital organs, the brain, and muscles. The muscles suffer the most. There is just not enough oxygen for those big leg muscles to push the pedal down and propel the rider, gear, and bike upward. Biking in this situation becomes an agonizing slog.

Lauren and Jay's highest mountain pass so far was in Tanzania at 5,000 feet. They are now cycling up to the Too-Ashu Pass at 10,500 feet, riding all day with steep elevations of 2,000 feet in just 50 kilometers. Twelve percent grade. "We are already in our lowest gears—have been for ages—so there's little that can be done but to pedal harder,"[3] Jay writes. A small raging river of snowmelt flows down the mountain as they crawl up through "deep violet gorges, up past dark, mysterious caves." They finally find a place to camp next to the river along with cows and sheep that graze along the banks. The next day the road gets steeper, and Jay considers getting rid of things in his pannier to lighten the load. "I pedal and wonder . . . just how much pedaling my body can do."[4]

On a break for some food, a storm breaks and throws down rain and then hail. Jay posts: "Thick pellets of slush. Numb fingertips. A mean charcoal sky and a steep slippery road. Vans rush by and splash cold water on our bikes and, our bodies, everything." They are 7 kilometers from the top and then 3, 2, 1. They have reached Too-Ashu Pass, elevation 10,500 feet, but up ahead is a tunnel boring into the side of the mountain. They had been warned about the tunnel and told not to cycle it. "Very dark, very lengthy, very bumpy and very loud."[5] The air inside the tunnel is poisonous from the diesel trucks where the exhaust hovers in the middle.

The tunnel has an eerie similarity to the one Thomas Stevens biked through in the Sierra Nevada Mountains on a big-wheel Penny Farthing on April 22, 1884. Stevens entered a dark railroad tunnel boring through the mountain just as a train entered the other side. In his book, *Around the World on a Bicycle*, he wrote, "I hear an approaching train and forthwith proceed to occupy as small a space as possible against the side, while three laboriously puffing engines, tugging a long heavy freight train up the steep grade, go past. These three puffing smoke-emitting monsters fill every nook and corner of the tunnel with dense smoke."[6]

Stevens then followed the track on his bicycle, passing under snow sheds built to keep the snow in the mountains from blocking the tracks. Trains passed him in these smoke-filled sheds while he pressed himself against the mountain side. Stevens followed the old California trail over the mountains and plains, passing shocked Indians, and eventually reaching Boston on August 14, 1884, after starting out from San Francisco. *Harpers* reported that "more than one third of the route followed by Mr. Stevens had to be walked. Eighty-three and a half days of actual travel and twenty days stoppage for wet weather."[7] Thomas went by steamer to Liverpool, biked across Europe, then cycling through Slovenia, Serbia Bulgaria, Rumelia, and Turkey and then Anatolia, Amenia, Kurdistan, Iraq, and Iran. In Afghanistan, he was taken prisoner, and then continued on through Asia by steamer and ended up in Japan, where, he wrote, "distance actually wheeled, about 13,500 miles."[8] After publishing his 1,000-page overwritten book, *Around the World on a Bicycle* in 1887, he was credited with being the first man to bike around the world.

There was no train coming from the other side of the tunnel for Lauren and Jay, but there were trucks and cars speeding into the smoky abyss that made no room for two cyclists. They weighed their options. It's hailing. It's cold. The only way through the mountain is to hitch a ride from some trucker and that's not happening. They are already breathing hard from the elevation. The old Soviet-era cars pump out lead-based exhaust, and there are no pollution controls. Just breathing is an effort, but they have no choice: "we turn on our lights, pull neck gaiters up over our faces, and pedal into the void."

The tunnel is dark, smoky, with loud cars zooming through on both sides. It is no place for cyclists, and this is one of those decisions that is questionable but it's too late. Abby, Jay's friend from HUD, six years later said about the risks of the trip. "Jay was living fully every day . . . and he took the consequences that went with it. That was his goal . . . even if that happened to be his last day, he was not scared of anything."[9]

But now, he and Lauren are in a smoky tunnel not designed for cyclists. There is simply no room, and the car exhaust hovers in the badly ventilated-bored out cavern. "I feel it first in my lungs," Jay writes:

A tightening, like air being sucked out of a paper bag. Like my airways are filling with something they shouldn't be. Something thick. Like I need a certain amount of oxygen to live, and this isn't enough oxygen to live . . . at thirty-two hundred meters the air is about a third thinner than down at sea level . . . were still cycling uphill . . . breathing hard. Short shallow breaths . . . carbon monoxide, carbon dioxide. Dust and dirt and diesel . . . a few fans drone overhead. It's a feeble attempt . . . they make noise mostly. A dull hum that reverberates through two miles of concrete and morphs into a ghostly howl . . . lights flicker and some trucks flash by. We keep close to the wall and brace ourselves against cavernous potholes and swerve around big mufflers banged loose from automobiles. . . . We continue to climb. My body feels weak. Cold in places and numb in others. We have been riding through this tunnel for just minutes, maybe ten, maybe fifteen. . . . I see a light and rush toward it.[10]

Lauren struggles behind Jay, feeling she is suffocating. She already is suffering from the high altitude and having trouble acclimating. People can take anywhere from a day to a week to get used to high elevations. Some never do. Now she is biking through a smoky noxious void gasping for air, every push of her pedal agonizing with loud trucks and cars zooming by with strobe-like intensity. Her bike light does nothing against the murky darkness, and she sees distant light beaming on the other side and pedals toward it. She feels she might vomit if she doesn't get some clean air soon.

They come out of the darkness into hail and pull over gasping for air as they hurriedly put on more clothes. Lauren vomits. Then Jay. They rest, then pedal on as the weather breaks, and they coast into a lush valley on the other side. They are both drained from the climb, the altitude, and the polluted air in the tunnel. They decide to stay in a hotel for the night and find out later that cycling through the tunnel isn't allowed. After showers, they check email, charge their phones, and discover Lauren's sleeping pad has a hole and will not stay inflated.

The Ala-Bel Pass is next. A 3,200-meter-high pass that is cold and snowy. They start up a highway the next day sharing the road with cars and trucks when it starts to rain. Lauren and Jay ride with their heads down but the rain soaks them anyway. A man pulls his gold sedan over and calls out to take a photo. *"Pozhaluysta! Please!"* Jay shakes his head, and they keep riding. Five hundred meters later, the gold sedan passes the cyclists and stops. The doors open and a large man gets out and starts miming taking a photo, saying *pozhaluysta pozhalysta.* Jay shakes his head as they ride past. The man frowns, and then reaches out to grab the back of his bike. Jay shouts at the man *"Nyet!"* No! A few minutes later, the gold sedan roars by, turns and stops, blocking their bikes. Two men emerge from the car and stand directly in front of Jay and Lauren. They stop their bikes. One man shouts *"Pozhaluysta!"*[11]

Lauren is in front, and Jay is worried. "I can't tell if it's an earnest plea or a cruel sneer," he writes later. *"Nyet!* I shout. 'Leave us alone!'"[12] Jay motions to Lauren, and she starts again, biking slowly past the glaring men, threading her way through. They watch her pass, then Jay starts and pushes down on his pedal. The men stare at him as he pedals hard to get between them. The man on the right leans forward, then pushes violently on Jay's shoulder and knocks him off the bike. He falls to the ground and hits the tarred highway, rolls, then looks up at the two men standing over him. Strangely, Jay thinks of the tunnel he just went through and the light at the end. Never go into the light, he tells himself.

Notes

1. Simplycycling.org, #37, June 28, 2018.
2. Ibid.
3. Ibid.
4. Simplycycling, #38, July 4, 2018.
5. Ibid.
6. Stevens Thomas, Around the World on a Bicycle.
7. Ibid.
8. Ibid.
9. Interview with Abby Miller by William Hazelgrove, August 19, 2024.
10. Simplycycling, #39, July 11, 2018.
11. Ibid.
12. Ibid.

23
THE PAMIRS, "THE ROOF OF THE WORLD"

JULY 17, 2018

Day 366 on the Road, Year 2, Day 1

Jay and Lauren passed the one-year mark. They have been cycling around the world for 365 days now. On Jay and Lauren's Simply Cycling blog, the comments are still there. Many have been scrubbed after the attack, but some have survived. On the entry where Jay gets pushed off the bike by the man in the gold sedan is an ominous warning:

> Perhaps westerners should realize, you armed our enemies, you destroyed our prosperity with decades of cruelty and indiscriminate killing, destroying our infrastructure, creating a power vacuum that engulfed the entire region. Your capitalism forced people who never knew such a system to suddenly have to fend for themselves after decades of prosperity. Then you want sympathy? Our lives clearly do not matter to the west. Look at your Mexico. Look at how you lock them away, allies, your friends. People who supported the American revolution and everything you hold dear, look how you betray them because of their inconvenience? You found your weapons of mass destruction after all. Not an aging ancient SU-25 rotting in Saddam's desert, but yourselves, in the mirror.[1]

After Jay was pushed off his bike and hit the ground, the men started shouting. Jay jumps up and begins shouting back in English, and the men yell in Kyrgyz.

Jay manages to splice together some Russian words that roughly translate to, *"you are not good!"*[2] The men laugh, and one man approaches Jay. His eyes glint with amusement. Jay writes in his blog:

> One man walks toward me and I yell louder. They seem eager for a fight, like they're just bored and this is a fun way to spend a late afternoon. Broken vodka bottles litter the roadside. I wonder if they've been drinking. One can only shout for so long when those they're shouting at don't speak the same language. So everyone quickly tires of raising their voices and Lauren and I figure it's not very productive to stick around. *Nyet!* we yell once more as we straddle our bicycles and pedal away. *Do not follow us!*[3]

The men quickly get in their car and begin to follow, and then the sedan pulls alongside Jay and Lauren. The man on the passenger side lifts his camera and starts filming them. "Pozhaluysta," he sneers. Jay pulls out his own phone and snaps a picture of the license plate, and the car speeds away. Jay in his blog doesn't say anymore, but the question remains, why were the two men filming Jay and Lauren? For now, though, the danger seems to have passed. They reach the top of Ala-Bel Pass, and its getting dark and colder. They put on more clothes and then start down the mountain and camp in a farmer's yard where Jay gets stung.

In his blog, he tallies up the misfortunes of the past few days. "Bee sting. A broken spoke nipple . . . mean men on the mountain."[4] And Lauren's air mattress will no longer hold air. Then Lauren's pedal falls off. In Kyrgyzstan, they find a man who welds the pedal back on and refuses to take money for it. A woman gives them a loaf of bread for free. They continue along the Uzbekistan border. They ask someone if they might camp in the forest behind their house. They offer their yard and give them food and a place to wash up.

"The world is a big place," Jay writes in his blog that night, addressing the two men in the gold sedan:

> Travel around it long enough and you're bound to find something a little nasty. Maybe someone who thinks it's funny to follow you in his car, to push you off your bike because you won't take a picture. . . . You can choose to focus on these things . . . but to focus on the bad is to ignore the good . . . for every pair of men blocking our path on a quiet mountain road there have been ten thousand willing to fix our pedals, to fill our panniers with freshly baked bread to offer us a safe place to spend the night.[5]

They reach the city of Osh and take a week of rest before taking on the Pamir Mountains. Jay records his impression of the city:

THE PAMIRS, "THE ROOF OF THE WORLD"

> It's Soviet-style, all big brutalist buildings and straight roads and an overzealous sampling of the grey-to-beige color palette. It's a bit hazy . . . and doesn't exactly enchant the senses in the way you might think an ancient Silk Road city would . . . there's a large bazaar with cheap nuts and decent hostel with a clean double room and a really excellent coffee shop with strawberry banana smoothies and homemade veggie burgers. . . . We unpack our things, settle in, and look forward to a long week off the bikes.[6]

It is here they meet Nathan and Sophie. The two couples had been conversing on WhatsApp, and it turned out a friend of Nathan and Sophie (Romaine), in France, was on his way and could deliver a new air mattress for Lauren. WhatsApp is a platform that provides instant messaging highly encrypted for security. Jay explains the use this way.

> Nathan, Sophie, Lauren, I, and about two hundred other cyclists are all part of a big WhatsApp group for people traveling the world—though mostly central Asia—by bicycle.[7] It's a place to ask questions (*does anyone know how long it takes to get an Uzbek visa?*), share tips (*the pass to Issyk-Kul is now cleared of snow*), or just socialize (*I'm in Tashkent for the next few days; anyone want to grab a beer?*)[8]

Through WhatsApp, the two couples meet up in Osh. Years later, after the attack, Nathan and Sophie wrote an article, "When Paths Cross: A Tribute to Jay and Lauren," published on bikepacking.com. They arranged to meet in a coffee house. In the article, Nathan writes:

> Jay and Lauren were easy to spot when we walked in. Panniers propped up against the table legs, buffs around their necks. We hit it off straight away and put the world to rights every day for over a week. Stories from travels and home often merging into philosophy and politics. Jay and Lauren were both intellectual, curious, and humble in different ways. They were likable and easy going. When Romain arrived, we decided to ride on together, heading towards the Pamirs.[9]

The five cyclists leave Osh and head for Tajikistan to finally bike the wild Pamir range of Tajikistan. Lauren and Jay have filled their panniers with food and water. Nathan, Sophie, and Romain start out, and they meet at the first campsite that night after climbing some of the first Pamir passes. Jay writes: "it's fun traveling as a pack . . . we take nice long lunch breaks and make delicious dinners."[10] The other bikers often ride ahead, but other times they ride in a line. Nathan writes:

Jay listened to Russian podcasts in his headphones to learn the language. Lauren listened to Taylor Swift, who motivated her to pedal the climbs . . . we mixed it up between riding together, chatting, and pointing out eagles circling overhead or beautiful rock formations, or sometimes we'd ride at different paces and reunite for lunch and to camp . . . we were treated to delicious cinnamon cakes for breakfast—far tastier than our soggy porridge in oat and boiled water.[11]

On the second day out of Osh, it is hard biking to the higher elevations. They set up camp next to a creek when an old Lada (Soviet-Era) sedan stops by them. Jay and the others think they might be told to move, but a family gets out and invites them to stay and share some food. A daughter strums a small guitar as they eat. "You can't plan for these encounters but when they happen, they can make an afternoon a day or even a trip. Bonds that are shaped by kindness and reciprocity,"[12] Nathan writes later. They continue the next day and climb and climb and climb. Over 5,000 feet in 50 miles, Jay notes. They ride in a line, and Lauren gets a flat. The other cyclists offer to wait, but Jay tells them they will fix it and catch up. The picture Lauren posts on Instagram shows thin blue crushed stone trails with enough room for one biker. They summit the pass and catch up with Nathan, Sophie, and Romain outside a guesthouse in the town of Sary-Tash before dark.

The majestic white-capped Pamir Mountains lord over the town and promise the ride of their lives, but everyone is exhausted from three days of cycling. They take a day's rest break. The guesthouse fills with cyclists:

> For some of us it was the start of our adventure through the Pamirs, others coming from the opposite direction were nearing the end and relished telling tales of exhausting riding, barren landscapes, and meagre diets. Kim and Rene, a Dutch couple, Tucker and Della, another American couple, and Aleksandra from Poland were all heading West along the Silk Road like us.

This is the first mention of Kim Postma and Rene Wokke, who will be with Lauren and Jay during the attack.

The town is a crossroads. Go right out of town for Tajikistan and go left for China. Jay notes that "while the road to Tajikistan is derelict and bumpy, the road to China is smooth and paved. . . . China is in the midst of a well-publicized global trade expansion, building roads all over the world, and Kyrgyzstan is just right next door. Sary-Tash, though tiny and unassuming, is the gateway from China to Central Asia."[13]

A day later, they turn right and bike toward Tajikistan. At the border, they stare at "the snowcapped mountain chain . . . enticing and ominous, inching

THE PAMIRS, "THE ROOF OF THE WORLD"

closer until it loomed directly above us at the Kyrgyz border post."[14] The border guard points to the sky, which is now ominous with thunderheads. The entry to Tajikistan is still a few kilometers up the mountain, which is a "a difficult windy pass that no customs official wants to be stationed atop."[15] Snow has begun to fall, and the wind has picked up. They decide to wait and camp under an abandoned slanted roof next to the border station.

Everyone crowds into Jay and Lauren's five-man tent they name "party place." A picture on Instagram shows everyone smiling in their sleeping bags inside the orange tent. In the morning, they are stamped out of Kyrgyzstan, and the road goes from paved to a rocky terrain and then turns into a rusty-red earth track to the Tajik border post. "Impressive sceneries of a vast ochre and silver plateau, crystalline lake and 7000-meter snowy mountains stretched before us," Jay writes, "We take it slowly. The road isn't so bad, but it isn't good either. We roll through the mud and bump along the stones and by the time we reach the steep switchbacks of the final pass, we're exhausted."[16]

At 13,000 feet, just 2,000 feet below the summit of the Rockies in America, Lauren begins having problems. Nathan notes in his article, "Lauren was sick with the altitude and didn't feel up to cycling the high pass ahead." The air is 20 percent thinner than at sea level with each breath bringing in a fifth less oxygen. Some people acclimate quickly, some don't. They consider their options. Jay and Lauren could camp, but sleeping at 13,000 feet elevation is not good. The body gets even less oxygen. The second option is to turn back, but this would involve going back down and getting back into Kyrgyzstan would be difficult. So, they settle on the third option, which is to get off the bikes and walk. Kim Postma, who would join Jay and Lauren in the Pamirs, said that going up the mountains, "they would walk a little bit, rest and then walk a little more." Jay writes the same: "Take a few steps. Take a break. Take a breath. Take a few more steps. Walk, rest, repeat." [17]

They go higher, and Lauren and Jay switch bikes. Jay's bike has less food and is lighter. He sees the iconic Marco Polo statue at the Tajikistan pass and goes back to help Lauren. "It's so blustery that the second I turn around the wind rushes so far down my esophagus that I get the hiccups."[18] He goes back down a few hundred meters and takes his bike from Lauren and together they get to the top. Czech cyclists are posing for photographs around the statue, but Lauren is still having trouble. Jay writes in his blog:

> Lauren is still having trouble breathing. Descent is really the only thing that's going to help. Still a bit out of breath, we get back on the bikes and race downhill to the Tajik border. It's not very far down, but it should be a good place to rest until Lauren catches her breath. We arrive and Lauren sits on the ground. She is shaking and hyperventilating. Cycling is an intensive activity. You ride up

a hill and of course you're out of breath. You're exposed to the elements and so of course you're hot, and sometimes cold, and once you stop you're most definitely colder than when you were riding. Oh, and plus, it's now snowing—of course it's snowing—and so there's certainly going to be some shivering.[19]

The border guards give Lauren hot tea, but her hands are shaking so much she can barely hold the cup. Jay goes into the customs booth with their passport and gets their entry stamps into Tajikistan. When he comes out, a crowd is around Lauren, who is becoming less and less responsive. Jay writes in his blog: "The border guards are looking concerned. Fellow cyclists are looking concerned. A few overlanders are shouting, panicked: *She needs to get down!*"[20] Essentially Lauren and Jay are mountain climbers now and subject to the same problems. High-altitude pulmonary edema (HAPE) is altitude sickness taken to its logical extreme. It is the condition that kills climbers every year on Mount Everest. It comes from an acute lack of oxygen. The first case was reported in 1891, when a young Dr. Jacott died from an inflammation of the lungs after climbing Mont Blanc. In 1902, Alistair Crowly described a case of a climber suffering from edema of both the lungs and his mind gone after an expedition to the Karakoram Range. Symptoms range from fatigue, breathlessness, and a cough that will produce a pink frothy sputum. Lauren was a long way from that, but no one wanted to take chances.

The problem is they are at 4,100 meters elevation on the Pamir Plateau and the closest town at lower elevation is Karakul. It is 5,500 kilometers from the border, and no way Lauren can bike it. The Czech cyclists have a vehicle, and they agree to drive Lauren to Karakul. There is only room for one with her bike tied to the roof. Lauren is loaded into the truck with her panniers, and Jay tells her he will see her later that night. Jay watches the truck disappear and then takes off on his own. Several comments on his blog questioned putting Lauren into a truck and not accompanying her, but, according to Jay, there was simply no room.

It is 5:00 p.m., and Jay doesn't want to sleep on the Pamir Plateau if he can help it. He will have to bike hard to reach Lauren. Lauren's colleague Kristen, from Georgetown, didn't look favorably on Jay's decision to put Lauren into a truck. Kristen worked with Lauren in Georgetown admissions for seven years and shook her head when I asked her about the long-term possibilities. "They were very different, and it would not have surprised me if it had not worked out long term. A last call the month before she died, Lauren had said 'it was hard and after a year it seemed a natural point to evaluate the trip,'" Kristen paused. "I know that she loved him and knew he was very passionate about doing this and she had an adventurous spirit, but this was incredibly physically demanding and dangerous . . . she was genuinely considering going home."[21]

THE PAMIRS, "THE ROOF OF THE WORLD"

Jay rides alone on the darkening mountain road with snow wisping in the air.

I ride fast. I ride relentlessly. I bump down the washboard descent and make peace with breaking spokes. I soar past other cyclists and shout a frenzied, *sorry* I can't stop to chat, behind me. It's beautiful on the Pamir but I don't stop to take any pictures. I don't stop for anything. I ride about forty kilometers straight, tearing up the second pass, and only slow when the vehicle that brought Lauren to Karakul approaches from the opposite direction.[22]

Jay screams *thank you* at the truck as he pedals toward Homestay Aguiden in Karakul, a guesthouse where they will be staying. He reaches Karakul sometime after seven. Romain, Sophie, and Nathan wave him down, and Jay shouts, "Where's Lauren?" Sophie gestures behind her. "She's ok. She's inside resting."[23] Jay goes into the guesthouse and finds Lauren still "weak and fatigued but with more measured breathing." By the next morning, Lauren is breathing fine and stronger. They take the next day off to let their bodies acclimate to the higher elevation. Sophie and Nathan take off on a different route through the Pamirs. They agree to meet in the capital of Tajikistan, Dushanbe. Lauren and Jay wave them off then go back in and lay down, rest, pass the time.

Three hours later, Nathan, Sophie, and Romain return. They had hit a snowstorm and were forced to turn around. Over lunch they decide to return to the guesthouse and wait out the storms. Fifteen cyclists stay in the guesthouse, and Nathan in his article mentions Kim Postma and Rene Wokke again, who will be with Jay and Lauren on July 29. A series of snowstorms pass through, and for three days they read and play games, and Jay shares his vegan chocolate.

Lauren hadn't recovered fully and is anxious about continuing. Molly Scalise recalled a hike she took with Lauren in Virginia. "It wasn't very long but Lauren kept asking when it would be over and stopped to rest several times . . . and I thought she wants to bike around the world?"[24] Lauren has been biking for a year and proved herself over and over. But everyone reaches their physical limit, and Lauren had reached hers. The next pass is Ak-Baital, which is the highest and fiercest pass. The altitude is 4,650 meters above sea level, which is a thousand feet higher than their last pass. Lauren is suffering from intestinal issues and her breathing has not fully recovered. Jay notes everyone seems to be suffering from some degree of intestinal issues related to altitude.

They plan to bike to the pass the next day, but Lauren's anxiety increases along with her stomach issues. She asks about getting a ride to Murghab, which is the next town on the Pamir Highway. The homestay hosts arrange a ride for her and her bike in an old Soviet ambulance being used as an intra-Pamir bus. Still Lauren wants to bike, but vomits into some Tupperware, and it's decided she will take the ride. This time there is plenty of room in the ambulance for Jay to go with her.

"I consider going," Jay writes. "But Laurens okay and Lauren will just be resting anyway and this stretch, from Karakul to Murghab is one of Pamirs finest. At daybreak the next morning. I wave to Lauren as her ride pulls away into a gorgeous golden sunrise. See you in Murghab."[25]

Jay sends Lauren on her way. There has been an undercurrent in the interviews so far. It is one that people stay away from like the undertow in the ocean. You have to be careful or the undertow can pull you under and out to sea. This undertow pulls strongly here. It is in the comment Jay's mother made, "that Jay didn't want Lauren to go on the trip . . . that she might slow him down. That he would have to worry about another person."[26]

There is something else everyone has carefully avoided. The second decision by Jay not to go with Lauren in the old ambulance brings to light another thought. Was Lauren an unsuspecting innocent sucked into the personality vortex of Jay Austin? The man who moved into a taped-off section of his apartment, refused to vote for a corrupt system, refused to pay his student loans, took off on a scooter across the country, moved into a Tiny House, then quit his job to go bike around the world. Shoving your girlfriend into an old Soviet ambulance in the Pamir Mountains in Tajikistan who is ill, stressed, anxiety-ridden, suffering from altitude sickness, a very long way from home, and, as Kim Postma would say several times, "frightened," and then leaving her so you can bike "this stretch from Karakul to Murghab that is one of Pamirs finest," brings up more questions.

In one sense, Lauren knew the risks and why should Jay be penalized that she's not strong enough to make it through the mountains. "The mountains are calling and I must go." The quote in the kitchen of Jay's tiny house is front and center. Lauren knew what Jay was about. They had been going out since 2012. Jay Austin was a pilgrim on a spiritual quest of adventure. This is obvious. Lauren of all people knew this. But another thought is not so pretty: a self-absorbed pilgrim on a voyage of self-discovery who doesn't consider his girlfriend needs care at this point. Lauren had hit her limit and maybe she should have gone back with her parents in Kazakhstan and allowed Jay to continue.

But she didn't, and Jay makes his decision and does feel some guilt as he writes:

> I am once again on my own. It's a strange feeling, having spent the virtual entirety of the past year with a person, to suddenly be alone. It is Day 366 on the road, Year 2, Day 1 and I'm not sure if it feels silly to have parted ways with Lauren just to cycle this stretch or silly to feel guilty for parting ways for just a day or two. Lauren will be in Murghab. Lauren will be safe I will be in Murghab soon.[27]

Then again, Lauren would have bristled at Jay going with her in the ambulance. She had gone to Beirut and Syria on her own. She had crossed the country to go to a school on the East Coast, thousands of miles away from family and friends, and then stayed there for a job. She had quit her Georgetown University job to bike around the world after thinking about it for a year. If Jay had offered to go in the ambulance, Lauren would have told him, *no*. She would have said, this is what you have been waiting to do, to bike the Pamirs. Because after traveling together for over a year and spending twenty-four hours a day together, they were almost married. Most couples would have been torn apart by a year of traveling on bikes and wild camping. Most certainly, Lauren would have told Jay, go! She would never hold him back. If that's not marriage, then it is certainly love.

Jay bikes the 134 kilometers alone to the 4,650-meter pass. It is one long barren wasteland to Murghab, and Jay follows the ambulance tracks in the dirt along with Nathan, Sophie, and Romain. They are headed for the town of Bartang along with two other cyclists, Della and Tucker. "Jay, you want to come along too," Nathan asks. "It's tempting," Jay writes. "A few more days in a lovely valley with these friends. It's tempting, but of course Nathans just kidding. . . . I give my five cyclists big hugs, see you in Dushanbe, maybe?"[28] In the article Nathan writes after the tragedy, "We lingered. Warm hugs, goodbyes, and see you soon. Eventually jay set off toward Al-Baitul Pass. We watched until he turned to a green dot on the horizon." [29]

They would never see Jay and Lauren again.

Jay later writes in his blog the final line from the movie, *Goodwill Hunting*, "I have to go see about a girl."[30] He rides quickly and rhapsodizes about traveling alone. "You take fewer breaks. You move at your own pace."[31] He wants to get to the lower elevations before nightfall and not be stuck at 4,650 meters. The road is a bumpy gravel and sand and goes back up. The desolation is intense, and the sky is black ahead. Jay leans forward and begins to climb toward the pass. "4100 meters. No switchbacks, just a long wicked uphill climb. I suck in and push hard, but my calves and my lungs and my heart can't handle these grades at this altitude. I get off my bike and begin to push over the stones."

The altitude is taking its toll on Jay as well. At 4,300 meters, it begins to snow, and he puts on his rain gear. At 4,500 meters, Jay passes five cyclists going the other way. He asks how far, and they respond and yell back, *Far! Very steep!* He reaches 4,600 meters.

> I am back to pushing. I can see the pass right in front of me but I cannot will my body to move toward it. My bike feels like a tank and my legs feel like they are ensconced in concrete. My lungs are like, wait, wait, wait, wait, what the hell is this? I have skydived from lower altitudes than this. It'd be a shorter walk to Everest than back to sea level.[32]

Still Jay cycles on. He sees a truck at the top of the pass. "I take five steps, stop, and measure my progress. . . . Under normal circumstances reaching this truck might take three minutes . . . and so it takes forty five." Finally, he reaches 46,540 meters. Ak-Baital. There are two signs. One going up and one going down. A shout comes from the truck. "Good job," a man calls. "You want some tea? Coffee??"

"No thanks. I just need to get down."

"You want a peach?"[33]

Jay takes the peach.

In the pictures Jay takes at the Ak-Baital Pass, it looks like the moon. Barren and bleak. Windswept. It's 4:00 p.m., and he is 80 kilometers from Murghab. He considers camping and going the next day, or he can try and get there before dark. He goes for it.

> My head is pounding. Every time I hit a pothole. . . . I feel a sharp pain in my cranium . . . down into the valley, into the wind, into the dry Pamir Plateau. Down, legs turning, gears turning, wheels turning and vibrating against the rough asphalt. Down, and then not so down, and then mostly just wind from all directions. 5PM, 6PM, 7PM. Sixty kilometers to go. Forty. Just twenty left.[34]

Jay rounds the mountain three hours later and sees a small lit town, "humble and diminutive in the distance." He takes on a headwind for the last 5 kilometers and heads toward the Pamir Hotel. He had told Lauren he would see her at the hotel the next day. Jay pedals toward the hotel and a child waves at him. He waves back and pedals on, but the child keeps on waving. The child then runs inside a guesthouse and comes back out and resumes waving. Jay stops and stares at the child. "I pull out my phone and take a photograph of this strange tall child desperately trying to get my attention. I look at the photo in the camera and zoom in. . . . I can't make out the details but . . . green Patagonia jacket. Shock of curly brown." [35]

Jay looks up and Lauren runs toward him.

On July 15, 2018, Jay posts again from Murghab, where he describes the town as "a dusty smattering of old Russian shipping containers repurposed into a small bizarre. Still at 3600 meters the air is too thin to stand up without getting woozy. 'A sun-bleached statue of Lenin down on the main street, arm outstretched in a theatrical fashion . . . there is a mountain backdrop.'"[36] But it is a third world country of the old Soviet Union. The electricity only runs for a few hours at night and then all is dark. Ever since the Russians left the town, it is dependent on small generators for electricity. Jay and Lauren end up at a small guesthouse with a standard outhouse. Jay is exhausted, and Lauren is "still recovering from bowel issues." They agree to take a few days and explore Murghab.

Jay's final blog post on the Simply Cycling blog is in Murghab, Tajikistan:

> Elevation: high. Very high. Too damn high to cook pasta properly. Too high for trees to grow. . . . Behold, Murghab. There is the mountain backdrop, which is pretty. There is the sky, which is very blue . . . a few basic guesthouses and homestays, sure. Drop toilets and bad dinners and thin mats on the floor. And then, in a league of its own, there is the Pamir Hotel. It is the gem of Murghab. Everyone stays at the Pamir Hotel: overlanders, Russian military, cyclists keen for their first taste of Western comforts since Osh or Dushanbe, depending on which direction they're headed. With a polished wooden lobby and a faintly Wes Anderson aesthetic, one's first steps into the Pamir Hotel certainly feel familiar. Here, for the first time in weeks, a bed. A hot shower. A flushing, sit-down toilet. . . . Despite the power lines running down the street, there is no electricity. The Russians took that with them when they left. Just generators, for a few brief hours per night. And outside those hours, all is still. No water heaters. No water pumps. No way to flush those fancy Western toilets when they fill up between the hours of midnight and six in the evening. At least there is a bed.[37]

Some Instagram posts later extracted from Jay's phone after his death fill in the gaps. A final Instagram post posted on July 25, 2018, describes his solo ride up to the pass. "Day 366, 4655 meters, 15272 feet. With the steep grades and thin air and intermittent snow, this was probably the hardest climb of my life. The last kilometer had me pushing my bike about five steps, taking a thirty second breather, then heaving forward another five. Really glad I did it. No need to ever do it again."[38]

Jay Austin is at the near end of his journey quest. Almost 100 years before, a man on a different journey quest, who didn't believe in evil either, with a philandering father, went looking for his nirvana in the Amazon jungle.

Notes

1 Simplycycling.Org, #40, July 8, 2018.
2 Ibid.
3 Ibid.
4 Ibid.
5 Ibid.

6   Simplycycling.org, #41, May 29, 2021.
7   Ibid.
8   Ibid.
9   Bikepacking.com, When Paths Cross A Tribute to Jay and Lauren, Beriot Nathan, Boyle Sophie, August 18, 2020.
10 Simplycycling.org, #41, May 29, 2021.
11 Bikepacking.com, When Paths Cross A Tribute to Jay and Lauren, Beriot Nathan, Boyle Sophie, August 18, 2020.
12 Ibid.
13 Simplycycling.org, #41, May 29, 2021.
14 Bikepacking.com, When Paths Cross A Tribute to Jay and Lauren, Beriot Nathan, Boyle Sophie, August 18, 2020.
15 Ibid.
16 Simplycycling, #42, May 29, 2021.
17 Interview with Kim Postma by William Hazelgrove, April 29, 2024.
18 Simplycycling.org, #42, May 29, 2021.
19 Ibid.
20 Ibid.
21 Interview with Kristen Robinson, April 12, 2024.
22 Simplycycling, #43, July 8, 2018.
23 Ibid.
24 Interview with Molly Scalise by William Hazelgrove, March 12, 2024.
25 Simplycycling.org, #43, July 8, 2018.
26 Interview with Jea Santovasco, March 21, 2018.
27 Simplycycling.org, #43, July 8, 2018.
28 Ibid.
29 Bikepacking.com, When Paths Cross A Tribute to Jay and Lauren, Beriot Nathan, Boyle Sophie, August 18, 2020.
30 Simplycycling.org, #43, July 8, 2018.
31 Ibid.
32 Ibid.
33 Ibid.
34 Ibid.
35 Ibid.
36 Simplycycling.org, #44, July 15, 2018.
37 Ibid.
38 Jay Austin Instagram post.

24
THE LOST CITY OF Z
1925

In 1925, Percy Fawcett accompanied by his son Jack and Jack's friend Raleigh went in search of a utopic city in the Amazon jungle. Percy had gone into the Amazon countless times to map out the unexplored region for the National Geographic Society. He had survived man-eating piranhas, poisonous snakes, insects that left deadly diseases in the skin, starvation, and hostile Indians. The Great Age of Exploration was still in full swing with Robert Falcon Scott perishing in British Glory trying to be the first to reach the South Pole only to be beaten by the Norwegian Roald Amundsen.

Percy had come from an aristocratic family with his father, Captain Edward Boyd Fawcett, being part of the Prince of Wales' inner circle. His nickname Bulb (for his inflated nose) belled his fatal weakness, a love for drink and philandering, which quickly emptied the coffers of the family fortune. Bulb spiraled down into dissolution. Neglecting his wife and children, he died at forty-five. Percy would later sum up his father as "a good man gone wrong."[1] Percy's mother did not fill in for his absent father. In a book, *Exploration Fawcett*, Percy summed up his childhood: "Perhaps it was all for the best that my childhood . . . was so devoid of parental affection that it turned me in upon myself." [2]

He found release in the Royal Artillery as a twenty-one-year-old lieutenant, and then he found his true calling as an explorer of the Amazon for the Royal Geographic Society. The last great unexplored region on earth was the Amazon. This hostile environment as large as the United States was the tabula rasa of Percy's soul as he mapped regions no man had ever entered. He discovered tribes of Indians who had never seen humans from outside the Amazon. Quickly he developed a radical way of building trust with the indigenous people who had come to regard the outsiders with suspicion. Percy believed showng kindness was the way to approach the remote tribes. Other explorers went into the

Amazon armed to the teeth. This was especially true after the discovery that the Amazon was critical to the burgeoning automobile industry.

Rubber was needed by Henry Ford in vast quantities for car tires. Model Ts were rolling off assembly lines in America like hotcakes. Everyone wanted a car, and Henry Ford was determined to give it to them, but he needed the black latex that came from rubber trees and the place where this rubber was most abundant was in the Amazon. The early men who found the rubber rarely survived or thrived.

> Wearing a miners lamp to help him see, a trapper would hack through jungle, toiling from sunrise to sunset, searching for rubber trees, then upon his return, hungry and feverish, would spend hours hunched over a fire, inhaling toxic smoke as he cooked the latex over a spit until it coagulated. It often took weeks to produce a single rubber ball large enough to sell. And it was rarely enough to discharge his debt.[3]

Trappers died of starvation, dysentery, or disease. The Peruvian Amazon Company was determined to pull out rubber from the Amazon, a wilderness that rivaled the American west in brutality, and turned to slave labor. Armed men went deep into the forest and kidnapped men and women and brought them back to service in the rubber trade. Terror was used as a weapon against the indigenous people. "To pacify and enslave the native population, it castrated and beheaded Indians, poured gasoline on them and lit them afire, crucified them upside down, drowned them, and fed them to dogs. The company's henchmen also raped women and girls and smashed children's heads open."[4] Once-friendly tribes now turned against the intrepid explorers and retaliated with poisoned arrows, while other explorers were found "buried up to their waists and left to be eaten alive by fire ants, maggots, and bees."[5]

Fawcett early on deplored the policy which created a slave trade and unlike other explorers believed showing the Indians he could be trusted was the best way to survive in the Amazon. He required all his men to agree to not fire their weapons at the Indians under any circumstances. Many saw this as sheer suicide, but Fawcett argued his nonviolent approach was not only moral, but was the only way for an outnumbered party to show it was friendly to tribes. Fawcett believed in the higher nature of the indigenous people, the essential goodness that only had to be coaxed out and that assuming evil intent was wrong.

This was put to the test when Fawcett's boats came under attack from a barrage of arrows. Percy ordered his men to put down their rifles while he took off the handkerchief from his neck and began waving it over his head. Still the arrows came, so Fawcett waded into the water and began walking toward the hostile Indians. He continued walking toward the shore when the arrows stopped.

THE LOST CITY OF Z

Percy stopped with his hands over his head until an Indian came out and guided him to shore. They led him away but then returned as friends. Fawcett believed fully that his nonviolent approach was the way to approach the Indians who had come to regard the explorers with great suspicion.

During his trips, he became enamored with the idea of a mythical Eldorado, an advanced civilization, which was said to exist deep in the Amazon. As far back as 1600, Sir Walter Raleigh claimed: "the kingdom which the conquistadors had heard about from the Indians was so plentiful in gold that its inhabitants ground the metal into powder and blew it through hollow canes upon their naked bodies until they be shining from foot to the head."[6] Yet no one had found it, though many tried. Fawcett through his expeditions had been steadily gathering evidence. "Digging up artifacts, studying petroglyphs, and interviewing tribes." Percy believed a sophisticated civilization existed deep in the Amazon, which he called the lost City of Z. He viewed it as a nirvana "in a valley . . . about ten miles wide and the city is on an eminence in the middle of it, approached by a barreled roadway of stone . . . the houses are low and windowless and there is a pyramidal temple."[7]

Percy would return home to his wife and children after each harrowing expedition and would enjoy the fruits of domestic life, but he was eternally restless and became more and more obsessed with finding the lost city of Z. By 1914, he had narrowed down the location of the mythical city, but the assassination of Archduke Ferdinand diverted his plans to return with the beginning of the First World War. Fawcett went to the Western Front and commanded an artillery unit that held its position when others could not. The hardships of the Amazon had held him in good stead, but after battles like the Sohm, Percy returned home suffering from shell shock. He became more consumed with the City of Z as "a glittering place seemingly immune to the rottenness of Western civilization."[8]

In 1920, Fawcett returned to the Amazon to find the lost city but was stopped when his leg became infected, and he had to return to the nearest outpost. It would take him until 1925 to secure funding to return. This time he was taking his twenty-one-year-old son Jack and Jack's best friend, Raleigh Rimmel, to finally find the fabled city of his dreams. Fawcett was now fifty-seven, and one newspaper declared, "not since the days when Ponce de Leon crossed unknown Florida in search of the waters of perpetual youth . . . has a more alluring adventure been planned."[9] The SS *Vauban* left port on January 10, 1925. For five months, dispatches came back from the Amazon by Indian runners that were sent all over the world by telegraph. Then the dispatches stopped. Fawcett said he might be out of contact for some months, but a year passed. Then two. Percy Fawcett and his son Jack and his friend Raleigh had simply disappeared. Never to be heard from again.

Books would follow. Then a movie showing the Percys' demise at the hands of Indians, who were not taken in by his nonviolent approach. Many said that Percy had come to believe in his own invincibility. This sad tale of 100 years before resonates with Jay and Lauren's journey. A man with a philandering father who abandoned his family. An indigenous people exploited by an imperialist power bent on extracting raw materials any way it can. A man looking for salvation in exploring, looking for a mythical world only to crash into a culture that will take revenge on anyone it can. In the final scene of the movie, waiting for their fate, Percy turns to his son, and says, "there is still so much in this world we don't understand."[10]

In four days, Jay and Lauren would cross paths with Hussein Abdusamadov. It is not a stretch for Jay Austin to have this same last thought.

Notes

1 Grann, David, *Lost City of Z*, Doubleday, NY, 2009.
2 Fawcett, Percy, Exploration Fawcett, NY, Henry Abrams, 2010.
3 Grann, David, *Lost City of Z*, Doubleday, NY, 2009.
4 Ibid., 89.
5 Ibid., 90.
6 Ibid., 11.
7 Ibid., 12.
8 Ibid.
9 Ibid., 12.
10 Paramount, *City of Z*, Movie.

25
SIXTY MILES TO DUSHANBE

JULY 28, 2018

Sixty miles to the capital of Tajikistan, Dushanbe. It was a mantra beating in Lauren and Jay's head as they cycle with their air pods singing and talking in their ears. Jay was listening to another podcast, and Lauren was listening to music, Taylor Swift, Coldplay, Nickelback. The two happiest days for any cyclist are when they get on the bike and when they get off. The anticipation of a ride is great and the thrill of being done with the endorphin high is better. They were done with the Pamir Mountains. The high passes had been conquered. For Jay, it was the pinnacle of the trip; the highlight of an amazing year's journey across twenty-nine countries in 377 days.

For Lauren, the accomplishment was that she had not quit. She had not gone home with her parents, she had stayed with Jay, and while the altitude had forced her to be transported over two passes, she had hung in there. And now they were headed for a city, Dushanbe, where regular life could return and assess what was next. India maybe. Home maybe for a while. It was all up in the air the way most of the trip had been.

They pedaled down the stark black two-lane. There was none of the beauty of the Pamir Mountains here. They were still in the mountains, but they were now on Highway A 385 in the Danghara District, which was outside the Pamirs. Alongside the highway were giant Orson Welles Martians holding up high-tension lines. The sandy shoulders of the two-lane highway break for unending short brush and rock and in the distance were the painted white peaks of the Pamirs. But this was all behind them now.

The heat had become intense with the sun radiating back from the black-tarred pavement. Biking on a dirt trail or a gravel road is much cooler than a highway. The heat sink of cities proves this over and over where the roads act like radiators. Biking in heat is an exercise in drinking water, keeping a steady pace, not overexerting. The objective is to stay as cool as possible. And now for the first time they were biking in a group. This was new. Biking with other people is a very different experience than biking alone. Biking alone is very Zen. Jay appreciated being alone. When he took off on his scooter across the country, it was a very solitary pilgrimage. He writes in his blog:

The notions of being alone and being lonely began to diverge in my head though I was perfectly comfortable being alone, climbing a remote mountain or rolling down an empty road with only my thoughts for company. . . . I needed to go, to be alone."[1] He quotes Emerson extensively in the Scooter Diaries. "But if a man would be alone, let him look at the stars."[2]

But the trip has changed Jay. The stress of traveling, the logistics, the day-to-day of close proximity with another person will either make or break a relationship. Even in the Scooter Diaries, Jay recognized that sharing an experience with someone was greater than sharing it alone. "I would not doubt that somewhere, on the outskirts of my mind, I was running away from loneliness, confident that the sights and sensations of a new location would keep my mind too occupied to feel that stinging sadness, the sadness of not being able to share such remarkable experiences with another." It was the same moment Chris McCandless had in his journey into the wild. As he lay dying in the school bus in Alaska, he wrote in his journal a sad realization that had come too late: "HAPPINESS ONLY REAL WHEN SHARED."[3]

Lauren had changed Jay Austin; where there was one, there were two now. But now, there were five other cyclists. Biking in a group brings another dimension to cycling. The speed of the group dictates how hard the cycling is. The conversations while cycling steal away from private thoughts. Even the safety of a group is different. Every cyclist has one thought when biking on a highway: *I hope I don't get hit from behind*. It is the ultimate blind spot. The sound of the approaching car is the first inkling of danger. The cyclist hugs the white borderline or gets as far over into the thin strip of asphalt as possible. To cycle is to have faith that another human being will not run you over with their car or truck.

The fear is amplified when a car or a truck approaches, and the engine becomes a roar and the whine of the tires a small train. A cyclist learns to tell a truck from a car very quickly. The diesel trucks are unmistakable, but the pickups can be discerned by the kiss of the wide tires on the hot pavement. And then the vehicle passes, and sometimes it is close and sometimes it is far. Sometimes a mirror extended out from a pickup will almost brush your shoulder. I don't wear air pods because I want to hear that approaching battering ram. Sometimes the truck or car is so loud and ominous that the cyclist goes off the highway and

SIXTY MILES TO DUSHANBE

comes to a stop on the shoulder. But if air pods are in, the cyclist hears none of this.

Now Jay is feeling good. Lauren is still faintly nauseous; the Pamir Mountains are over, but they are still cycling at high altitudes in a mountainous region. Their only goal is to get to Dushanbe where they could take a break in the capital of Tajikistan. Fellow cyclists Kim Postma and her longtime companion Rene Wokke from Amsterdam were also looking forward to warm showers and a soft bed. It had been several weeks before, sitting on a bench under a shelter, when Lauren and Jay approached them. "You could just tell they were American," Kim later recalled. "It was hot, and the young woman asked if they could share the shelter and then when they left the woman said to me, thank you for sharing the shelter. Very American."[4] Rene and Kim were on a trip from Thailand to Iran. They had decided to travel through Tajikistan to avoid Afghanistan because they thought it was too dangerous. They had traveled to more than 130 countries on their bikes.

Two weeks later, they met Jay and Lauren again in the Pamir Mountains. Jay's blog doesn't mention Kim or Rene, but Kim was there when Lauren took the ambulance. "When we met in the Pamirs, they talked about why they were doing this, share the world meet new people. He wanted to change his life more than she did and this trip was to make that transition." Kim's impression was that Lauren was frightened a lot of the time in Tajikistan. "She had problems with her stomach. She couldn't eat. She talked about her parents and her sisters a lot and really missed them and said she would like to go home by Christmas and Jay would continue. But when she said this, Jay said, we will see about our budget."[5]

They were later joined by Marie Clarie, fifty-nine, and Markus Hummel, sixty-two, a Swiss couple, and eventually Guillaume Kazabat, a young, bearded Frenchman. They are seven now biking along the Pamir Highway. Over the next few days, the couples became close and planned to rent an apartment in Dushanbe, where they would enjoy wine and good food. "It was all paradise in our heads," Kim said, nodding, and recalls when they summited a 14,000-foot pass in mid-July with Jay riding ahead and then coming back and pushing up Lauren's bike so she could walk. "I remember she was having panic attacks," Kim continued. "I think it was the stress of the altitude." They celebrated at the top of the pass. "Ya . . . we were all so happy."[6]

Kim Postma pauses in our interview six years later. She is leaning back in a chair in her living room. She looks at the laptop camera. "I think now . . . that we were being watched the days before the attack. You know, odd things happened. Two days before the attack we were interviewed on the road by a radio station. A man leaned out of a car with a microphone." She shakes her head. "That had never ever happened before." On the internet is a random video of Kim and Rene, Marie Claire, and the French cyclist Guillaume biking through a town in Tajikistan days before the attack. It is a hot dusty day, and the video shows the cyclists with their loaded-down bikes. "I didn't like that town," Kim replied when I brought up the video. "There was something dangerous about it."[7]

In the video, the cyclists look tired and stop at an intersection with the wind kicking up the dust around them. Rene stares ahead and Kim and Guillaume wait behind him. The fatigue of biking nonstop is evident and something else, boredom. Biking continually every day becomes boring. Biking long distances becomes boring. Especially when loaded-down bikes struggle to go 10 miles an hour. It is hot as well, but what is most evident is that the cyclists stand out as people from another country.

The Tajikistanis stare at them from stores and the sidewalks. They are Western Europeans on expensive bikes loaded with expensive gear. It is dangerous to stand out. During the investigation after the attack, it was determined that the terrorist leader, Hussein, stumbled upon the group of cyclists and stalked them for two days. His ISIS operative Qori Nosir, the religious man who had radicalized Hussein as a young man, approved the plot the day before, saying the attack on Americans would bring international attention.

This would back up Kim's suspicion they were being watched. At a campsite in an orchid where a Tajik farmer had brought them all tea, they are interviewed again, this time by a television station on the day before the attack. It is an eerie last glimpse of Jay and Lauren as the video rolls. Lauren is tan and smiles and speaks on camera and describes the people they are cycling with. "We met on the road—two Americans, two from Switzerland, two from the Netherlands, and one from France. We are having a wonderful time in Tajikistan."[8] Lauren with her fresh face, warm brown eyes, pulled back hair, looks like what she is, a beautiful young woman on the trip of a lifetime. Jay is interviewed in a sleeveless T-shirt and a light beard. He is tan and lean, almost skinny from biking for over a year. He laughs and speaks in halting Russian. He looks like a young man drinking in all that life can give him. But the video is troubling. It is never confirmed the interview was related to the attack, but for Kim the interviews are ominous. It is a last glimpse of Jay Austin and Lauren Geoghegan for all time.

Notes

1 Austin, Jay, Scooter Diaries.
2 Ibid.
3 Krakauer, Jon, *Into the Wild*, Anchor Books, NY.
4 Interview with Kim Postma by William Hazelgrove, April 29, 2024.

5   Ibid.
6   Ibid.
7   Ibid.
8   Radio Free Europe, Tajik Cyclists Attacker Was Influenced By Others, https://www.youtube.com/watch?v=yC8e8b5XXIM&t=43s.

26
COLLISION
JULY 29, 2018

Year 2 on the Road, Day 12

July 29 began as a hot day. Jay and Lauren and the other cyclists have gone from freezing in the mountains to sweating on the highway. Their water is running low, and they stop at a gas station to fill their water bottles from a spicket. The day before Hussein Abdusamadov went into a town and purchased several kitchen knives. When interviewed on camera in the *New York Times Weekly* video *Collision* after the attack, the proprietor shows what he sold Hussein. They are not only large kitchen knives but also sharpened meal cleavers with wooden handles used to hack up thick beef.

The cyclists are milling around at the gas station when a white South Korean Daewoo sedan pulls in. An olive-skinned man with short black hair gets out and approaches Kim Postma. She is filling her bottle from the spicket. "He was very pushy and spoke English very well," Kim says quietly in her living room. "He said, don't you like Tajikistan? Who are you? You must say you like Tajikistan."[1] Hussein would later tell the *New York Times* reporter, Rukmini Callimachi, he just discovered the cyclists at the gas station, but his phone messages and the approval from Qori Nosir days before prove he had been stalking them for two days.

Hussein then approaches Jay while he is topping off his bottle. "He begins asking him questions. Where do you come from? Where are you from, he asks and keeps badgering him with questions. Jay answers in Russian and laughs. He is evasive, saying he was from Russia, Tajikistan, then finally admits he was from the United States," Kim recalled. "I am here with my friends and brothers,"

Hussein says, pointing to the car full of men. "He is still badgering Jay with questions and eventually Jay told the man to leave us alone then."[2]

Hussein gets in his car and drives away. They finish filling their water bottles, and everyone gets back on their bikes and continues on the two-lane Highway A 385. They are now close to the village of Safobakhsh in the Danghara District just 100 kilometers south of Dushanbe. Skeletal powerlines are on one side. It is getting warmer, and they are biking uphill. It is 3:30 p.m. Kim Postma in our interview speaks very slowly, her eyes steady on the computer camera. "We were going very slowly with our air pods in. We were cycling in a row, Jay and Lauren in front, then it was Markus and Marie Claire, then there was me, and behind me was Rene. Guillaume had stomach problems, and he had fallen far behind."[3]

In a picture of the group taken shortly before the attack, Jay has a baseball cap on and wearing blue shorts and a gray T-shirt. Lauren has on a floppy hat, but she will put back on her cycling helmet. The road is boarded by large stones. Rene is standing, and Kim Postma has her arm raised. It is hot, and this is a water break. Guillaume the French cyclist is last in the line. They begin again and ride slowly in the heat. Once again, Guillaume falls behind.

Over the previous weeks, Hussein Abdusamadov, thirty-three, has recruited four young Tajikistan migrant workers. Zafar Safarov and Asomiddin Majidov, both nineteen-year-olds, two relatives of Hussein, who had just come back from Russia two days before the attacks. The others were brothers, Jafariddin Yusupov, twenty-six, and Asliddin Yusupov, twenty-one. Jafariddin was radicalized by Hussein in Russia and had convinced his brother to join the plot. The younger brother had served in the army. In a video posted before the attack, they sit in front of an ISIS flag on a hilltop in black T-shirts pledging allegiance to Jihad. Their demeanor is not that different from young men pledging a fraternity. They hold up one finger as they chant. In the phone videos recovered after the attack, their voices are that of excited young men. They have never killed anyone before. They are amateurs. They are poor. They are radicalized for this one attack. They have knives, steel handle meat cleavers, and instructions. Interviews with the four terrorist parents later reveal little. The father of one of the young men, Juma Safrarov, is shown a picture and identifies his son Zafar in the Islam State group video. "It's easy to deceive a child. I'm sure someone influenced him and led him down such a path,"[4] he says.

The four men and Hussein are now trailing the cyclists in the Daewoo sedan and steadily increasing the speed. In a recovered phone video shot from inside the Daewoo sedan, the engine roars, and someone shouts *"May the peace, mercy and blessings of God be with you. Praise be to God Lord of the Universe. Blessings and peace on the Prophet Muhammad and his family and his companions to Judgement Day!"*[5] The car accelerates. A still frame from the video shows the first cyclist in front of the car, Kim Postma. Then the camera falls to dash level as a woman screams and someone says, "the guys should see this."[6] Hussein then drops the phone.

Kim has her air pods in and feels a fist hit the side of her leg.

"I got hit by the car first and fell," she relates slowly, clutching her hands. "But I wasn't injured and so I got back up and tried to stop cars in the road. Rene, he was screaming, because he just saw me get hit by the white car then I saw the car driving on." Kim pauses. "Driving on and hitting the others in front of me." She shakes her head. "The other cars, the ones driving past, no one stopped." [7]

In pictures later taken of Jay's bike by the State Department, the back wheel rim is pushed in and mangled, but the bike is surprisingly intact. When a cyclist is hit, the force is transferred to the rider. In videos of cyclists hit by cars, the cyclist absorbs the energy and is propelled off the bike. After hitting Marie Claire and Marc Hummel and knocking them down, the terrorists zero in on Jay and Lauren. They are riding furthest ahead with distance between them and the group. Jay is listening to a podcast. Lauren is listening to music. They are the most exposed outside the pack of the riders. Like a plane in a dogfight, the sedan zeros in from behind on Lauren first.

The force of the blow knocked Lauren unconscious. She never knew what hit her. The bowling ball indentation and drops of blood in the cracked windshield of the Daewoo sedan are later identified as a bike helmet smashing into the windshield. Lauren was propelled up and over the hood of the car and into the windshield where she rolled off to the side. Jay is now in front of the car that drives directly toward him. He is blind and deaf to what has happened behind him. Jay is staring down the highway with the mountains in the distance. A scream might have penetrated his air pods. A sixth sense of commotion, the world shifting. He might have turned and seen the white missile. The Daewoo sedan crashes into his back tire, breaks his leg, and launches him like a human cannonball onto the sloping gravel shoulder. Kim "recalled seeing Jay hit by the car, having accelerated upon reaching Jay. She saw him being knocked from his bike, flying a distance from the road onto the shoulder, but the shoulder sloped downward, so she didn't see Jay land on the ground."[8]

At this moment, if the Daewoo sedan had left, all might have survived. But now, the white South Korean sedan has stopped on the searing blacktop. The sun is blazingly hot overhead. The four young Tajikistan men jump out of the car as Hussein stays in the car to videotape. The men spread out like soldiers holding meat cleavers and large kitchen knives. The victims are on the side of the highway and on the road as the killers approach with sun-glinting blades.

Further back on the highway, Kim Postma runs across the hot pavement, still trying to stop passing cars. Kim shakes her head slowly. "No one would stop, they just kept driving."[9] In a grainy video shot from a passing car, the drivers weave between the bodies on the road. "I looked up the highway and saw very horrifying things. After they hit everyone, then I see the car stop and the men get out with the knives."

Kim holds up her hand clutching an imaginary knife.

It seemed each of them had a person they were assigned to attack. Rene was standing and some guy ran up to him and starts stabbing him with a knife in his belly. He stabbed and stabbed and stabbed. They begin stabbing everyone then. Marie Claire was stabbed in the back, and she is sitting on the ground, screaming over and over, *"They are killing us . . . they are killing all of us!"*[10]

Markus Hummel had been knocked from his bike by the car. Kim paused. "Marcus, he has his throat cut as he lay on the ground. Marie Claire, she is still in the road and goes into shock." The cars on the highway continue to weave through the opera of death on the sunny highway. I ask Kim a question, and she nods. "I could see Lauren was lying in a fetal position on the black pavement of the highway. She was in the road." From others, the sequence of Lauren's last moments is put together. She is not moving as a man runs toward her with a meat cleaver. She never sees the man who ends her life.

Jay is on his back on the shoulder of the road in the hot sun. In Hussein's phone video, recovered from the police, he is not far from Lauren. It looks to be 10 to 15 feet. He is conscious and feels the pain of his broken leg. He sees a dark-haired man approach him, holding a knife and a meat cleaver. The man attacks in a fury of slashing and stabbing as Jay tries to block the thrusting blades. The man continues slashing and stabbing. Later, many of Jay's wounds will be described as defensive.

Seconds have passed. Not minutes. Kim is standing in the highway as a blond-haired man continues to thrust his knife into Rene's stomach. She recalls the scene in a faraway voice. "I was on the other side of the highway and Rene is standing and I see the guy you know, just standing and stabbing him with a knife in his belly."[11] She moves her hand in a thrusting motion. "He stabbed and stabbed and stabbed." Kim pauses. "And then the man he stopped stabbing Rene, and he turns and looks at me with this big bloody knife. He stares for a moment and then runs across the highway toward me."

The blond-haired man, later identified as Zafar, crosses the highway toward Kim holding the knife out. She backs away as he approaches with the gleaming blade. In the phone video shot by a passing driver, Kim runs up onto a sandy access road. Kim pauses in our interview, then composes herself. "I walked backward you know as he approached and kept walking back and back and then I shouted something like, *what do you want . . . what do you want.*" Kim paused again, shakes her head slowly. "Then two meters in front of me, he suddenly turned around and ran back to the car . . . the leader or somebody shouted come back . . . that was my escape. . . . I guess they were calling him."[12]

Kim recrosses the highway to Rene, who's standing with bright red blood flowing from his stomach. A grainy phone video of the attack will rocket around the world, and many will interpret the video as the main attack, but it is the end of the attack. In Hussein's phone video, the four men run toward him as he shouts, "*Run! Let's go, sit down, we're leaving!*"[13] The four men have all rejoined Hussein in the car, and there are shouts of "*Drive brother Drive!*"[14] on the captured video. In the same video, later extracted by the police, a man is seen running from Jay's body. He is holding a knife and behind is Lauren lying curled up on the highway. The video taken by a passing car now shows Hussein's car turning around for a final pass. The white car passes Lauren lying in the road and Jay in a crumpled mass off to the side. The car is headed for Kim Postma.

Kim pauses and wipes her eyes. "So I was running to Rene you know, he has blood coming down when he shouted, *'look out look out!'* because the car was coming back high speed and trying to hit me."[15] In the Hussein-captured phone video, someone shouts, "Lets hit the woman!"[16] Kim starts to run. "I ran back across the highway and they hit Rene with the car." Kim touches the top of her head. "I saw him fly up into the air and come down on his head."[17]

In the phone video, Kim runs away, then a blurry figure flies up into the air. The man filming from his car grunts when he sees Rene become airborne. Kim pauses in our interview for a long moment. She looks up. "And then the men they are gone, they just drove away."

Kim pauses again. "That was it."[18]

The attack by Hussein and the four radicalized young Tajikistanis had taken less than five minutes. Four people lay dead or dying on the sun scorched highway. Jay Austin, Lauren Geoghegan, Markus Hummel, and Rene Wokke.

Markus Hummel was sixty-two.

Rene Wokke was sixty-one.

Lauren Geoghegan was twenty-nine.

Jay Austin was twenty-nine.

People begin to stop their cars.

Notes

1   Interview with Kim Postma by William Hazelgrove, April 29, 2024.

2   Ibid.

3   Ibid.

4 *New York Times*, Rukmini, Callimachi, ISIS Says It Killed 4 Cyclists in Tajikistan, July 30, 2018.
5 Ibid.
6 Ibid.
7 Interview with Kim Postma by William Hazelgrove, April 29, 2024.
8 Santovasco, Jea Reflections on the Death of My Son, 53.
9 Interview with Kim Postma by William Hazelgrove, April 29, 2024.
10 Ibid.
11 Ibid.
12 Ibid.
13 *New York Times*, Rukmini, Callimachi, ISIS Says It Killed 4 Cyclists in Tajikistan, July 30, 2018.
14 Ibid.
15 Interview with Kim Postma by William Hazelgrove, April 29, 2024.
16 *New York Times*, Rukmini, Callimachi, ISIS Says It Killed 4 Cyclists in Tajikistan, July 30, 2018.
17 Interview with Kim Postma by William Hazelgrove, April 29, 2024.
18 Ibid.

27
THE AFTERMATH

JULY 29, 2018

The hot wind rolls down from the heated mountain side. The violence of the moment was replaced by eerie calm. People groaning, crying, shouting for help. The hot sun is now unbearable with the heat radiating off the black tar of the highway. Blood running onto the pavement, then trickling red into the sand on the side of the road. The last cyclist, the young Frenchman who fell behind with stomach issues (Guillaume), rides up with his gears clicking. He slows to a stop. The cries and groans reach him. He stares at the battlefield. Too much to take in. Shock. The silence is broken by cars stopping, doors opening, people running into the scene of carnage.

Kim Postma paused in our interview, breathed deeply, then began again:

There was this quiet after the terrorists left. I ran to Rene and he was still breathing, but the final blow by the car had given him a massive head wound. I remember it was so hot in the sun, and I wanted to block him. I was shouting *help us* because we are sitting in the road in the sunlight and I am shouting, *give us shelter*.

Kim recalled:

At one point I was trying to stop his bleeding sitting on the side of the road. A Belgian truck driver he stopped, he spoke Dutch and helped me stop the bleeding from Rene's stomach with a T shirt he pulled out of his truck, but his head was bleeding too.

Kim paused again. "Here we are in this road and the heat was coming up from the pavement you know, and it was so hot and I'm shouting, help, *help us*, do something, and we are still in the full sunlight with Rene."[1]

A later picture of Marie Clarie shows her sitting up with a woman trying to bandage her back and Markus's body at her feet. There are no pictures of Lauren and Jay except the later police photos. They are far up the road away from the people helping Markus, Marie Clarie, Kim, and Rene. Lauren and Jay had turned back into the two solitary bikers they started the trip as. They were different even in death. When I asked Kim if anyone went over to help them, she shook her head. "No people refused to go look at Jay . . . Lauren and Jay . . . they were gone. They wanted to help the living."

Guillaume, the French cyclist, is the only witness before help arrived. I asked to interview him later, but he refused in a reply on Instagram. I asked Kim about the French cyclist. "He had no idea what happened. He saw dead people and blood. He gave me my phone later. He was in shock, and he felt guilty because he thought we were waiting for him." But what Guillaume saw was unbelievable. Rene Wokke was lying on the ground with Kim bent over him with a severe head wound and blood gushing out of his stomach. Markus Hummel lay at Marie Claire's feet with a gushing mortal slash in his neck. In the Associated Press photo, Marie Clarie is sitting up while a woman bandages her back. Markus Hummel appears to have on a red shirt but when the photo is blown up his shirt is completely red with blood and his face bone white. Marie Clarie has blood down her back and on her legs and has succumbed to deep shock with stab wounds in her back and a nonexistent memory of events. Guillaume then saw the crumpled body of Lauren in a fetal position on the highway and on the sandy shoulder was Jay.

Guillaume walked across the black highway onto the sandy shoulder and stared down at Jay. What he saw would haunt him forever. In police photos, Jay's eyes are slightly open, but he's so butchered and covered in blood, he is hard to recognize as a human. Guillaume said that when "he got to Jay he could tell he was already dead. He found Jay lying on the ground on his back, that his arms were to his sides and that his head was slightly tilted to the left."[2] The carnage made Guillaume never want to think of it again. He turned and didn't look back.

Now it is the quiet of the dead. It is natural to wonder what the last thoughts of people are before they die. If Jay was still alive after the knife attack, then his last thoughts had to be for Lauren. What happened to her? Was she alive? In Hussein's phone video, both Jay and Lauren can be seen not that far apart. Jay's HUD friend, Abby, pointed out that if Lauren had died and he survived, Jay couldn't have lived with himself. And as Jay lay in the bright hot sun, did he have the final communion he had always craved? In *The Scooter Diaries*, Jay wrote about a mystical experience after taking some hallucinogenic grass and seeing the Joshua Tree in the Mojave Desert. The tree was named by Mormon settlers who had just crossed the desert and saw the tree's unique shape as a sign of faith and hope. Jay wrote:

> I felt as though I was pulling myself up over a wall, about to glimpse what was atop it, an experience I had felt many times before, but this time was different, this time, I had a hold of the wall's top ledges, this time I was hoisting and pulling and throwing myself onto it, this time I had actually arrived at the top. And it was glorious. I cannot, and could not, ever accurately describe what happened then. In an instant, the universe was inside me, and I could feel every fiber of it, every particle of matter. Every single thing made sense, and nothing made sense, and I felt everything, and I felt nothing. In an instant, I felt every answer to every question I've ever had, and then, nodding in the ultimate realization, the answers vanished with the questions in tow, leaving me not with any practical answer whatsoever, but leaving me without the questions I had battled against for decades. I couldn't even remember what the questions were. All that was left was quiet, peace. In that instant, my rational mind cynically doubted what was happening, chocking the experience up to a misfired synapse or a mistaken overdose of dopamine. But at the very next instant, another wave of truth hit me, and I began crying, torrents of tears running down my face, not sadness, not happiness, just awe. This is it. I was terrified, I was thankful, I was devoid of emotions and filled with every one of them. I was ready. And so I waded into it, into the metaphysical ocean before me, and felt a peace and a truth I had never felt before, and it persisted, and the deeper in I waded the stronger it felt, and the harder I felt it, and I cried so hard I had to pull to the side of the road for practical fear of physically crashing at the actual moment of this actual moment. Waves of realization broke atop me. I realized that my wish for all the puzzle pieces of the universe to click together into something that made sense hadn't happened in an instant; I had been putting the puzzle together for years, and it was only that morning that I realized what I was putting together, how close I was to being complete, and with each piece set into place, the next became exponentially easier, until with one final click, it was done. Complete. And complete was the right word for how I felt: my search, my quest, my life.[3]

And in that moment, before Lauren was hit by the Daewoo sedan, was she thinking about going home to take a needed break from the trip? She had proven herself. She had been biking for over a year through deserts and high-elevation mountains, been chased by elephants, caught in storms, ridden old ferries in the middle of the night, endured sickness and loneliness, seen amazing acts of kindness, acts of anger, of brutality, ridden through dark carbon monoxide-infested tunnels, and camped outside in areas people would not even walk through. She had done it. Whatever it was. She had done it. Maybe she thought of Jay, of her mother and her father, all those birthdays in the backyards with her father barbecuing hamburgers and hotdogs with a pinata, and her favorite cookies her mother baked at Christmas, and the Saturday runs to Winchell's donuts, or going to Mexico with her mother, or being that natural leader, or the weekly family meetings, or was she thinking in those last moments about Georgetown friends, or the time she spent working for Congressman Adam Schiff, attending fireworks on the fourth of July, having Ethiopian food in kitschy Georgetown restaurants. Maybe she wound back and thought of Jay. For if marriage is a meeting of the souls, then they were married. As married as two people can be. And maybe she thought about all those moments; for if life is a collection of stars, then they must burn brightly before the dark.

The FBI later said only ten minutes elapsed before help arrived and the terrorists left. In pictures of the scene, there are ambulances and cars blocking the road. People are everywhere. Pictures of the bikes lying in the dust on the side of the road show little damage. Jay's bike with the crushed rear rim has the most damage. The driver of the Daewoo sedan clipped the cyclists until he reached Jay and Lauren. He hit them head-on. Kim Postma had stood up with only a few scrapes after she was hit. The force of the car knocked the cyclists down, but didn't kill them. Marie Claire was able to walk and get into an ambulance. Jay Austin would have survived. The later autopsy would determine his leg was broken, but death came from the knife and cleaver attack. Lauren might have survived as well from the car hitting her from behind.

Then again, Hussein could have planned it this way. The car wasn't to kill but to immobilize the cyclists. The killing would be by the four men Hussein had recruited in the last few weeks. When they bailed out of the car, their mission was to kill, but they were not trained killers. They were young migrant workers from Tajikistan who had to stab and chop another human being to death. The blond-haired man, Zafar, who attacked Rene Wokke was thrusting a knife into his stomach, but Rene remained standing. Zafar didn't slash his throat or stab him in the chest. He stabbed Rene in the stomach repeatedly and then ran toward Kim Postma. He could have knocked Kim to the ground and slit her throat, but he approached with the knife held out like a bad movie.

Kim Postma faced her attacker and shouted, *"What do you want?"* Was this too much for the young jihadist? Did the tenuous grip of radical Islamic fervor slip away. Either way, Kim Postma survived, but few others did. The phone video of the attack conveys none of the horror. It is too distant, too blurry. The car scoots around like an errant Pacman knocking small gray figures into the sky. The only sound is the man who exclaims loudly when Rene flies into the sky. But the

THE AFTERMATH

horror is the aftermath. A doctor later told Jay's mother, her son died from loss of blood and then a heart attack. Jay was stabbed approximately ten times, but he was also chopped with a cleaver eight times.

According to Kim Postma, Lauren was frightened in Tajikistan, but she was biking toward Dushanbe, where a room, a shower, a comfortable bed, dinners out awaited them. It was the last big hurtle. Once out of the mountains, she could lose the altitude sickness and that foreboding that started with her last hug with her mother. If there is such a thing as destiny, then maybe Lauren felt the tap on her shoulder then. She and Jay were in the same universe with the destiny to enter eternity at the same time.

When Kim Postma saw the car crushing her fellow cyclists and men bailing out of the car with meat cleavers, it's amazing she didn't just run into the fields and keep running. But she didn't. She ran across the highway and helped Rene. The physical distance of Lauren and Jay from the others is evident in the pictures. The truth is no one was helping them, because it was assumed they had died.

Kim was still trying to save Rene with the truck driver. At some point, they were put into a car and drove "to what we might call a hospital," she explained in our interview.

> I don't know what it was. A man said he was a doctor, and they took Rene away and they pushed me away and I just sat there and waited. Marie Claire came into the building on a stretcher, and she was lying on her side but she couldn't talk. She was deeply in shock. There were so many police people, and they spoke Russian, and they kept asking me questions I didn't understand.[4]

Eventually, Kim and Marie Claire are in another ambulance and taken to a hospital that looked more modern. There is no information on who transported Jay and Lauren to the hospital. Kim tried to find out what happened to Rene while caring for Marie. "Marie Clair was still in shock," she said haltingly in our interview. "She kept asking *what happened what happened what happened* . . . and I tried to explain to her about the attack, but she couldn't understand. They took her away for surgery and when she came back, I sat with her for hours not knowing what happened to Rene."[5]

Finally, someone called Kim from the Netherlands. Kim closes her eyes and is quiet, then she speaks. "They said Rene had died and he was shocked because he thought I knew." She shook her head slowly. "I started shouting and screaming you know and became very angry. No one at the hospital no one would tell me anything."[6] Kim then got in touch with officials in the Netherlands. The German ambassador became involved, and a doctor appeared, and told Kim he would help her.

"He said he would take me to Rene . . . so I follow him down these stairs." The doctor took Kim down to the morgue in the basement of the hospital. Kim paused. "It was very dark and cold, really shocking, all these steel drawers," she said slowly. "The doctor, he began to pull open these drawers and the first one was Markus Hummel." Kim pauses, and closes her eyes. "So, then he shut that one, and we went to the next drawer." Kim nods slowly and reaches out. "And he pulled the drawer open and there was . . . Jay. They only pulled it out a little way so I could just see the face, none of you know, the wounds . . . so they closed that one, and then he pulled another drawer." Kim is silent. Pauses. "And that was Rene."[7]

The next drawer would have been Lauren. This is the only information as to where their bodies were brought. Kim was severely shaken and wanted to stay with Rene's body, but the Tajikistan police told her that wasn't possible. Her life was in danger as the only survivor of the attack. She was a witness to a terrorist attack and could identify the men who had murdered Jay and Lauren, Markus and Rene. The Tajikistan government insisted she leave the country.

"They said you are the only survivor and they will come after you, everyone said I was at risk now."[8] In a game of James Bond maneuvers, Kim was smuggled out of the hospital with the help of Guillaume, the French cyclist, and a person from the German embassy. Kim paused in the interview. "I didn't want to leave Rene, but they kept saying you must go and (Guillaume) he was in shock. He had no idea what was going on." A diversion was created with Guillaume and Kim arguing, and "in that fuss I escaped through the emergency staircase downstairs where they then blindfolded me and put me in a car. The driver took me to a safe house of the embassy. Nobody knew except the ambassador, the woman of the safehouse, and I was not allowed to tell anything to my friends and relatives at home."[9]

Kim stayed in the safehouse for two days and then flew home to Amsterdam in the early morning. During our interview, we talked about Jay and Lauren, and how things might have ended up differently. Kim had spoken with Lauren's parents soon after the attack. "They wanted to hear everything you know about their daughter in those last two weeks . . . was she happy. What was she like? I tried to tell them everything I could. I had nightmares every night for a while." Kim nodded slowly. "But the therapy did its job."[10]

Kim and Rene had started a book, and now she had the motivation to finish it. "When they wanted all the interviews I said fine. You mention my book and I will give you the interview," she said, smiling. We talked about the Mideast, and Kim said she could understand how the attack happened. "It was very much bad luck you know . . . wrong place wrong time, I don't feel angry, they were such losers. They attack and only kill four and let two get away." Kim shakes her head. "Losers."[11]

It is the end of our interview, and Kim is quiet. The years are there now. Events of six years before are beginning to fade again. "You know, one of the things I remember and many things I cannot remember, is the beers in my panniers exploded all over my clothes after I had been hit." Kim smiled mildly. "So, in the hospital until I changed my clothes I smelled like beer the whole time."

I asked her if she thought Jay and Lauren would have ended up together. Kim tilted her head and was quiet for a long moment. "Lauren was very open and wanted to meet people and curious about other people, she wanted to do the trip." Kim paused again. "Jay . . . he was a thinker you know, but they were in love, they were really in love as a couple." She nodded slowly: "Yes, they were happy with each other." [12]

Notes

1. Interview with Kim Postma by William Hazelgrove, April 29, 2024.
2. Santovasco Jea, Reflections on the Death of My Son.
3. Austin, Jay, The Scooter Diaries.
4. Interview with Kim Postma by William Hazelgrove, April 29, 2024.
5. Ibid.
6. Ibid.
7. Ibid.
8. Ibid.
9. Ibid.
10. Ibid.
11. Ibid.
12. Ibid.

PART IV
HOME

28
UNITED STATES
JULY 30, 2018

People found out in different ways. *The New York Times* ran a front-page article: "ISIS SAYS IT KILLED 4 CYCLISTS IN TAJIKISTAN."[1] I read the first few lines over breakfast, *"A car ran down a group of cyclists in the Central Asian state of Tajikistan over the weekend, killing four people from the United States, the Netherlands, and Switzerland."*[2] Soon every major newspaper carried the story of the two Americans murdered in Tajikistan. NPR released a feature on July 31, 2018, "DC Couple Killed in Tajikistan Attack Were Biking Around the World Together."[3] ABC News on July 31 led with "2 American Cyclists among 4 Dead in Tajikistan Attack Claimed by ISIS." The BBC story released on August 1 featured pictures of Jay and Lauren and the other bikers on the Pamir Highway under the headline "Tajikistan Attack: Four Cyclists Mown Down Are Identified." In the article Markus Hummel is quoted, as stating that biking the Silk Road was *"a dream come true."*[4] Kim Postma is listed as a survivor with an occupation listed as a fifty-eight-year-old hospital administrator. Jay's blog is quoted, *"Life is short and the world is big and we want to make the most of our youth and good health before they're gone."* Lauren's parents released a statement, *"Praising their daughters enthusiastic embrace of life's opportunities, her openness to new people and places, and her quest for a better understanding of the world."*

By August 15, the *Washington Post* was already speculating on the wisdom of cycling in Tajikistan. "Were the American Cyclists Killed in Tajikistan Naïve for Traveling There."[5] This will be echoed in the blogosphere for years to come. "Their deaths are senseless and tragic but could have been avoided if they had used more judgement in planning their travel itinerary," one commenter on the article wrote. This line of questioning would spiral into a juggernaut of taunting people who believed Jay and Lauren were entitled millennials who should have known better.

CBS This Morning featured pictures and quotes from Jay and Lauren and interviewed Molly Scalise. Molly found out about the attack after she received a Facebook call from Lauren's sister. "I didn't know what Jays status was and didn't know any details. So, I started calling all our friends and searching the internet to see what we could find out. I think it was the next day we found out Jay had been killed as well and that it was terrorists." [6]

Molly's house became the hub for friends to grieve and find out information. A follow-up story in the *New York Times* appeared on August 7, 2018: "A Dream Ended on a Mountain Road The Cyclists and the ISIS Militants," by Rukmini Callimachi, who eventually produced the video documentary *Collision*. This would be followed by more stories in NPR, *Outside Magazine*, CBS News, BBC, *Washington Post, People*, ABC, *Daily Mail UK*, *Global News*, and many others.

Lauren's childhood friend, Kendall, found out just before she was to move to Atlanta for a teaching position. "We had packed everything into POD containers and the only things we had left in our 650 square foot apartment was a futon and a suitcase." On July 30, 2018, Kendall left for an errand and returned to find her husband waiting for her. Her mother was calling, and she didn't want Kendall to be alone. Kendall wipes her eyes during our interview. "So, we just sat there and waited, and I thought something had happened to my father because he was in and out of hospitals with various conditions. My husband was white as a sheet and then my mother called."[7]

Kendall pauses, her eyes getting glassy, leaning close then back.

"My mother said Lauren Geoghegan is dead. Jay is dead too. They were hit by a car and we don't have any details. I think I reeled back and screamed '*no no no.*'" Kendall pauses, shuts her eyes. "For the next three days I stayed in bed in the empty apartment on the futon . . . only to rise and vomit and fall back in bed." Kendall is quiet for a moment. "Then I would get up and go to the computer and just kept hitting *refresh refresh refresh* to get any information. When I talked to Lauren's mother all she could say was . . . *my baby my baby my baby*."[8]

Kendall pauses, wipes her eyes again "I was in this other world and somehow three days later I got on a plane and moved to Atlanta into an empty townhome and started a new job. I felt like I was on drugs in this detached state."[9] Kendall's first email to her new boss was asking to go home for a funeral; she wrote a eulogy on the plane.

Kristen Robinson, Lauren's friend and coworker at Georgetown, found out when Molly called her. "There were no details at first just that she died. I was eight and a half months pregnant and trying to keep my blood pressure low. Molly asked if I would pass the news along and after a few days we convened to put together some pictures her mother asked for." Kristen paused. "After a while I couldn't read about the incident itself . . . it was too much."

Tifffany Del Rio found out about the attack in Georgetown. "Molly called me and said Jay and Lauren had been killed in Tajikistan. I was at home and pregnant. My husband thought we had lost the baby, because he comes home and his wife is crying in the doorway." She pauses during our interview. "I didn't want to go to work and have people coming to my desk while I'm crying." Tiffany wipes her eyes. "I think if that had not happened, Lauren would have had a family. That's what I think about. When I get off this computer with you, I'll go pick up Cheerios and she will never be able to do that." Tiffany shakes her head. "I envisioned Lauren getting old and having kids. Jay . . . I envisioned in some foreign country getting hit by a truck at fifty."[10]

Jenn Cribbs, Jay's colleague at HUD, found out when Abby Miller called her. "I saw Jay getting hurt or in an accident . . . or something like that, but not terrorists. I mean they really killed the wrong Americans. Jay and Lauren had walked away from the system and were questioning the values of bourgeois life. They were the last people who should be seen as representative of American life . . . and then." She paused again. "And then you are left what does it all mean . . . how capricious the whole thing is."[11]

Jay's mother, Jea Santovasco was on her back porch when she heard the phone ringing in her New Jersey home. The answering machine picked up as Jea listened to a foreign voice. The woman spoke for several minutes before Jea picked up the phone in her office. The room had been Jay's bedroom and his brothers before their mother converted the room into an office for her appraisal business. The woman calling was Beth Androv from the US Embassy in Dushanbe Tajikistan. The woman asked Jea to identify herself and then Jea knew immediately the call was about Jay. "I can't say for sure whether I knew Jay was dead at that very moment," she wrote later. "I really don't think so, but rather that he was hurt. I thought for sure she would say that he had an accident, fell off his bike, that he was hospitalized, but would be okay." The woman asked Jea to identify herself and then she told Jea her son was in an accident; then she said, "Jay was dead . . . he was hit while cycling by a hit and run driver." She said it just like that. My thought was this cant' be hit and run . . . it has to be a terrorist attack." When Jea asked about Lauren, she told Jay's mother that Lauren had died too. At some point, Jea hung up and stood silent in her dead son's bedroom. She didn't move and slowly turned around. Then she screamed.

Jay's mother, after receiving the news her son had died in Tajikistan, called her daughter. She suggested she email Jay or call him. There might be a mistake, and the information might be wrong. His mother learned President Trump was supposed to call to offer condolences. He never did. She fielded inquiries from CNN, ABC, CBS, *The New York Times*, and MSNBC. But for now, there was still hope. Jay's sister pointed out there were multiple cyclists, and the rescuers didn't speak English. Jay might not have been one of the victims. The denial of the disaster was strong early on, so they waited for a response from Jay's cell phone. It never came.

Lauren's parents received the call from the Charge De Affairs in the afternoon of July 29, 2018. They did not say Lauren had died and they didn't say it was a terrorist attack. Hours later, on Sunday afternoon, another call came from the head of the embassy that it had been a terrorist attack and Lauren was dead. Lauren's mother said she wanted to go to Tajikistan and get Lauren, but the FBI told her not to come. A week later, on Saturday, a 757 Turkish airliner pulled up into the Tarmac at East LA airport. The hand of a powerful senator might have gotten Lauren back in record time. Senator Adam Schiff, whom Lauren had worked for and who would read her eulogy, could have made sure the wheels of government for once worked efficiently.

A coffin was unloaded and taken to a local funeral home in Glendale. Lauren Geoghegan had gone off a year before a bright young woman on a trip to bike around the world and came back in a coffin unloaded on a drizzly morning. It was staggering to think this light of the world was no longer there. Her childhood friend, Kendall, said Lauren's mother went and looked at the body closely in the funeral home. When Kendall asked how she could do that, Lauren's mother replied she wanted to spend as much time with her as possible and look at every inch of her and experience what she felt and feel what she felt.

On the day Jays mother found out, she stared out her back door; it was a sunny, placid day. The normalcy of the day seemed absurd to her now. Two friends slept over, and then her daughter arrived, and then her son. His mother spent a lot of time in the bathroom, physically ill. That night, she fell asleep on the futon on the back porch. The darkness of her backyard was deep. She was facing a door out to her back deck when a vision began to materialize in the air. The image was several feet tall and a foot wide and shimmered in the darkness. Jea would later write, "There were specks of stars in the black sky at the very top and the center of the image had a cast of blue over it. I thought how odd that the countless number of stars gathered only in this one spot in the sky." A road appeared without streetlights with land spreading out on both sides." From the left side of the road, from out of the complete darkness, Jay walked onto the road. He walked toward me, very gingerly as he normally would and I could so perfectly see him in his entirety, from his head to his feet. He was wearing dungarees and the sneakers that he does and his shirt was mostly white with a faint plaid with thin stripes of red . . . he got right up to me and crossed his legs at his ankles like he would and cocked his head . . . smiled that half devilish smile. .and just said, "Hey" like he would . . . and then he was gone. It was all gone."

His mother could still see the oblong shape of the road and the open country under a pale moon. She would later interpret the vision to mean Jay had wanted to let her know he was alright.

Jay's body had been taken to a funeral home in Queens after flying into JFK. His will had specified he be cremated at the place of his death, but Tajikistan didn't allow for cremation. His mother arranged to see Jay's body at the funeral home but was told he was in a funeral home in Manhattan. She was then directed to Greenwood Cemetery, where she was to return the next morning to get Jay's ashes. She was told that the body was in a decomposing state, and she couldn't view her son. She settled for viewing a small tattoo on his arm of the Little Prince.

She would later receive a form letter from the White House when she asked about getting the autopsy report released for Jay and Lauren. When the autopsy arrived, she was in shock at the amount of times and places her son was stabbed. She later took the report to a doctor who estimated that Jay bled out slowly and that it could have taken possibly twenty to thirty minutes for Jay's heart to stop beating. The police report from Tajikistan has never been released, and it was only through the *New York Times* documentary *Collision* the photo of Jay Austin on the side of the road is visible. It is a very hard photo to look at and confirms what the autopsy describes.

Legacy site was created for Lauren and a scholarship was set up in her name. The video montage of Lauren is beautiful and celebrates her life. During the funeral held at her high school, Immaculate Heart, Congressman Adam Shiff gave the eulogy. It is surprising. Here was a politician who gives speeches for a living, yet when he spoke of Lauren Geoghegan, he had to stop multiple times.

> The journey Lauren took is not for the faint of heart or the fearless . . . but for the one who can overcome their fear for whom there is something worth knowing despite the risk. Lauren wanted to experience the world and its people, and this was more powerful than fear. More valuable than money, more immediate and essential than the allure of a predictable day or job . . . it is how Lauren and Jay lived that moves us. How their example jars us and how the lethargy and complacency forces us to see the beauty around us . . . question what is really important. . . . Laurens life forces up to open our eyes and see the magnificent all around us . . . they chose not to live their lives that way . . . they chose to believe in the goodness of others . . . we cannot determine what we will come across in life . . . we live with the expectation of good. That is how Lauren lived and that is how she expected us to live. . . . They chose . . . to approach life as good as courageous people do. We can decide to live with the expectation of good. Life is short. Her life was tragically short . . . her example impels us to step out of our routine and to see the beauty around us and in others . . . to live lives of constant amazement.[12]

Jay's Memorial was on Saturday, August 11, 2018, at Crispus Attucks Park on U Street Northwest in Washington, DC. It was a hot day, and people stood in a circle and spoke about Jay with the cicadas whining in the background. Jay's friend Ryan Koronowski found out about the attack through the news and experienced utter shock and disbelief. "We went to Molly's house to talk about them. The same place Lauren had lived. I shared some passages of The Scooter Diaries that I ended up reading later at the memorial service in Crispus Atticus Park. People just sharing memories."[13]

Jay's sister Jude also read a section from Jay's Scooter Diaries:

Many people I am told, lead perfectly happy lives free from nagging questions of what it all means and how to escape the trivial meaninglessness of an existence that will end and how to come to terms with the inevitable heat death of the universe. I am unfortunately not one of those people. No, though I am grateful to live a life colored by a particularly positive disposition, I have been haunted from a young age by existential questions and philosophical questions which I have no answer. As an intuitive, feeling, judging, introvert. . . . I am perpetually in search of an answer, a coherent truth that will piece everything together, that will connect the entire universe and all its mysteries, despite the logical rational realization that such a thing cannot possible exist.[14]

On May 31, 2019, the town of Manalapan planted a Quaking Aspen in honor of Jay on what would have been his thirtieth birthday. His mother had chosen the Quaking Aspen because it "symbolized fearlessness, having the confidence and competence to allow us to live beyond physical pain, suffering and worry but rather to focus on the joys in life, the importance of focusing on one's goals and aspirations in life."[15]

On November 12, 2022, a bench was dedicated to Lauren's memory at Georgetown University. The bench is brown wood with a gold plaque that reads:

Lauren Anne Munoz Geoghegan C"10
WHEN SOMEONE ASKED ME WHAT THE GREATEST THING I HAD CONTRIBUTED TO THE WORLD WAS, I SAID MY LOVE
TIMSHEL

Notes

1 *New York Times*, Rukmini, Callimachi, ISIS Says It Killed 4 Cyclists in Tajikistan, July 30, 2018.

2 Ibid.

3 NPR, DC Couple Killed in Tajikistan Attack Were Biking Around The World Together, July 31, 2018, https://www.npr.org.

4. BBC Tajikistan Attack: Four Cyclists Mown Down Are Identified, August 1, 2018.
5. *Washington Post*, Chang, Elizabeth, Were the American Cyclists killed in Tajikistan naïve for traveling there? August 15, 2018.
6. Interview with Molly Scalise by William Hazelgrove, March 12, 2024.
7. Interview with Kendall O'Connor by William Hazelgrove, March 6, 2024.
8. Ibid.
9. Ibid.
10. Ibid.
11. Ibid.
12. Legacy site for Lauren Geoghegan, Congressman Adam Schiff eulogy.
13. Interview with Ryan Koronowski by William Hazelgrove, May 6, 2017.
14. Austin, Jay Scooter Diaries.
15. Santovasco Jea, Reflections on the Death of My Son.

29
EVIL ON THE ROOF OF THE WORLD

On March 7, 2024, four men in fatigues with AK-47s entered the Crocus City Hall in Moscow. The band *Picnic* was to play to a sold-out show. The four men opened fire and then set the concert hall on fire. One hundred and forty-five people were killed and 551 wounded. The four men were found to be Russian migrant workers from Tajikistan who had been radicalized by ISIS K. The state department warnings that Lauren and Jay read didn't consider the cauldron of terrorists incubating in the decimated country that is Tajikistan.

According to the UN, more than 80 percent of Tajikistanis live below the poverty line. Many Tajikistanis skip meals so their children can eat. Unemployment is rampant and two million men a year seek employment outside the country, mostly in Russia. "The new Tajik generation has lost all belief in the future," said Muhyiddin Kabiri, leader of the Islamic Renaissance Party. The thirty-year iron-fisted rule of Tajikistan's President Emomali Rahmon gives Tajikistanis a clear choice: a secular dictatorship or the Islamic State. The mothers of three of the suspects of the massacre said that salaries are too low to pay rent or to afford permits to work. "Let them answer who bought the weapons, who gave them their equipment. My son didn't have money for a gun."[1]

Into this extreme poverty came two cyclists from the United States, who spent more on their bikes and equipment than the average Tajikistan would see in a year, where the income is estimated by the World Food Program as less than $1.33 a day, and an estimated 30 percent of the population is malnourished. At the time of his death, I was told Jay Austin had close to a half million dollars in his bank account. Jay had essentially retired from American life and had worked at HUD to build his escape vehicle. His Tiny House shows a man with a singular vision, which was to leave American life and live life on a simple scale. The man who traded bitcoin and crypto on his way across Europe is different from Chris McCandless burning his money on his way to living off the grid. Jay refused to pay the student loans he had taken. He was accused of not paying his rent for six months on his Tiny House. He could have done both or stayed at HUD and had the loans forgiven, but in his mind, he was leaving, and there was not a moment to lose.

On their journey around the world, Jay was so fixated on their expenses that they fought over extra drinks and *Gummy Bears*, and Lauren hid a scarf she had bought. But in Jay's mind, the nugget of gold he carried with him was their freedom. Jay had planned his life as a boy and then planned his escape from that life as an adult. The zealot is not perfect. William Faulkner once said, "Writers have walked over the back of a lot of old ladies to get where they want." This might be said of Jay Austin. He was determined, calculating, smart, and he had plotted his escape from American middle-class life. The four years he planned to travel around the world was just the beginning. It was clear he was never going back to work, and what's more, he didn't have to.

The people with whom Jay and Lauren shared tea and food in Africa, Europe, and Central Asia seemed quaint with their perfect Old World minimalist lifestyle. The truth was the Tajikistanis and others were barely hanging on. "I cook once a day in the evening. We eat half of it for dinner and leave the rest for the children's lunch the following day," Maryam, a school janitor, said. "I make hot tea and put lots of sugar in it. It helps too. If I ate lunch, we wouldn't have enough food for the kids."[2] To Jay and Lauren, the nineteenth-century lifestyle of the country people harkened back to a simpler way of living. What comes to mind is E. M. Forester's quote in his novel, *Howards End*: "literature is for a man with a full belly." The Tajikistanis didn't have full bellies, and they must have stared at Lauren and Jay with fascination and envy. Here were the rich Americans they had heard about all their life. And in fact, in comparison, Lauren and Jay were rich.

Like Barbara and Larry Savage, who biked around the world in the 1970s, or Cheryl Stray, who hiked the Pacific Northwest Trail in the 1990s, or Chris McCandless, who plunged into the Alaskan wilds, or Thomas Stevens, who took a big wheeler bike around the world in 1887, Jay and Lauren belong to that group of people who leave their former lives behind to crash into the unknown. It is a very American ideal to become someone else by transforming yourself through experience. If America gives anything to people, it is their choice to become whoever they want.

Jay and Lauren's decision to quit their well-paying jobs in Georgetown and go around the world on bikes belongs to the group of people who dare to pit themselves against the elements, if not the world. Jay upped the stakes by declaring he would prove through his sojourn that people were good and evil did not really exist. The fact that Chris McCandless and Jay Austin both changed their names is something for psychologists to consider. The online rancor that greeted the death of Lauren and Jay was predictable. "Evil is a social construct, huh?" wrote one commenter on Jay's blog, "then I guess these two morons died in a construction accident." "Thanks for exiting this world and not reproducing your stupid fucking idiocy," wrote another.

Many people blamed Jay and Lauren for their own deaths. They were pilloried for being too trusting, too naïve. "Be assured," Christian evangelist Franklin wrote in a Facebook post about the murders, "evil does exist in this world."[3]

In the year 2025, most people lead risk-averse lives. Lauren and Jay did a very public thing. They quit their jobs in Washington DC and went on a biking trip around the world with no return date. It is unthinkable to most people that two highly educated young professionals would pursue a journey through parts of the world most people would only dare from the balcony of a cruise ship. In the final scene of *Amadeus*, the life of Wolfgang Amadeus Mozart, his protégé and executioner, Salieri announces in the insane asylum: "I speak for all mediocrity."[4]

Jay and Lauren were anything but mediocre and proved it by daring to live authentically. And if you peel away the rancor that came trickling in over the internet, it is mediocrity outraged. How dare these people attempt to go around the world after throwing away their jobs and savings and professional futures. And Jay threw gasoline on the fire by declaring he didn't believe in evil. The commenters are smug in their assertion that the risk of going to a third-world country like Tajikistan was stupidity personified. But Jay and Lauren knew exactly what they were doing and found something in each other that was greater than the parts.

A flame of adventure lit up both their collective dreams. The tragic outcome only throws into relief what an incredible and brave undertaking their journey was. Jay was a zealot. There is no doubt. He was an idealist. He was an off-the-grid kind of guy who believed absolutely in minimalism and vegetarianism, and questioned the American way of life of working and retiring after thirty years. He was forever trying to do the moral or right thing to a fault. As his friend Abby said, "he could be the most obnoxious white man on the planet." He was bright. He was progressive. And he was going to take his beliefs to their logical conclusion. He just happened to find the love of his life along the way.

Lauren Geoghegan wasn't looking for answers. She did not have $500,000 in the bank. In fact, she was dependent on Jay in the latter part of their trip. His approach to their spending can seem shallow with the money he had in the bank. But Jay was used to a tightly contained world, and if the trip did anything, it changed him. Lauren found her answers early on. Love. That was what she exported. She was just that person. And she loved the man who had come to Washington and changed his name and worked for HUD and lived in a tiny house and taught her to cycle and then said with a flick of the wrist: let's go bike around the world. Bold and daring, even romantic. And so, they did. They began a trip that 99 percent of the population would never even think about doing.

And there were problems all along the way. Lauren and Jay were both strong opinionated people. They both had the habit of not backing down from a fight. They had been dating on and off for the last five years, and some doubted they would end up together. But sparks in a storm coalesce, and they lit each other up with an intangible energy; so they took off.

Jay was changed by Lauren. He did see two was better than one by the end. It was during their journey of meeting amazing people and enduring hardships and danger they became married. Marriage is not a document. It's not even living together. It is something that happens to two people when their souls become fused. Their wedding was their trip, their reception, and their honeymoon. They were together 24/7 and that will make or break any couple. Somewhere, their collective destinies became intertwined forever.

And when they entered that highway the last time on July 29, 2018, they were one. When the terrorists came for them, their collective destiny was set. Jay's mother said a medium told her their souls rose up together over their bodies. Lauren was religious. She did believe in God. Jay was spiritual. I think he saw God all around him. But when the tragedy occurred, they were together. Why these two cultures should crash together on a mountain road on July 29, 2018, is left to the ages. Politics. Culture. A privileged pair of bikers from Washington DC crashing into the orbit of young men with nothing to lose. Fodder for radicals who can scoop them up and direct them. The perfect foot soldiers for a movement. And so, the great catastrophe happens. Two extremely talented people were wiped out by people with nothing to lose. And the trolls move in and say they got what they deserved, but millions know their story, while the cynics sit in their collective darkness, the darkness of mediocrity.

Seventy years ago, Jay and Lauren might have headed out onto the road and crossed America in a car the way Jack Kerouac and Neal Cassidy did in the 1940s and produced the novel *On the Road*. A hundred and fifty years ago, they might have headed west in a covered wagon and looked for their destiny with the risks that came with settling the frontier. But in the year 2017, the world was different; the last frontier was the world, and so Jay and Lauren wanted to circle the earth on bicycles and leave behind their testament of adventure. We are fascinated by people who throw life aside to embrace adventure, and at the same time, when disaster occurs, we shake our heads and question if they were foolish. But when we learn about these people, their stories, their wants, their needs, their humanity, their story, it enriches us.

In one of Jay's final posts in the Scooter Diaries, he wrote:

> We all get but one life to live, one blank canvas on which to paint our masterpiece. Perhaps some can live with subtle texture, a simple pattern, the routine and repeated shapes of a routine and repeated life, and if that

wallpaper may satisfy its creator, let it be so without the slightest hint of judgment or scorn from myself or any other. But for me, nothing but the brightest canvas will do, a screaming mess of passion and paint splatter, vivacious variety, every last inch of my narrow dimensions covered with the dirt and grime and blood and tears of well-worn life. And if, after it all, my piece comes to nothing more than a sopping, dripping, sorry excuse for a coherent, proper, ordered existence, so be it—for at least I picked up the brush and tried my hand at it at all.

In one of their Instagram pictures, Jay and Lauren had just reached the Indian Ocean. They are sitting on the beach side by side. They are looking into the wide blue expanse. Lauren's curly brown hair is flowing back, and Jay has a baseball cap on and sand on his back. They sit by the ocean and take a deserved break from biking. It is a moment in time. Their arms are back, and they are together the way any two lovers are. They are on the adventure of their lives. So, they stare into the ocean, together, into their collective vision of eternity.

Notes

1 Radio Free Europe, Tajik Cyclists Attacker Was Influenced By Others, https://www.youtube.com/watch?v=yC8e8b5XXIM&t=43s.
2 Ibid.
3 Simplycycling.org.
4 Movie, *Amadeus*, Milos Forman, Director, 1984.

30
ENDINGS

On March 16, 2020, The 219th Legislature of the State of New Jersey passed Concurrent Resolution No. 161 condemng the terrorist attack on Lauren and Jay, "which constitutes an affront to American values of tolerance and freedom, values embodied, and expressed so eloquently by Mr. Austin and Ms. Geoghegan."

The four Tajikistanis recruited by Hussein who attacked Jay, Lauren, Rene Wokke, Markus Hummel, Marie Clarie, and Kim Postma were killed by Tajikistan police. They attempted to escape into Afghanistan but were followed by villagers with sticks and clubs who saw the shattered windshield with speckled blood. "The windshield was dented in but not shattered,"[1] one of the villagers recalled. The police believe they were headed for the Afghanistan border when they confronted them on a hillside. The police fired a warning shot. The four men turned and attacked with the meat cleavers and knives. All four men were eventually shot dead, and Hussein was captured and sentenced to life in prison. A photo soon after his capture shows a man brutally beaten by the police.

After he was sentenced, the *New York Times* video magazine, the *Weekly*, interviewed Hussein in 2022. Hussein's movements in late July of 2018 are shadowy. His cellphone gave investigators clues to his coordinating with his ISIS contacts. In the *New York Times Weekly* interview in prison, he confirms he is part of the external wing of ISIS. ISIS worldview is a supremist one. It dehumanizes anyone who does not adhere to their narrow interpretation of Islam. When the interviewer Rukmini shows Hussein a picture of Lauren and Jay on her cellphone, Hussein doesn't react.

"Can you explain to me why you killed them?"[2]

Hussein pauses in his blue jumpsuit and blue cap with the four-armed men with facemasks behind him. He is handcuffed and considered extremely dangerous even though he is serving a life term. "We had pledged to commit Jihad," he says looking down. Jihad is defined simply as "a struggle to fight against the enemies of Islam."[3] Hussein explains that when he was in Syria and Iraq, he received orders to commit a terrorist attack in Belgium. They were supposed to attack the

European Parliament, but his documents to enter the country did not arrive in time and he was ordered to commit a terrorist act in Tajikistan. He recruited four other young men to carry out the attack, but he needed a target.

"When Muslims are being killed everywhere we must try to kill non-believers wherever we find them. When they stop killing Muslims, we will stop too."[4]

Rukmini points out that Jay and Lauren had not killed anyone and believed people were inherently good. Hussein shrugs, "We received an order and followed it . . . we had no plans to talk to them." Rukmini then asks how he chose his victims. "We saw them in the territory of Danghara and attacked them." Rukmini asks about seeing the cyclists at a gas station the day of the attack. "Yes, I talked to them. I asked them where they were from. I asked them what nationalities they were, and they told me they were Americans." Rukmini confirmed these were the people he was talking about on her phone. "They said they were Americans and laughed. Americans had to be killed."[5]

Rukmini then asked Hussein if he felt any regret. "When Americans kill Muslims, they don't regret it. We're the same way. We will continue." Rukmini asks what he sees when he looks at her. "I see a Christian person. A person who isn't a Muslim." Rukmini persists and asks if he has anything in common with the people he killed. "No there was nothing in common. They are humans and so are we. We didn't have anything else in common."[6]

Hussein died in prison a year later. Prison authorities said he was trying to radicalize other prisoners to Islam. Qori Nosir, who masterminded the plot, was sentenced in Russia to life in prison for committing terrorist acts. The State Department risk assessment for Tajikistan remains elevated, but each year thousands of people bike the Pamir Mountains on the highway known as the Roof of the World. Some of them, undoubtedly, are couples who quit their jobs to bike around the world.

Notes

1 *The Weekly*, *Collision*, Callimachi, Rukmini, *New York Times*, Documentary 2019.
2 Ibid.
3 Ibid.
4 Ibid.
5 Ibid.
6 Ibid.

31
THE WALDEN PONDO COFFEE HOUSE

The leaves of Georgetown have now all turned. It is fall, and the students have returned once again to Georgetown University. They stream past the woman eating her lunch quietly on the wooden bench with the gold plaque. The air has that snap with the promise of a winter to come. Kristen Robinson sits on the bench and looks out. She has children now. A daughter and a son. Her daughter's middle name is Lauren. "I sit on the bench quite often,"[1] she told me in her interview. "I feel her presence often and feel closest to her when I am out in nature." She pauses. "Sometimes I'll be eating a chocolate chip cookie and picking out all the chips and I'll tell my daughter, Lauren did this and try and keep the memory alive for my kids. . . . I told my kids in age-appropriate ways she had passed. I mourn every day that the world lost one of its brightest lights."[2]

Kristen, Kendall, Molly, Tiffany, and Ryan have moved on with families and children. Now in their mid-thirties, they are in the thick of family life. Kendall with her kids in the other room shakes her head.

> I think of all the boring things Lauren won't get to do. It didn't take a lot to make Lauren happy. Whenever I think I'm not a great mother or not making enough money, I think I get to be here and she doesn't. It makes no sense. I mean the whole moral arc of the world where good prevails and they would have married and had that coffee house on near the Pacific.

She grows quiet. "Whenever I have a question, I close my eyes and think what Lauren would say. She loved sunflowers and I got my son Dillon a sunflower tattoo in honor of Lauren. It makes no sense . . . good will prevail." She pauses. "Maybe they would have gotten this coffee house in the pacific northwest . . . assuming everything worked out."

Molly Scalise now has children and still lives in Georgetown and balances a full-time job with raising a son. "I think about Lauren all the time and recently started taking drum lessons. For me it is scary, but I thought if Lauren had the courage to go around the world, I could at least take drum lessons in their honor." Molly pauses. "I don't know if they would have gotten married, there was talk about leaving the East coast and going out West, maybe having kids. Lauren wanted to have a family." Molly nods slowly. "I can say this, they had a love for being in the world and a love for each other."

Jay's Georgetown friend Ryan has a son who is five years old and born one year after Jay and Lauren died. His middle name is Austin. Ryan told me, "You know initially I don't think Jay wanted to have a family, but I think with Lauren that changed. He loved playing with our daughter Jocelyn."[3] Jay and Ryan's nights out to *the Saloon* or having Ethiopian food are over. The watering holes are filled with undergraduates, and Lauren and Jay's generation has moved on to children, homes, and apartments in Georgetown or the suburbs. When I ask Ryan about the effect of Jay and Lauren's death, he pauses. "It has made us more cautious. . . . I mean we have kids now. It changes you."[4]

Jay's close friend who he met in graduate school, Tiffany, smiles. "I think I will always remember Jay barefoot and wanting to run across the Brooklyn bridge." She has children now, and I can hear them in the next room. "I take my son rock climbing in honor of Jay because he used to do that at HUD where he would go over his break to a rock-climbing gym." She pauses:

I always worried about Jay on these trips and then this happened. The strange thing is that if Jay were here, he would wonder what happened to his killers. He would want to know what shaped them, these young men without opportunities. I don't know if Jay believed in marriage, but maybe he and Lauren would have married. I would have loved for them to come back to Georgetown.

Tiffany pauses: "Jay was like a brother to me, we were close, but I felt like he was always looking for something."[5]

In an interview with Abby, his friend from his days at HUD, she said when she got the call from a friend, she just knew it in her bones. Jay was dead. "Fucking Jay. Now you are just dead." She paused. "The memorial was surreal for Jay in Crispus Atticus Park in Georgetown. Everyone was standing in a circle. A lot of people from the government. Lauren's mother. She was the only member of Lauren's family who came. Jay's mom and his siblings. People saying things." Abby trails off, shakes her head. "Jay was living fully every day, that was his goal, even if that happened to be his last day. I don't think he was ever going to be doing one thing very long. He was not going to do what most people in the US do." Abby nodded slowly. "The way Jay lived was so in your face . . . you either loved him or hated him."[6]

Lee Para, his Tiny House partner, was more philosophical:

> He died at the top of the mountain. He lived his life the way he wanted to. I think Lauren would have returned home after Tajikistan and then gone back for the last leg of the trip in South America. Jay said that after Africa he might have stopped if it hadn't been for Lauren being there. She got them invited into a lot of places he could not have done alone.

Lee paused in her home in Mexico and nods slowly: "I think he lived with magic, and he didn't want that magic to disappear."[7]

It is hard to know what would have happened upon Jay and Lauren's return had they lived. A clue though is found in a blog post at the end of Jay's Scooter Diaries.

> And this brings me to one final adventure . . . the birth of a café. Though the last thing this city, my city, any city needs is another place selling coffee, what my surroundings severely lack . . . is a gathering place, one with seats and open doors, a place for community and conversation and yes hot beverages for garnish. I do not wish to be a business owner . . . for profit money, expansion . . . and so Walden Pondo for what else would it be called? Will be a nonprofit donation-based establishment serving simple teas and simple foods, serving the community, an aspirational model of fair, responsible, ethical development, More to come, all of it, always, more to come.

So, there was a method to Jay's madness. The coffee house. After the great around the world adventure, they would land in California and open *The Walden Pondo Coffee House*, where organic brews would be served up and people could come and converse in an open, friendly European-style café. Lauren or Jay would man the espresso machine between taking orders and preparing food and eventually someone would ask about their trip around the world, and they would explain what an amazing journey they had years ago. But now they had settled and were starting a family, but who knows maybe one day they might travel again and cycle the world, or at least part of it. But this of course, is a dream.

And now, Kristen Robinson has finished her lunch and left. The bench at Georgetown University is empty. Leaves fall. Snow will descend. Time passes. The thought associated with the memorial bench is someone in the future will see Lauren's name and the quote and will wonder who she was and what type of life she lived.

In the spring, after the snow melt, they might Google Lauren's name and find out about Jay and Lauren's story and their amazing trip. They may read the articles, their Simply Cycling blog, the Instagram posts that compose their living legacy. They may even read this book. And they might, in the end, be inspired by two people who saw no obstacles in life, but only possibilities.

Notes

1 Interview with Kristen Robinson by William Hazelgrove, April 12, 2024.
2 Ibid.
3 Interview with Ryan Koronowski by William Hazelgrove, May 6, 2017.
4 Ibid.
5 Interview with Tiffany Del Rio by William Hazelgrove, March 16, 2024.
6 Interview with Abby Miller by William Hazelgrove, April 30, 2024.
7 Interview with Lee Para by William Hazelgrove, March 26, 2024.

ACKNOWLEDGMENTS

This book could not have been written without the willingness of friends and family of Jay Austin and Lauren Geoghegan to be interviewed by an author who they did not know but with a desire to tell the story of two remarkable people. So, I thank Bob and Elvira Geoghegan for allowing me to ask questions about their daughter, Lauren Geoghegan, and Jea Santovasco for allowing me to ask questions about her son, Jay Austin and the use of her informative book, *My Stories Since the Death of My Son Jay Austin: An American Murdered by Terrorists While Cycling the Globe*. To the friends and colleagues of Jay and Lauren: Molly Scalise, Tiffany Del Rio, Kendall McCarthy, Ryan Koronowski, Abilene Miller, Kristen Robinson, Jude, Lee Para, and Jenn Cribbs, I thank you for giving me insight into Jay and Lauren. To Kim Postma, I am in great debt for returning to the scene of the attack as I probed the one survivor who could talk about it. More information about Jay and Lauren's amazing journey can be found at simplycycling.org

APPENDIX

Jay's Reading List

Travel

On the Road, Jack Kerouac

Zen and the Art of Motorcycle Maintenance: An Inquiry Into Values, Robert Pirsig

Blue Highways: A Journey Into America, William Least Heat Moon

Wanderlust: A History of Walking, Rebecca Solnit

Into the Wild, Jon Krakauer

The Wild Trees, Richard Preston

Fear and Loathing in Las Vegas: A Savage Journey to the Heart of the American Dream, Hunter Thompson

Philosophy and Such

Small Is Beautiful: Economics As If People Mattered, E. F. Schumacher

Thus Spake Zarathustra, Friedrich Nietzsche

The Happiness of Pursuit: What Neuroscience Can Teach Us About the Good Life, Shimon Edelman

The Man Who Quit Money, Mark Sundeen

In Search of Time: The History, Physics, and Philosophy of Time, Dan Falk

The Singing Neanderthals: The Origins of Music, Language, Mind, and Body, Steven Mithen

APPENDIX

Novels, Letters, and Poetry

The Rebel: An Essay on Man in Revolt, Albert Camus

The Plague, Albert Camus

The First Man, Albert Camus

The Stranger, Albert Camus

A Happy Death, Albert Camus

Democracy in America, Alexis de Tocqueville

East of Eden, John Steinbeck

The Grapes of Wrath, John Steinbeck

The Death of Ivan Ilyich, Lev Tolstoy

Don Quixote, Miguel de Cervantes

Ulysses, James Joyce

The Fifty Greatest Love Letters of All Time, David Lowenherz

Love and Other Difficulties, Rainer Maria Rilke

Poetry of the Taliban, Columbia University Press

Le Petit Prince, Antoine de Saint-Exupéry

Countries Jay and Lauren Cycled Through

South Africa
Namibia
Botswana
Zimbabwe
Malawi
Mozambique
Tanzania
Egypt
Morocco
Spain
France
Italy
Austria

Romania
Greece
Turkey
Kazakhstan
Serbia
Kosovo
Montenegro
Albania
Macedonia
Bulgaria
Istanbul
Tajikistan

BIBLIOGRAPHY

Interviews

Molly Scalise
Bob and Elvira Geoghegan
Jea Santovasco
Tiffany Del Rio
Kendall McCarthy
Ryan Koronowski
Abby Miller
Kim Postma
Jude Delatela
Kristen Robinson
Lee Para
Jenn Cribbs

Books

Fawcett, Percy, *Exploration Fawcett*, New York, Henry Abrams, 2010.
Fiennes, Ranulph, *Lawrence of Arabia*, New York, Pegasus Books, 2024.
Fitzgerald, F. Scott, *The Great Gatsby*, New York, Simon and Schuster, 1925.
Grann, David, *The Lost City of Z*, New York, Knopf, 2010.
Kerouac, Jack, *On the Road*, New York, Penguin, 1955.
Kinzler, Stephan, *All the Shah's Men*, Nashville, TN, Turner Publishing Company, 2003.
Krakauer, Jon, *Into the Wild*, New York, Anchor Books, 1997.
London, Jack, *White Fang*, New York, The Macmillan Company, 1906.
Santovasco, Jea, *My Stories Since the Death of My Son Jay Austin*, Independently Published, 2023.
Stevens, Thomas, *Around the World on a Bicycle*, Boston, Macha Press, 2016.
Strayed, Cheryl, *Wild*, New York, Atlantic Books, 2014.
Thoreau, David, *Walden*, New York, Thomas Crowell and Company, 1910.
Twain, Mark, *Huckleberry Finn*, New York, Readers Library Classic, 1885.
Vacher, Marguerite, *Nuns Without Cloister*, New York. University Press, 2010, 345.

Publications

Outside Magazine.
New York Times, Isis Says It Killed 4 Cyclists in Tajikistan, July 30, 2018.
Washington Post, Chang, Elizabeth, Were the American Cyclists Killed in Tajikstand Naïve for Traveling There? August 15, 2018.
Bikepacking.com, When Paths Cross, A Tribute to Jay and Lauren, Beroit, Nathan, Boyle, Sophie, August 18, 2020.
Washington Post, Jay Austin, Leading the way Toward Government Innovation, April 21, 2015.
Reason, Krainin, Todd, Washingtons Beautiful, Illegal Tiny Houses, December 2014.
New York Times, MacFarquhar, Neil, an ISIS Terror Group Draws Half Its Recruits from Tiny Tajikistan, April 18, 2024.
Daily Mail, Moore, Hannah, American Couple Killed in a Terror Attack in Tajikistan, August 2018.

Blogs, Media Websites, and Social Media

Tajik News Service.
US Department of State.(.gov), https://travel.state.gov>traveladvisories>traveladvisories
Simplycycling Blog.
Jay Austin Various Blogs.
Scooter Diaries.
Lauren Geoghegan Instagram.
Jay Austin Instagram.
Movie, *Amadeus*, Milos Forman Director, 1984.
NPR, DC Couple Killed in Tajikistan Attack Were Biking Around The World Together, https://www.npr.org July 31, 2018.
BBC Tajikistan Attack: Four Cyclists Mown Down are Identified, August 1, 2018.
Secura Online Article Cycling in South Africa, www.secura.co.za>5 Best Safety Tips for Cycling in South Africa.
Reason Magazine Jay Austin Killed in Tajikistan Tiny House Innovator.
Koronowski, Ryan, Two Bikers Killed by ISIS Militants A World Away, Were My Friends, WBUR, August 2018.
Legacy Site for Lauren Geoghegan Congressman Adam Schiff Eulogy.
Radio Free Europe Tajik Cyclists Attackers Was Influenced By Others, https://www.youtube.com/watch?v=yC8e8b5XXlM&t=43s
Asia Plus, Gaisina, Liliya, All About life of Jay Austin who was Killed by Terrorists in Danghara, July 31, 2019.
BBC NYC Bike Path Killer Sayfullo Saipov Convicted of Murder, https://www.bbc.com/news/world-us-canada-64421338
Eurasianet, Tajikistan: Ringleader of ISIS Inspired Killings of Cyclists Dies in Prison, https://eurasianet.org/tajikistan-ringleader-of-isis-inspired-killings-of-cyclists-dies-in-prison
Youtube Tajik Cyclists Attacker was Influenced by Others, https://www.youtube.com/watch?v=yC8e8b5XXlM&t=43s

BIBLIOGRAPHY

Independent, Callimachi, Rukmini, How A Couples Dream Trip Ended in Tragedy at the Hands of ISIS, August 17, 2018, https://www.independent.co.uk/news/long_reads/isis-terror-attack-cyclists-tajikistan-holiday-jay-austin-lauren-geoghegan-a8489421.html

Tinyhousetinyfootprint.com, Jay in a Matchbox Tiny House, https://www.tinyhousetinyfootprint.com/roll-with-me/jay-in-a-matchbox-tiny-house

The Standard, Gardner, David, Murdered by ISIS Round the World Cyclist Couple who Wrote of Kind Lovely People in Travel Blog, https://www.standard.co.uk/news/world/murdered-by-isis-roundtheworld-cyclist-couple-who-wrote-of-kind-lovely-people-in-travel-blog-a3902316.html

RadioFreeEurope, Tragedy in Tajikistan: Most Humans Are Warm Friendly People Who Wish US No Harm, https://www.rferl.org/a/tragedy-in-tajikistan-most-humans-are-warm-friendly-people-who-wish-us-no-harm-/29401621.html

Releifweb Tajikistan: Poverty is Biggest Threat to Peace, June 28, 2002, https://reliefweb.int/report/tajikistan/tajikistan-poverty-biggest-threat-peace?gad_source

Asia Times, Escobar, Pepe. Pamir Highway: The Road on The Roof of the World, https://asiatimes.com/2019/12/pamir-highway-the-road-on-the-roof-of-the-world/

RadioFreeEurope, Many Tajiks Forced To Skip Meals as Poverty Deepens Survey Shows, https://www.rferl.org/a/tajikistan-covid-poverty-economy-survey/31031706.html

Spectrum News, Associated Press, Victims from Belgium Describe NYC Bike Path Attack at Trial. https://ny1.com/nyc/manhattan/news/2023/01/11/victims-from-belgium-describe-nyc-bike-path-attack-at-trial

Radio Free Europe, From Presidential Lyceum To Jihadist Drifter: The Mutable Path of an Accused Terrorist Ringleader in Tajikistan, https://www.rferl.org/amp/tajik-cyclists-attack-abdusamadov-terrorist-ringleader/29435946.html

Documentaries and Movies

The Weekly, Collision, Callimachi, Rukmini, *New York Times,* Documentary 2019.
Lost City of Z, Paramount.
Amadeus, Paramount.

INDEX

Abdusamadov, Hussein   107, 138, 141–3, 166, 173–4
Accursed Mountains   124
Adventure Cyclist   5
The Adventures of Huckleberry Finn (Twain)   116
Afghanistan   7, 141–2, 147
Africa   16, 68, 84–5, 92, 105–6, 130, 132
Airbnb   109, 136
Air Quality Index   145
Ak-Baital Pass   157, 160
Ala-Bel Pass   148, 152
al-Baghdadi, Abu Bakr   107
Alexander Supertramp   91. *See also* McCandless, Christopher Johnson
Amazon   163–5
American Nazi Party   20
Amundsen, Roald   163
Apartheid   29
Armstrong, Lance   146
Around the World on a Bicycle (Stevens)   5, 146–7
Arquillos   88

Barcelona   65, 86–7, 101
bike hijackings   14
biking   5, 16, 25, 27, 32, 42–3, 67, 86, 121, 146, 167, 170, 181, 201

Boneyard Studios   77–8
Botswana   13, 41–2, 44, 55
Brooklyn   47, 49
Buffalo Bill   115
bush camping   42

Callimachi, Rukmini   173, 190, 203–4
Camus, Albert   77
Carter, Jimmy   106
Cassidy, Neal   200
Central Asia   137
City of Z   165
Civilian Conservation Corps   20
Clarie, Marie   180, 182–3
Clarke, Clinton C.   127
Collective Security Treaty Organization   142
Collision   143, 173, 190, 193
couchsurfing   30, 32, 109, 112
Cribbs, Jenn   49, 51–3, 77, 130, 191
Crowly, Alistair   156
Curbed DC   79
cycling   15, 24, 27, 32–3, 67, 112, 118, 146, 148, 151, 154–5, 168, 170, 189

Daewoo sedan   173–5, 181–2
Delatela, Jude   47–8

INDEX

Del Rio, Tiffany   61–3, 101–2, 123, 191, 206
Department of Housing and Urban Development (HUD)   1–3, 16, 22, 47, 49–52, 75, 77, 92, 103, 130, 197, 199, 206
Diversity Immigrant Visa   105
Doctor Zhivago   94
Dushanbe   141, 157, 167, 169, 183
Dwell Magazine   76

economic crisis   13
Education of a Wandering Man (Lamour)   95
Eisenhower, Dwight   106
Eldorado   165
Elephant Sands   43
evil   8, 70, 83
Exploration Fawcett (Percy)   163

Family Happiness (Tolstoy)   94
Faulkner, William   198
Fawcett, Percy   163–5
FBI   48, 105, 182
Ferdinand, Archduke   165
Fitzgerald, F. Scott   115
Flavor Maize Snack   43
Ford, Henry   164
Forester, E. M.   198
Franklin   199

Georgetown   19–20, 22, 61–2, 101, 132, 205–6
Gordon, George   19
Great Age of Exploration   163
Great Depression   75
Great Karoo Desert   17, 27
Great Recession of 2007   76

Harpers   147
Hemingway, Ernest   116
Hensley, Henry   50–1

high-altitude pulmonary edema (HAPE)   156
Highway A 385   167, 174
Hollywood Hills   21
The Homeless Children's Playtime Project   22
homosexualism   41
Howards End (Forester)   198
Human Rights Watch   145
Hummel, Markus   176, 180, 189

income disparity   32
International Monetary Fund   13
Into the Wild   127
Into the Wild (Krakauer)   75–6, 91–2, 102, 127
ISIS   203
Islamic militarism   142
Islamic Radicalism   142
Islamic Renaissance Party   142, 197
Istanbul   135–6

Jeffers, Robinson   95
Jihad   174, 203

Kabiri, Muhyiddin   197
Kahn, Loyd   75
Kalahari Desert   41
Karakul   156–7
Kazabat, Guillaume   174, 180, 184
Kazakhstan   145, 158
Kerouac, Jack   102, 200
King, Carol   63
Koes   28–9
Kohalimov, Gulmurod   142
Koronowski, Ryan   64–6, 193, 206
Krakauer, Jon   92–3, 95–6

Lake Malawi   57
Lamour, Louis   95
Lawrence of Arabia   106
Ledger, Keith   21

London, Jack 93
loneliness 23, 84

Macedonia 135–6
malaria 58
McCandless, Christopher Johnson 6, 75–6, 91–6, 102, 168, 197–8
Miles from Nowhere (Savage) 39
Miller, Abby 2–3, 16, 50–3, 191, 199, 206
Miller, Abilene 52
Mississippi River 116–17, 119
Model Ts 164
Montenegro 122, 124
Morocco 2, 38, 69–71
mountain biking 99
Muir, John 93, 136
Mukami National Park 67
Murghab 157, 160–1

Nakhaudov, Hussein 141
Namibia 32
Nathan, Beriot 153–5, 157
National Geographic Society 163
nervous disease 115
neurasthenia 115
New Orleans 23
The New York Times 109, 143, 189–90, 193, 203
Northern Rhodesia 55
Nosirhoja Ubaidov. *See* Nosir, Qori
Nosir, Qori 141, 143, 170, 173, 204
The Not So Big House (Susanka) 75
NPR 189
Nxai Pan National Park 42

O'Connor, Kendall 3, 19–22, 123, 190, 192

Office of Strategic Planning and Management 50
On the Road (Kerouac and Cassidy) 200
Operation Ajax 106
Outside Magazine 93

The Pacific Crest Trail 127–9
Pacific Northwest Trail 198
Pamir Highway 136, 157, 169, 189
Pamir Mountains 137, 145, 152, 154, 158, 167, 169, 204
Para, Lee 77–9, 207
PCT 129–31
Penn, Sean 92, 127
Penny Farthing 5, 146
Peruvian Amazon Company 164
Picnic 197
pollution 38
Pope Manufacturing Company 5
Postma, Kim 123, 154–5, 157–8, 169–70, 173–7, 179–80, 182–4, 189
Potomac River 19

Rahmon, Emomali 142, 197
Raleigh, Walter 165
Reason Magazine 77
Rimmel, Raleigh 165
Robinson, Kristen 4, 21, 156, 190, 205, 207
Rockwell, Norman 20
Roof of the World 204
Rota 38
Rousseau, Jean Jacques 30
Royal Geographic Society 163

Saipov, Sayfullo Habibullaevic 105, 107
San Fernando Valley 20
Santovasco, Jea 47, 50, 191

INDEX

Satan 106
Savage, Barbara 35–9
Scalise, Molly 3, 19–20, 63–4, 101–2, 123, 157, 190, 206
Schiff, Adam 21, 181, 192–3
The Scooter Diaries 22, 168, 180, 194, 200, 207
Scott, Robert Falcon 163
Serbia 135–6
Shah, Mohammad Reza 106
Shelter (Kahn) 75
Sierra Nevada Mountains 146
Simply Cycling blog 8, 31, 151, 161, 208
So Far Away (song) 63
South Africa 13–4, 16–17
Spain 38, 71, 83–4, 86, 89, 101
Stevens, Thomas 5–6, 8, 146–7, 198
Stray, Cheryl 127–32, 198
Sundown City 20
Susanka, Sarah 75
Swift, Taylor 154
Switchboard 50
Switchboard movement 50
Sykes Picot Agreement 106

Tajikistan 6–7, 31, 38, 51, 107, 142, 153, 169, 182–3, 189, 197, 199, 204
Tajik Soviet Socialist Republics 141
Tanzania 67
Thanksgiving 68
"the Matchbox" 2, 48
Thomas, Jonathan Taylor 21
Thoreau, Henry David 75, 91, 93

thru-hiking 128
Tiny House 8, 22, 48, 61–2, 75–9, 93, 102, 137, 158
Tiny House Community 77–8
Tiny House movement 75–7
Tiny Houses (Walker) 75
Tolstoy, Leo 94
Too-Ashu Pass 146
Tour De France 146
Trump, Donald 191
Turman 106
Twain, Mark 116–18

UN 197
unemployment 13, 197
United States 106
US Embassy 106

Verdugo Mountains 20

Walden (Thoreau) 75, 91
Walker, Lester 75
warmshowers 30, 55, 57, 68, 87, 100, 109
Washington 19–20, 25, 61
Washington Post 49, 62, 75, 189
The Weekly 203
WhatsApp 153
Wild (Stray) 127, 132
Witherspoon, Reese 127
Wokke, Rene 154, 157, 169–70, 174, 176, 179–80, 182–4
World Food Program 197

Yellowstone National Park 23

Zambia 55

ABOUT THE AUTHOR

William Elliott Hazelgrove is the national best-selling author of ten novels and fourteen narrative nonfiction titles. His books have received starred reviews in Publisher Weekly Kirkus, Booklist, Book of the Month Selections, ALA Editor's Choice Awards Junior Library Guild Selections, Literary Guild Selections, and History Book Club Selections, and optioned for the movies. He was the Ernest Hemingway Writer in Residence, where he wrote in the attic of Ernest Hemingway's birthplace. He has written articles and reviews for *USA Today, The Smithsonian Magazine, Daily Mail*, and other publications, and has been featured on NPR's All Things Considered. *The New York Times, LA Times, Chicago Tribune, CSPAN*, and *USA Today* have covered his books with features. More information can be found at www.williamhazelgrove.com.